Sports in the Pulp Magazines

Sports in the Pulp Magazines

John Dinan

McFarland & Company, Inc., Publishers
Jefferson, North Carolina, and London

> The present work is a reprint of the library bound
> edition of Sports in the Pulp Magazines, first published
> in 1998 by McFarland.

LIBRARY OF CONGRESS CATALOGUING-IN-PUBLICATION DATA

Dinan, John, 1929–
    Sports in the pulp magazines / John Dinan.
      p. cm.
    Includes bibliographical references (p.) and index.

    ISBN 978-0-7864-4047-4
    softcover : 50# alkaline paper ∞

    1. Sports journalism — United States — History. 2. Popular literature — United States — Periodicals — History. 3. American periodicals — History — 20th century. 4. American periodicals — History — 19th century. I. Title.
PN4784.S6D56   2009
070.4'49796'0973 — dc21   98-26758

British Library cataloguing data are available

©1998 John Dinan. All rights reserved

No part of this book may be reproduced or transmitted in any form or by any means, electronic or mechanical, including photocopying or recording, or by any information storage and retrieval system, without permission in writing from the publisher.

Cover art ©2009 Wood River Gallery

Manufactured in the United States of America

McFarland & Company, Inc., Publishers
  Box 611, Jefferson, North Carolina 28640
    www.mcfarlandpub.com

Table of Contents

Preface   1

1. Introduction   3
2. The Magazines   7
3. Sports in the Pulps   33
4. The All-Sports Pulps   63
5. Street & Smith's Sport Story Magazine   103
6. The Pulp Writers   130
7. Editors, Artists and Readers   158
8. The Passing of the Pulps   179
9. Appendix: Sports Pulp Titles   192

Index   197

Preface

Pulp historians and sports fiction historians have managed to virtually ignore more than 20 years of sports fiction in more than 100 different pulp magazines, including more than 50 pulps devoted exclusively to sports fiction. Ron Goulart in his *Cheap Thrills* devotes a paragraph to the subject. When Quentin Reynolds wrote his history of Street & Smith he was similarly neglectful; not more than a few sentences were devoted to the several Street & Smith sports pulps, including the long-running *Sport Story Magazine*.

In his history of baseball fiction (*Baseball by the Books: A History and Complete Bibliography of Baseball Fiction*), Andy McCue covers dime novel sports fiction, series book sports fiction, juvenile and adult sports fiction, but devotes not a word to pulp sports fiction in spite of the claim of "completeness" in the title of his book.

The Grant Burns book *The Sports Pages: A Critical Bibliography of Twentieth-Century Novels and Stories Featuring Baseball, Basketball, Football, and Other Athletic Pursuits* contains no material from the sports pulps. Michael Oriard's *American Sports Fiction, 1868–1980* provides only superficial coverage of the sports pulps — a few pages.

In *The Handbook of American Popular Culture* (edited by M. Thomas Inge) the pulps are covered as are sports, but there is no mention of the sports pulps under either entry.

If all this is not enough to demonstrate the absence of research into the sports pulps, one has only to look into the world of current-day pulp collectors or researchers and their interests. What are their interests? The hero pulps, the rare titles (like *Strange Suicide Stories* or *Civil War Stories*), the outré weird menace or horror pulps, detective pulps with some of the big-name writers (Chandler, Woolrich, Hammett, MacDonald, et al.), or the early works of writers who later would earn a larger reputation than could be provided by writing for the pulps (like Louis L'Amour). Certainly not the sports pulps. Which brings us to the purpose of the present work: to make a good beginning toward filling the pulp sports information void which exists in spite of the efforts of the popular culturists, the pulp collectors and researchers, and those who research the history of sports fiction.

1

Introduction

The Pulp Magazine

There is a scene in *The Maltese Falcon* where Sam Spade (Bogart) is asked that question about the bird; just what is it? Spade's answer: "The stuff that dreams are made of." This is precisely what a pulp is; a dream machine which transports the reader to the darkest jungles, the coldest regions of outer space, or the inner motivation of a major-league pitcher who is working a three-and-two count for all the marbles.

As a physical entity the pulp magazine wasn't that much to look at, except for the cover which, in the hands of the best pulp cover artists, triggered the reader's imagery and set the stage for the adventures yet to come. The pulps came in three basic sizes: 7 × 10 inches, 8½ × 11 (called bedsheet) and 5½ × 7¼ (digest size), and typically included 128 numbered pages made of the cheapest pulp paper stock. The rumor that one could get a splinter or a severe case of pulp lung from the decomposing paper has not been substantiated.

Most — some four million magazines a month — were published in New York City and printed in the now non-existent Myrick Building at 29 Washington Street in Springfield, Massachusetts. From here they went to the neighborhood variety store where they were stacked on multi-level wire racks, presenting an amazingly colorful phantasmagoria of cowboys, hard-boiled dicks, bug-eyed monsters, superheroes saving gorgeous gals, super Feds saving the United States from evil invaders, villains, unspeakable horrors, blazing .45s and six guns, Tarzan, the Shadow, Doc Savage, the weird and unimaginable, and the on-field dramatics of baseball, football, basketball, boxing, and dozens of other sports.

Most pulps cost a dime, chump change even in the tight times of the Great Depression. You put your dime in that little rubber-stippled mat on top of the glass case and took your pleasure home where the adventure began. But first, you might scan the whole magazine; you might even send off for the Johnson & Johnson catalogue of low-priced necessities like sneezing powder, a joy buzzer or a whoopie cushion, or even one of those eight-page Tijuana Bibles if you thought you could intercept the mail before mom or dad got to it.

And then, finally, to the pulp story, the pleasure delayed. There were things happening in the pulp story that didn't happen elsewhere. You could go to the Texas Panhandle, the dark side of the moon, the jungles of Africa or Yankee Stadium — as a player in each of these dramas. For a kid growing up in the 1930s that wasn't half bad considering your family, like most, didn't own a car and you didn't know anyone, nor did your parents, who had ever flown in a plane ... of all things.

The play's the thing. The pulp story was formula — and some warned that the pulps would rot our brains — but what it did was allow a kid who had never been out of his city limits to expand the limits of both his world and his imagination. Not bad for a dime!

In the end, the ignominy of it all — the inevitability of being discarded or, worse, hung on a nail in the outhouse — meant that the half-life of a pulp magazine was but a few days. But fresh off the newsstand it opened new doors. Like Bogie's Falcon, it was the stuff of dreams.

Sports and Magazines

Over the period 1865–1885 American interest in sports grew steadily.* Increasing leisure was a factor and magazine coverage of spectacle sports (racing, baseball, and boxing) and recreational sports (bicycling, hunting, fishing and baseball) increased accordingly.

---

*Mott, Frank Luther, *A History of American Magazines, 1865–1885, Volume III.* Cambridge, MA: *The Belknap Press of Harvard University Press, 1957.*

1. Introduction

General sports periodicals included *Spirit of the Times,* the *National Police Gazette* and the *New York Clipper.*

Brentano's *Aquatic Monthly and Sporting Gazetteer,* begun in 1872, featured yachting, rowing and swimming sports reporting. In 1869 a short-lived magazine (*Onward*) devoted its coverage entirely to croquet, and some of the magazines of the day (*Sporting Life, Turf, Field and Farm*) reported the results of cricket games. One could read of lawn tennis games in *Wheelman.*

The biggest sport event of the period (John L. Sullivan's defeat of Paddy Ryan in nine rounds on February 7, 1882) was reported in the *Clipper, Police Gazette* and *Day's Doings.* All-American college football selections were yearly *Collier's* features from 1891 to 1948.

From 1885 to 1905 a number of magazines covered spectacle and recreational sports,* the biggest events of the era being the last bare-knuckle fight immortalized by Whitman, and Sullivan's loss of his heavyweight title to James J. Corbett in 1892.

Yachting, the sport of the rich, was covered in *Cosmopolitan, The American Yachtsman* (1887–1908) and *Motor Boat* (1904–present). College football became popular; Harvard, Yale, Princeton and Pennsylvania at first, and later, several Midwest teams. Games were covered in *Nickell Magazine, The Pathfinder,* and *Arena. The Golfer* (1894–1906) was the organ of the U.S. Golf Association. *American Golf* (1900–1902) and *Golfer's Magazine* (1902–1931) survived on the spread of country clubs, and a number of tennis publications came and went: *Bulletin* (1894–1897), *American Lawn Tennis* (1898–1901) and *Lawn Tennis* (1901–1903).

There were a number of bicycling magazines, foremost among them *The American Cyclist* (1890–1898) and *Good Roads* (1885–1931). *Harper's Bazaar* and *Vogue* put out bicycle fashion editions every spring.

Other participant sports then popular were bowling (*The Bowler's Journal*: 1893–1934) and hunting and fishing (*Sports Afield*: 1887–present, and *New England Sportsman*: 1899–1941). *Western Field and Stream* began publication in 1896 and dropped the "Western" part of the title when it moved to New York in 1898.

With the exception of the Frank Merriwell saga which started

---

*Mott, Frank Luther, A History of American Magazines 1885–1905, Volume IV. Cambridge, MA: The Belknap Press of Harvard University Press, 1957.

in 1896 (*Tip Top Weekly*) there were no magazines of this period publishing sports fiction of any type on a regular basis.

From 1905 to 1930 a number of mainstream magazines were published; among them were *The American Mercury, The New Republic, Good Housekeeping, Time,* etc. Few of these covered sports events and only one had sports fiction, and then on an irregular basis. *Everybody's Magazine* had been around since 1899 and lasted through March 1929, after which it combined with *Romance*, under the title *Everybody's Combined with Romance*. During the 1920s it featured a number of regular pulp writers (E. Phillips Oppenheim, Rafael Sabatini, etc.) but little sports fiction. Through the middle twenties it featured extensive sport reportage, but from 1926 this material was cut back significantly.*

During this period the science fiction and detective pulps were achieving enough popularity to spawn genres which would last to the present day. While these magazines rarely featured a sports plot/milieu, some pulp writers experimented with combining sports with science fiction or detective/mystery themes, in some cases with a fair amount of success.

Mott, Frank Luther, A History of American Magazines: Sketches of 21 Magazines 1905–1930, Vol. V. Cambridge, MA: The Belknap Press of Harvard University Press, 1968.

2

The Magazines

The First Pulps

The first pulps were the general fiction magazines of the turn of the century. Magazines like *Ainslee's, All-Story, Argosy, Blue Book Magazine, Munsey's Magazine, McClure's Magazine, Pearson's Weekly,* etc. provided exciting stories by the likes of Edgar Rice Burroughs with his adventures of Tarzan starting with the October 1912 issue of *All Story*. Other important popular writers of the day to write for these magazines included Bertha Bower, H. Bedford-Jones, H. G. Wells, Kipling, Twain, Harte, and Conan Doyle.

The father of these general fiction magazines was a man named Frank A. Munsey. A man of unbridled ambition, he told his story in one of his magazines on the occasion of the 25th anniversary of his first publication. The first issue of *The Argosy* was published December 2, 1882, and its feature pieces were holdovers from the dime novel era: Horatio Alger and Edward Ellis. Five months later *The Argosy* was in the hands of a receiver; Munsey was broke. Borrowing money, Munsey got *The Argosy* back on its feet, and, with the help of advertising revenues and an advertising campaign of his own doing, the magazine grew. In May of 1887, *The Argosy* reached a circulation of 115,000 copies, from which Munsey was netting a tidy profit of $1500 per week. In February 1889, Munsey produced a new magazine: *Munsey's Weekly*. In the fall of 1891 he changed its title to *Munsey's Magazine,* described as "the burden-bearer" of his publishing house, which at the time consisted of two newspapers and six magazines: *Munsey's Magazine, The Argosy, The Scrap Book, The All-Story Magazine, The Ocean,* and *The Railroad Man's Magazine.*

Michael Oriard, in his book *Reading Football* (subtitled *How the Popular Press Created an American Spectacle*)* argues that the game of football was a product of early magazines like *Outing, Harper's Weekly, Outlook, Independent, Collier's,* and the juveniles, *St. Nicholas* and *Youth's Companion.* Together with the daily newspapers (mainly the three New York papers—*Herald, World, Times*), Oriard says, these magazines transformed college football into a cultural phenomenon which integrated the hopes and ambitions of the young adult male with such concepts as dominance, violence and heroism, within the socio-economic milieu of immigration and its racial implications. While these papers and periodicals were creating a public appetite for college football through the 1880s and 1890s, the *Police Gazette* supported the working-class "manly art of self defense" while demeaning college football as "silly, pretentious and hypocritical."

The amount of magazine and newspaper space devoted to sports topics in turn gave a synergistic boost to college football which, in turn, provided grist for the print trade mill. All of this was fundamental to the evolution of sports from now-and-then material in the general fiction pulps at the turn of the century to the complete sports pulp magazines of the 1920s, '30s, '40s and '50s.

The history of these early general fiction magazines is a complex theater of titles dropped, combined, and revived to best meet the costs of sales, postage and distribution. For example: In 1908 Munsey combined *The Live Wire* into *The Scrap Book.* In 1912, *The Cavalier* was absorbed by *The Scrap Book,* and in 1914 *The Scrap Book* was taken from this marriage of convenience, combined with *All-Story Weekly,* and retitled *All-Story Cavalier Weekly.* How much of a success was Munsey in his chosen field of publishing? In the November 1911 *Pearson's,* the editor quotes retired U.S. Steel president Charles M. Schwab to the effect that Munsey was the largest single shareholder of record in U.S. Steel.

Baseball fiction was everpresent in the Munsey general fiction magazines. Pulp collector/researcher Al Tonik sent me the following list from his pile of old *Argosy* pulps:

---

*Reading Football: How the Popular Press Created an American Spectacle, *The University of North Carolina Press, 1993.*

2. The Magazines

Argosy–All Story, Aug. 31, 1929: "The Third Strike" by Herbert L. McNary.

Argosy, Sep. 17, 1932: "The World Series Murders" by Herbert L. McNary (part 5 of 5).

Argosy, Oct. 6, 1934: "The Duplex Chucker" by James W. Egan.

Argosy, Aug. 29, 1936: "The Speed King" by George Bruce (part 1 of 4); the next three parts were provided in the Sep. 5, Sep. 12 and Sep. 19 issues of *Argosy*.

Argosy, Apr. 30, 1938: "Rubber Arm" by Martin McCall.

Argosy, Sep. 17, 1938: "Yannigan's Choice" by Holmes Alexander.

Argosy, June 3, 1939: "The Wingless Wonder" by Judson H. Phillips.

Mr. Tonik describes his collection of *Argosy* pulps as "meager"; in his small sample, baseball fiction is well represented.

Munsey was not only the father of the general fiction pulp magazines; with the publication of *The Railroad Man's Magazine* he started the trend toward single-subject or single-character pulps. Americans had always been in love with the old coal-fired steam trains and Munsey would capitalize on this from the early 1900s well into the middle of the century. *The Railroad Man's Magazine* was followed with *Railroad Magazine*, and in 1929 he published *Railroad Stories*, the most popular of the series.

Other publishers got the idea and soon one would find single-subject magazines in seven categories (in addition to railroad material): Westerns, Love/Sex, Detective/Mystery, Science Fiction/Fantasy/Horror, Air/War, Hero pulps (The Shadow, Doc Savage, etc.) and Sports. As America edged toward World War II, the single-material pulps would increase in popularity to the point where they dominated the pulp magazine market.

The pulp magazine earned its sobriquet "pulp" from the cheap pulp mash from which its pages were produced. By the time the single-subject pulps came along in the 1930s their format had been established: 7 × 10 inches, and 128 ragged-edged pages of pulse-pounding purple prose topped off with a garish, glossy cover designed to entice the unwary to part with 10 cents.* Their pages were

---

*Page length varied plus or minus ten pages or so, prices could run to 25 cents, and digest-size pulps of the late 1940s and 1950s measured 7¼" × 5¼".

laced with ads for BB guns, whoopie cushions, nose straighteners, a new Charles Atlas body, radio skills ("You don't have to leave home to learn jobs like these"), false teeth and a cure for piles.

There was a pulp magazine for every taste. In addition to the foregoing genres there were titles like *Strange Suicides, Spy Novels Magazine, Speakeasy Stories*, as well as amalgams like *Spicy Mystery Stories*. It was the most exciting era in the history of popular fiction in the most exciting era in the history of popular fiction in the most exciting period in modern American history, spanning two World Wars and the Great Depression.

Sports activities, individual and team, based on skill, strength, speed and an element of chance, have come to dominate American leisure both as active and passive pursuits. Football's Superbowl is the glaring example of sports as passive entertainment on a grand scale, with literally millions watching the television broadcast. College football and basketball, the Olympic games, major-league baseball and basketball and professional boxing are not far behind in terms of the viewer headcount. A click of the television remote and there you are. The ease with which this is done cannot be matched.

In an earlier day, sports as leisure meant going to the corner store and purchasing one of the 50-plus sports pulp magazines which featured the major American sports and such minor (in terms of participants) sports as ice boat racing, dog sledding and fencing. Yes, there was the radio, but radio broadcasts were confined almost exclusively to baseball games.

The advantages of the sports pulp were portability (one could take it almost anywhere, and read it sitting, standing or lying down in the corn shed) and availability. In 1934, the National Recreation Association conducted interviews of 5,000 Americans to determine what they did in their spare time versus what they wanted to do. The results indicated that they wanted an active leisure but, in fact, their leisure time was largely confined to listening to the radio and reading. Those who were sports minded were reading one or more of the sports pulps.

Sports fiction in the pulp magazines covers the period starting with the general fiction pulps and ending with the digest magazines of the early 1950s. Volume is of great interest when looking at the pulps and certainly so for the pulp writer. He was a man who could turn a western into a science fiction tale or a sports story with a few well-placed modifications. He would have been ten times as productive in the word processor era. At ¼-cent per word, such skill was vital to success. Tom Curry, a man who in his time wrote sport, western, detective, etc. pulp fiction, did so with a basic formula: "The general theme must be that the hero, being young, handsome, strong, personable, and being endowed with great moral courage and character, as well as being an expert (batter/fielder, cow puncher, space explorer, etc.), must face the most hazardous, challenging circumstance and defeat the enemy in a physical confrontation."

Harold Hersey's description of sports pulp plotting is similar to Tom Curry's:

> We have the athletic hero engaged in adventures of the prizering and out of it, on the baseball field, in football, basketball, etc. He is always victorious at the close of each story. God help the poor fellow; he must ever win against every obstacle. He is denied the privilege of failure, and, in consequence, the greater privilege of growth. He must remain the complete, utter juvenile, just as Gilbert Patten fashioned him from his original mind when he wrote the Frank and Dick Merriwell stories for so many, many years. This formula defies change except in rare instances where genius spilled over the narrow confines of the sporting fraternity's curiously conservative minds.*

In addition to the fiction, there is much reportage in the non-fiction segments (usually called "departments") of these magazines which is of interest to the modern sports historian.

The objective of this book is to identify all of the magazines in this genre and examine the contents of the leading magazines in some detail; an effort, it is hoped, which will contribute to the pulp era information base, and the knowledge of sports fiction and non-fiction as it existed in the popular pulp sports magazines of the first half of the twentieth century.

The General Fiction Pulps

Between the early 1890s and the World War I era, some of the best popular fiction ever to grace a newsstand was being produced.

---

*Hersey, Harold, Pulpwood Editor, New York: Frederick A. Stokes Company, 1937. Hersey was one of the leading figures in the pulp publishing business.

Talbot Mundy was turning out great adventure sagas for *Adventure*. Under the pen name N. Bean, Edgar Rice Burroughs would start his writing career with "Under the Moons of Mars" in the July 1912 issue of *All-Story*. In the October 1912 *All-Story*, Burroughs' "Tarzan of the Apes" would start a decade-long relationship between him and the magazine. Bertha Bower was writing for *The Popular Magazine*, and H. Bedford-Jones, that master of the sweeping historical novel, would be writing for *Adventure* and *The Cavalier*. H. G. Wells could be found in *Pearson's*, Kipling in *McClure's*, and Twain, Harte and Arthur Conan Doyle in *The Strand*. William Hope Hodgson wrote some of his great sea/horror stories for *Blue Book*, a magazine that would long hold a reputation as perhaps the best of all pulp magazines from a quality consideration, and Willa Cather would write for *Popular* and edit *McClure's*.

Most of these magazines had a common format: 7 × 10 inches, 200 pages (plus or minus 20 or so), and a number of slick pages in the front and back of the magazine mostly devoted to ads. The ads pitched everything from Cream of Wheat to Iver Johnson pistols and Pabst Extract — The Best Tonic, an ad picturing a lady of the day reclining on her sofa over an M.D.'s testimony:

> My wife being in a low state of health has received marked benefits from Pabst Extract. It never fails to secure a night's sleep for her when she takes it while being tired and nervous.

This was the golden era not only of popular fiction but of patent medicines as well. In this same issue (September 1907 *The Argosy*) there are endorsements of Coca-Cola by Napoleon Lajoie, and ads for folding bathtubs and musophones.

Over the years the pulp magazine ads have been a source of interest if not wonderment, and some of the ads were intimately entwined with our wonder years. One such is the one-pager of Johnson Smith & Co. of Racine, Wisconsin. This company's ads included such delights as X-ray tubes, whoopie cushions, a flip-book Hotsy Totsy dance, stink bombs and wooden nickels. Most of these items sold for a dime or so; the pleasure in ordering one and waiting for its arrival was often diminished by its poor quality after the promises of the overblown ad copy.

The September 1907 *The Argosy* mentioned above contained one complete novel, six serial stories and sixteen short stories, which was typical fare in these magazines. The April 25, 1914, *All-Story Weekly*, for example, carried one novel, four serial stories, and five short stories. The July 26, 1913, *The Cavalier* carried four serial stories, two novelettes, six short stories and some poetry. In the years before World War I some of these magazines carried theater-related material in their slick sections.

Adventure, a general fiction pulp which first appeared in November 1910, was very popular with the male audience. While *The All-Story Magazine* tried to capture both male and female readership, magazines like *The Argosy* and *Adventure* were targeted exclusively to a male audience, especially *Adventure*. For example, the January 1913 issue carried about 20 pieces of fiction with titles like "The Sniper of Boulder Hill," "King Corrigan's Treasure," and "A Pair of 38's," and three short non-fiction pieces in which presumably personal-experience adventures were told in narrative fashion. The content was popular and *Adventure* would enjoy a run which lasted to the end of the pulp era in the early 1950s. Its style would be imitated by later pulps such as *Action Stories* and *Short Stories*.

Another *Adventure* feature which would be copied was its Camp Fire department. Introduced in its May 5, 1912, issue as "A meetingplace for Readers, Writers, and Adventurers," it contained letters discussing the relative merits of various firearms and other such manly subject matter, typical of which was "A Life on the Seven Seas," in which "A. E. Dingle Tells the Campfire the Tale of His Adventures," which took Mr. Dingle to France, Russia, Norway, Sweden, Greenland, Spain, Portugal, Italy, Egypt, the Holy Land, Arabia, India, China, Japan, Mauritius, the Islands of the Indian Ocean, East Africa, Australia, South Africa, etc. It well may be that Mr. Dingle never left his living room but he wrote great copy and the market for vicarious adventure was an expanding one as evidenced by *Adventure*'s longevity and its imitators.

Cover art had not yet advanced (?) to the garish apogee achieved in the 1930s and 1940s and tended more to realism; simple portrait-like renditions. There were exceptions, mostly found in the *Adventure*-like pulps where scenes of pirate wars or barroom brawls excited the male hormones. N. C. Wyeth's covers for *The Popular Magazine* and *McClure's* and Herbert Morton Stoops' *Blue Book* covers and interiors (under the pen name Jeremy Cannon) represent the best of this art.

The names of many outstanding writers of the day can be found in these magazines: Rafael Sabatini, H. Bedford-Jones, John Buchan, Edgar Rice Burroughs and Talbot Mundy are but a few. If one liked his buckles swashed, the general fiction pulps were the way to go.

The father of the pulps, the man who invented them, Frank A. Munsey, was not beloved. In his book about the pulps, *Cheap Thrills*, author Ron Goulart quotes a eulogist's observations: "Frank Munsey contributed to the journalism of his day the talent of a meat packer, the morals of a money changer and the manner of an undertaker."

What Munsey did have was unbridled ambition. In an autobiographical piece in the December 1907 *The Munsey Magazine*, he talks about his job running a Western Union Telegraph Company office in Augusta, Maine:

> As Augusta was the capital of the State, and as I lived at the hotel where most of the legislative and other State officers stayed, I very soon acquired a pretty good knowledge of the strong men of the entire commonwealth. Their lives had scope; mine had none. I chafed bitterly under the limited possibilities of my environment, where ambition, and energy, and aspiration counted for little. My very soul cried out for an opportunity to carve out for myself a bigger life.

That bigger life would start with *The Argosy*; the twenty-fifth anniversary of its origins being the occasion for Munsey's self-congratulatory biography: "The Story of the Founding of the Munsey Publishing House."

The history of these early magazines is a complex one. Driven by sales figures, postage rates, publication and distribution costs, these magazines were merged, dropped, combined and dissolved to meet the bottom line, as noted earlier in this chapter. This process would continue into the comic book era: the pulp *Adventure*, for example, evolved to *Adventure Comics*, which in turn became *Action Comics* and later became *Detective Comics*. Munsey also states in his autobiographical article that America's two oldest magazines, *Goldey's Ladies Book* and *Peterson's*, were "absorbed" by *The Argosy*, a process described in "The Magazine in America" which refers to Munsey as "the Grand High Executioner of Journalism."

Blue Book, which was *The Monthly Story Magazine* until 1905, is a source of some great adventure stories in the style and tradition of *Adventure* and *Short Stories*. Fred Glidden, who wrote under the pen name Luke Short (in the old West, Luke Short was a gambler-gunfighter contemporary and pal of Wyatt Earp and Bat Masterson), wrote Western fiction for both *Adventure* and *Blue Book*. Short wrote of a West with which he was familiar — the American Southwest and Rocky Mountain areas. His fiction, action packed in the pulp tradition, was the basis for many Hollywood films, including "Blood on the Moon," "Ride the Man Down," "Coroner Creek," and "Silver Rock."

Perhaps the greatest western writer of all times, Frederick Faust is credited with an output of 30 million words over a 20-year period which started with his work in *Blue Book, Adventure, Munsey Magazine, All-Story Weekly* and *Short Stories*. Writing under a dozen and a half pen names, mainly Max Brand and Evan Evans, Faust is still in print and the scope and impact of his work can be gauged by the record of one of his stories which had humble pulp origins: it was later printed as *Destry Rides Again* (selling over a million copies), and was three times produced as a film: in 1932 featuring Tom Mix, in 1939 with Jimmy Stewart, and again in 1954 with Audie Murphy.

In addition to adventure and western, romance and mystery were common subjects, and a common threat through all of this pulp fiction was the series character. The advantages of having a series character were clearly stated by Leslie Charteris, creator of "The Saint," aka Simon Templar:

> The advantages were evident; instead of fragmenting his creativity on a variety of heroes, the writer could concentrate on building and enlarging one — and every reader who was captured by that one would be sent back in search of the earlier stories he had missed as well as being a pre-sold customer for the next, far more than if he merely happened to like the author.

It was a simple formula but one which would prove to be successful in the general fiction pulp magazines. In a series about the series characters of the general fiction pulps, Robert Sampson describes the exploits of such characters as *The Argosy*'s Peter Moore; the Tarzan of *All-Story* and *Blue Book*; *Adventure*'s comic cowboy, Hashknife Hartley; Jimmy Dale, aka the Gray Seal, of *People's Magazine*; Colonel Terence O'Rourke of *The Popular Magazine*, and literally dozens of others.

What is of interest here is the fact that the most popular of the pulp magazines would prove to be the series characters with their own, titled magazines, such as *Operator 5, The Shadow,* and *G-8 and His Battle Aces.* While the general fiction pulps carried an abundance of series characters, they were never given the status of having their own magazine. While this would come later in the pulps of the 1930s and 1940s, the precedent for successful single-character popular fiction was established in the dime novels.

The dime novels were the popular literature of the last 40 years of the nineteenth century and competed with the general fiction pulps in the early years of the twentieth century. Made possible by technological advances in printing and papermaking and distributed by ever-widening railway networks, the dime novel became the first mass-produced, mass-distributed popular reading material. The early dime novels were issued every two weeks in formats ranging from pocket size to newspaper size, and in paperback and hardcover editions before becoming standardized in the classic "yellow-back" format which was advertised as "a dollar book for a dime." They would, however, continue to change format but the 100-page pulp-paper magazine with its orange-colored cover woodcut would be the most familiar. The subject of the cover woodcut was more often than not a series/hero character like Frank Merriwell, Diamond Dick, Nick Carter, or Old King Brady.

Single-character adventure, sports, western and detective heroes were the staple of the dime novels. Some of these characters, such as Nick Carter, would survive the dime novels, flourish in the pulps and find a life in the paperbacks. Some were the stuff of American legend.

In his dime-novel anthology, *Eight Dime Novels,* author E. F. Bleiler describes the army of "faceless hacks who could emit novels as freely as a queen bee lays eggs," the most interesting of whom was described as "The Great Rascal" by his biographer Jay Monaghan. The Great Rascal, aka Ned Buntline, aka Edward Zane Carroll Jackson, led a flamboyant life as sailor, soldier, firearms designer, prohibitionist and co-founder of the Know-Nothing party, and became famous for his Buffalo Bill dime novels. Buntline, if not the inventor, was the man who fictionalized the workaday Buffalo Bill (he was a meat procurer for a railroad crew) to mythic proportions.

William Gilbert Patten, alias Burt L. Standish — father of Frank and Dick Merriwell, was in the grand tradition of dime noveleers. At one time he did a series of westerns under the pseudonym Wyoming Bill. He "earned" this sobriquet by virtue of having been a passenger on a train that passed through Wyoming. Patten's mark was made in sports fiction with his archetypical all–American boys: Frank and Dick Merriwell. While his sports fiction is dated, it survives in the American consciousness (one still hears on occasion of a player who "pulled a Merriwell," meaning he overcame impossible odds to prevail) and in special collections such as Brown University's collection of Merriwell dime novels (John Hay Library).

So, though the precedent was there for headlining the series character, thus raising him to heights he would not achieve if blended in with a dozen other genre fiction pieces, the early general fiction pulps chose to ignore the possibilities of the single-character series hero.

The most talented of the writers of pulp fiction were able to make the transition from the general fiction pulps to the hero pulps and from one genre to another. Typical of this group was Tom Curry, a man whose career ranged from *American Magazine* and *McClure's* to *Black Mask* and *Texas Ranger Magazine*. Curry sold fiction to more than 300 magazines. His first story was "Diamond in the Rough" which appeared in *People's Favorite*, March 1921. He later became a *Black Mask* regular, the best of the detective fiction pulps, appearing with Dashiell Hammett and Erle Stanley Gardner. Curry would also write for *Argosy, Detective Fiction, Rio Kid Western, Sea Stories,* and *Short Stories.*

In 1936 (the 100th anniversary of the founding of the Texas Rangers) Tom started a mini-career producing 85 *Texas Rangers* stories under the house name of Jackson Cole, a name he shared with other *Texas Rangers* writers, Leslie Scott and Walker Tomkins.

In 1939 editor Leo Margulies, having seen the popularity of *Texas Rangers,* asked Tom to start a new western series. Tom played around with a few ideas before hitting on the concept of a fictional character in actual historical circumstances; thus was born the Rio Kid. October 1939 was the first appearance of the Kid, aka Bob Pryor, former Civil War captain and soon to be cohort of a series of historical Western American characters. A popular character with Western fiction fans, some of these Rio Kid stories were reprinted in paperback in 1972.

In addition to all this writing, Curry also wrote sports stories for Street & Smith's *Sport Story Magazine*. He died at his home on October 7, 1976 after a pulp writing career that spanned nearly 50 years. He wrote for the digest *Zane Grey Western* in the 1960s under his own name and as Romer Zane Grey.

The Genre Pulps

The early, family-styled pulps would give way to the new, genre-formatted pulps which were aimed at specific markets, much as non-fiction magazines are marketed to today's casual reader. Just as *Vogue, Computer Life* and *Playboy* are targeted to very narrowly-defined markets, so *Western Story, Love Stories* and *Astounding Science Fiction* were narrow-band audience pulps.

The new pulp looked to groups of people who were taken by the Western or the new science fiction of Hugo Gernsback. Similarly, the lonely store clerks of the country took to *Love Story* and the wannabe detectives were absorbed by a new brand of "hardboiled" detective fiction in *Black Mask* and *Dime Detective*. There were new pulps for railroad buffs, fans of the rodeo, the sports minded, and those interested in the Civil War. In short, there was a pulp for every conceivable taste, including horror, autopsies, and war on the sea, ground, or in the air; there were, too, adventure stories, ghosts, and super heroes.

When the dust settled, the new pulps were clustered into clearly recognizable genres, the most popular of which was the detective/crime/mystery genre with 234 different titles. The second most popular genre was the western, with 177 titles. There were 115 love titles, 106 science fiction/fantasy titles, 75 hero pulps, 60 aviation/war titles, followed by sports (53), western romance (30), weird menace or horror (25), spicy/saucy titles (24), and 59 general/miscellaneous titles.*

A brief look at these genres will show how the new pulp had changed from the old general fiction pulps which tried to be all things to all people.

---

*These figures are from The Pulp Magazine Index: Explanations and Disclaimers *in the #12/13 issue of* Pulp Vault.

The Detectives

There were more than 100 different pulp magazines which had the word "detective" in their titles and a number of other magazines that were detective pulps but which did not describe themselves specifically as such (*Gangland Stories, Clues, Gang World, Public Enemy, The Underworld*, etc.). The best of these magazines offered a new, exciting variety of fiction which would continue to be popular: the hard-boiled private eye story. Some argue that these stories were never done better than in their original pulp style by the masters of the genre: Dashiell Hammett, Raymond Chandler, Lewis Nebel, Paul Cain, Roger Torry and George Harmon Coxe, to name but a few.

The hard-boiled dick of the pulps came in all sizes and shapes and ran the gamut of occupations: railroad and hotel dicks, ex-cops, ex-gangsters, photographers, reporters, D.A.s, M.D.s, and the clergy. The most popular, soon to become the stylistic model, was the ex-cop in private practice, and the most popular private eye was Dashiell Hammett's Sam Spade.

Sam Spade evolved as a character from a nameless detective that Hammett featured in his work in the pulp *Black Mask*. Called by the name Continental Op, Hammett's detective was unlike the cerebral sleuths Dupin, Poirot, and Queen. More along the lines of an NFL running back, he generated results through the use of three basic talents: physical strength — the ability to absorb punishment and keep going; submission of his personal needs to those of his client; and a mental toughness which allowed him to confront danger with confidence.

Hammett and Chandler were the big names who made their first mark in the detective pulps but there were hundreds of others in the dozens of detective pulps produced over the first half of this century. Some, like Joe Archibald's Willie Klump, had long runs (*Popular Detective*). The pulps also introduced some variations on the character of the P.I., including the lady P.I.

The most popular lady P.I. of the pulps was Bertha Cool. Bertha was in charge of a two-person agency and weighed in at a cool 300 pounds. Writing under his A.A. Fair pseudonym, Erle Stanley Gardner got a 30-novel run out of this character, a run that lasted through 1970. The Bertha Cool character has generally been recognized as the first lady P.I., but the fact is she was not.

Gardner and Cleve Adams were writer/friends in the 1930s and not only wrote for the same pulps but frequently had stories in the same issues. A big market at that time for both writers was *Clues Detective Stories*. As early as January of 1935, Cleve Adams was writing about his lady P.I., Violet McDade, in *Clues*, and we can be certain that Gardner was familiar with this character four years before the first appearance of Bertha Cool. Violet McDade ran an agency, as did Bertha Cool, and was a larger-than-life creation like most pulp characters, skilled in the use of a brace of .45s and high-speed driving. The Violet McDade stories ran in *Clues* through 1938, the year Gardner produced his first Bertha Cool story: "The Bigger They Come."

The last lady P.I. of the pulps was the creation of Sven Anderton in a November 1951 issue of *Famous Detective*. Described by the police as a scrawny gargoyle, Edna Pender was one of two principals in the P.I. firm of Ware and Pender. Further described as big of bosom and feet and bowlegged, Miss Pender was deferred to as "boss" by male partner Ware. Edna Pender grew up in a shanty town and learned to hate the cops she had "plenty of trouble with as a kid." That she had the P.I. qualities was clear from her response to the news that a hood of her acquaintance was killed: "No great loss." She worked out of a fancy suite of offices, drove a bullet-proof Buick, owned a truck farm, and had the chutzpah to negotiate a fee for Ware and Pender services with none other than J. Edgar Hoover. The Ware and Pender stories appeared in *Famous Detective* through 1956, a year when the majority of pulps had long since stopped publication.

The Weirdos

Horror Pulps (dubbed shudder by some, weird menace by others) offered a kind of fiction which differed from the *Weird Tales* story, but for a variety of reasons they would never achieve the commercial success of *Weird Tales*. The *Weird Tales* story was based in fantasy and the supernatural; at one time it was subtitled "Tales of the Bizarre and Unusual," subjects which had great appeal if we can judge by its 30-odd-year life. The average life span of a horror title was a few years at best.

Henry Steeger (1903-1990), president of Popular Publications from 1930 to 1972, was considering the reformatting of *Dime Mystery Book Magazine*, a pulp which had begun publication in December 1932 but was floundering in 1933. Sales were down and Steeger, looking for an elixir which would revive the magazine, took inspiration from a trip he had taken to Paris, where he visited the Grand Guignol Theater.

The Grand Guignol Theater presented live shows which featured simulated acts of mutilation and torture, using the most bizarre human practices in these scenes from Dante's vision of Hell. Steeger observed that the more gruesome the act, the better the audience liked it. And so, with the advent of the October 1933 *Dime Mystery Magazine*, Popular Publications initiated its own Grand Guignol, with companion pulps *Terror Tales* and *Horror Stories* to follow suit in 1934 and 1935.

Robert Kenneth Jones, in his history of the genre (*The Shudder Pulps*), describes the typical content of these pulps as sex-sadism with luscious females on the covers suffering the usual ignominies: "whippings, roastings, and mad-virus inoculations." Those who administered these "ignominies" were deformed dwarfs, half-man half-beast creatures who inflicted the type of handiwork described in the second and last issue of *Real Mystery Magazine*:

> When the girl was turned over on her back, an even greater desecration was discovered. Her lips had been sewed together with heavy thread so that her screaming would be muffled and faint, and the maiden's wide-staring eyes told mutely of the further horrors she must have had to suffer. Her abdomen showed plainly the marks of a mutilating knife, while one of her virginal, firm little breasts had been completely amputated, and the other breast cut and slashed until it had become a ragged mound of blood-spewing horror.

Whew!

And as it goes in the pulp world, other publishers soon followed suit with their own versions of the weird-menace tale and for a time this strange market flourished. Titles such as *Sinister Stories*, *Startling Mystery*, and *Uncanny Tales* followed and traces of the weird-menace influence would show up in the detective genre (*Gangland Detective Stories*) and in science fiction pulps (*Dynamic Science Stories*).

Perhaps the greatest attraction of these magazines was the garishly brutal sex-sadism scenes on their covers. The masters in this field, Walter Baumhofer, Norm Saunders and Jerome Rosen, did for the reader what the Grand Guignol did for the Parisian theatergoer — provide a brief vision of Hell. Most of Rosen's pulp covers for the *Wu Fang* and *Dr. Yen-Sin* pulps showed the weird-menace influence of his *Dime Mystery* work, with Fu Manchu lookalikes inflicting standard shudder pulp tortures on scantily-clad females.

Both writers and artists sought to outdo one another in depicting these pulp horrors as the genre approached critical mass:

> In wooden boxes half-filled with straw, ranged along the wall, there were now eight whimpering infants, all squirming and pitiful in their pain. Each was strangely bandaged with dirty rags. The legs of some were tightly wrapped so that muscles would quickly atrophy and queer deformities result. There were others with bellies squeezed to the diameter of a man's wrist. Several wore wooden cups fastened over their skulls with openings through which bones might later bulge as the infants grew.

Pushing further and further for more outrageous themes, Arthur Burks, who had a reputation for producing quality *Weird Tales* fiction, must have been a bit short when he cranked out "Mates for the Morgue Master" in the December 1939 *Mystery Tales*. With this story of necrophilia ("I shook her again, calling her name. Then I remembered I had roused her from the dead. I began to stroke her body with swift, hot hands. I kissed her on the lips, and almost wept when there was no response.") the public tolerance was being severely tested. If the torture of infants and necrophilia were not enough, cannibalism would finish the job:

> With a straining squeal of avid lust, he leaped suddenly forward, seized the warm, soft body of the girl and buried his face against her soft thigh — the girl's straining throat gave forth an ear-splitting howl of absolute anguish as he did so! And when the idiot straightened up again, his mouth and chin were running with Paula's red blood, and on the soft roundness of her upper leg there appeared a deep, ragged hole, gushing crimson.

This scene was the second, and last, piece of horror fiction by Holden Sanford and helped to usher in the end of the shudder pulps. There was a war on the horizon and its promise of real horrors, as already seen in the Spanish Civil War, the Japanese incursion into

China, and Mussolini's rape of Ethiopia, over-shadowed the fantasy horror of the shudder pulps.

Today, because of their unusual content and outrageously conceived cover art they are avidly sought by collectors, and what Harry Steeger observed of the Grand Guignol Theater is true of the shudder pulps: the more gruesome the act, the better the audience likes it.

Weird Tales was a more palatable genre magazine. It produced a brand of fantasy fiction that was popular with the public, and managed to produce some major genre writers as well. Between 1923 and 1954, 279 issues of *Weird Tales* included stories by Robert E. Howard, August Derleth, H. P. Lovecraft, Ray Bradbury and Robert Bloch. Two new forms of fantasy fiction appeared as well: the sword and sorcery story and Lovecraft's Cthulhu Mythos, both of which have outlived their pulp roots.

Of *Weird Tales*, historian Sam Moscowitz has said:

> Some magazines have a soul. *Weird Tales* was such a magazine. Few periodicals inspire such loyalty from its authors and such devotion from its readers.*

More than any other genre, the horror/weird pulps not only eschewed sports and games of any kind, they reflected the disdain expressed by H. P. Lovecraft in a February 3, 1932, letter to James F. Morton:

> Meaningless spotted pasteboards, carved castles and horses' heads, little balls flying in the air, big balls kicked and grappled by future bond salesmen and bankers, little balls knocked around with sticks in the hands of unimaginative manufacturers and senile plutocrats, horses goaded into foam while describing frantic circles that land them exactly where they started out ...
> ...glory of sport ... rah, rah, rah.†

The Bug-Eyed Monsters

Science fiction has been called the soul of American technology. Its prominence in today's film industry represents an amazing

---

*Moskowitz, Sam, Introduction to Worlds of Weird, *Pyramid Books, 1965.*
†Lovecraft, H.P., Selected Letters 1932–1934, *August Derleth and James Turner, editors. Arkham House Publishers, Inc., 1976.*

climb from relative obscurity in the pulp magazines; this kind of fiction was read only by a handful of devotees (often referred to disparagingly as nerds et al.).

In its first incarnation in *Amazing Stories* (1st issue, dated April 1926) science fiction was pure space opera. According to Brian Aldiss (*Space Opera: An Anthology of Way-Back-When Futures*), space opera is full of "melodrama, dreams, and a seasoning of screwy ideas," not to mention a plethora of bug-eyed monsters, affectionately referred to as BEMs by the devoted. Space opera is for fun. Science fiction is somewhat heady, concerned as it is with complex societal conditions further complicated by conflicts arising out of psychological/political/scientific circumstances which have been extrapolated from solid science using logically-plotted stories.

In the introduction to *Space Opera*, Aldiss says that "space opera was born of the pulp magazines, flourished there, and died there." He couldn't have been more wrong! In 1973, Alan Ladd, Jr., then a junior executive at Twentieth Century–Fox, was approached by George Lucas. Lucas was trying to sell Ladd a movie idea he had recently, and unsuccessfully, pitched to Universal Pictures. Mr. Lucas was asking for a minimum of ten million bucks to back a space opera. Fortunately for young Ladd, he decided to bankroll the film which was released in 1977. *Star Wars* became an instant success of galactic scale.

The modern version of the space opera first appeared in the pages of *Amazing Stories*. While there were earlier such stories in the dime novels and in hardcover by numerous hands including Jules Verne, a man who has been called the "inventor" of science fiction (Peter Costello's biography, *Jules Verne — Inventor of Science Fiction*), there are stories which could qualify as such in ancient Greek literature; stories involving such science fiction topics as utopian societies and moon trips. The modern science fiction story did appear in various general fiction magazines before World War I (*Science Fiction by Gaslight*), but it was Hugo Gernsback's *Amazing Stories* that would define modern science fiction, or at least take the first few steps in that direction by packaging this fiction in magazine format and by selling it to a six-figure-sized audience on a monthly basis. He can truly be said to have created the science fiction market. *Amazing Stories'* format differed from that of the pre–WWI general fiction magazines in that it was *all* science fiction.

Science fiction was published after the pulp era as well as in the years preceding it, but the golden years for the science fiction pulps were circumscribed by Day in his *Index to the Science Fiction Magazines: 1926–1950*, a compendium of more than 50 different science fiction pulp magazines.

The Heroes

The popularity of hero pulps has not diminished over the last four decades. A few of the pulp hero characters (most notably Doc Savage and the Shadow) are familiar to the general public and a number of pulp heroes have had paperback reprints in one or more editions (*Captain Future, Doc Savage, Doctor Death, Dusty Ayers, G-8 and His Battle Aces, Jim Hatfield, Operator 5, The Shadow* and *The Avenger*, to name a few). Collectibles in their own right (mainly as reading copies), these reprints have not affected the appetite for their pulp originals.

Hero pulps with large runs include *The Avenger* (24 titles), *Bill Barnes, Air Adventurer* (61), *The Black Bat* (62), *Dan Fowler (G-Men Magazine)* (112), *Doc Savage* (181 titles, plus new material by Will Murray), *G-8 and His Battle Aces* (110), *KI-Gor (Jungle Stories)* (59), *The Lone Eagle* (66 titles, several in *The American Eagle* and *American Eagles*, and one in *Sky Fighters*), *Operator 5* (48), *The Phantom Detective* (170), *Secret Agent X* (41), *The Shadow* (325), and *The Spider* (118).

Hero pulps with low runs include *The Angel Detective* (1 title), *Anthony Hamilton (Famous Spy Stories)* (1), *Big Chief Western* (3), *Captain Combat* (3), *Captain Hazzard* (1), *Captain Zero* (3), *Cash Gorman* (2), *Dan Dunn* (2), *Dr. Yen-Sin* (3), *Don Diavolo* (5), *Flash Gordon (Strange Adventures Magazine)* (1), *Hopalong Cassidy* (3), *Ka-Zar* (3), *Matalaa (Red Starr Adventures)* (4), *The Man in the Red Mask* (2 titles in *Red Mask Detective*, one each in *Red Hood Detective* and *Movie Detective*), *Nick Carter* (3 titles in *The Shadow Magazine*), *The Octopus* (1), *The Pecos Kid Magazine* (5), *The Scorpion* (1), *The Secret Six* (4), *Sheena Queen of the Jungle* (1 title and 1 in *Jungle Stories*), *The Silver Buck* (1 title and two each in *Red Star Western* and *Silver Buck Western*), *Tailspin Tommy* (2), *Terrence X O'Leary's War Birds* (3) and *The Wizard* (4).

The B-Western hero of the silver screen, Buck Jones, had a limited-edition pulp magazine, and at one time a Tom Mix pulp was discussed but never produced; and every now and then a "new" pulp hero character is discovered and reported in one of the several pulp fanzines. Two examples of this are Dr. Coffin, who appeared in several issues of *Thrilling Detective*, and the Whispering Monk who appeared in but one issue of *All Detective Magazine*.

The hero characters are of great interest to those who research the history and lore of the pulps as they embody those slam-bang stories which, when not dismissed out of hand, were blamed for inducing current psychological and/or societal problems, just as the title character in *The Music Man* blamed the "trouble in River City" on the dime novel.

The Railroad Pulps

The railroad pulps were the first single-subject pulp magazines. Americans have always been in love with the old coal-fired steam train and when Frank Munsey published the first of the railroad pulps in 1906 (*The Railroad Man's Magazine*) he was hoping to cash in on this fascination. *The Railroad Man's Magazine* was one of six identified in Munsey's market analysis of the 1893 magazine market and the first pulp targeted to a very narrow target audience. The others (*Munsey's Magazine, The Argosy, The Scrap-Book, The All-Story Magazine,* and *The Ocean*) targeted general audiences. This was the early period of the pulp era, a time when probably any title would succeed.

The Railroad Man's Magazine would be followed by Munsey's *Railroad Stories*, the most popular of the railroad pulps, in 1929. In between these two publication dates, *Railroad Magazine* was first published.

During the Great Depression the railroads transported both those who had the fare and many who didn't. It was the job of the railroad dicks to see to it that those who didn't were summarily dumped from the train. *Railroad Detective Stories*, a pulp which is only rumored to have existed, told these stories.

The *Railroad Stories* department "On the Spot" gave readers a chance to comment on the accuracies of the non-fiction articles:

> The Virginia Central Railroad, 38 miles long, operates as an interchange between the C&O at Orange, VA, and the RF&P, the

> ACL and the Southern at Fredericksburg, VA. It was incorporated in 1856 as the Orange & Gordonsville Railway, later becoming the Potomac, Fredericksburg & Piedmont, and then the Orange & Fredericksburg. In 1925 this road was changed from narrow to standard gauge and became known as the Virginia Central.

Fiction in the railroad pulps was generally well-written and always fact-based. When the facts were not accurate there was always a reader ready to correct the mistakes or oversights, as in the foregoing.

The idea of a single-subject pulp took hold and it wasn't long before sports were of more interest than railroads. There would then be dozens of sports pulp titles on the newsstand and only one of the railroad titles (*Railroad Magazine*).

The Cowboys

From the turn of the century through the 1920s, western fiction was found mainly in the general pulp magazines such as Frank Munsey's *Argosy*, *Adventure*, *Popular*, *Short Stories* and *Blue Book*. These magazines carried a variety of fiction genres and publishers and editors soon discovered America's love affair with the so-called "oater," a discovery which led inevitably to the all-western pulp magazine.

Western Story Magazine was converted from dime-novel format to pulp format in 1919 and carried in its 144 pages, one novel, two serials, three short stories, one Western fact article, and a number of departments covering western geography, mining, letters to the editor, and lists of missing persons submitted by friends and relatives.

> Jackson, Madeline Hope: Mother's maiden name was Ruth Barrett. Last heard from at Torrington, Wyoming. Please write to your father, Clyde D. Jackson, Edgerton, Wyoming.

Western Story was not the only all-western pulp to start up in the 1920s. Others included *West*, *Frontier*, *Cowboy Stories*, *Ace High*, *Ranch Romances*, *Western Adventures*, *Triple-X Western*, *Lariat* and *Northwest Stories*. *Western Story* was the best of the lot, producing consistent quality fiction by William Colt McDonald, Fred Glidden (Luke Short), Hugh Cave, Walt Coburn, W. C. Tuttle, and the king of Western fictioneers, Frederick Faust.

Faust, the most prolific if not the most talented of western writers, produced a flood of western fiction under multiple pen names, the most popular of which was Max Brand. *Western Story* also had some of the best pulp cover artists, among whom Gerry Delano and Nick Eggenhoffer stand out.

Wild West Weekly, another popular western published in the 1920s, took the Young Wild West of the dime novels and transformed him into Billy West, young part-owner if the Circle J Ranch in Montana's Bitterroot Mountains. Cleary patterned after the dime-novel prototype, the popularity of *Wild West Weekly* did not derive from this imitation but would arrive with more timely pulp characters such as Sonny Tabor (loosely based on Billy the Kid) and *Kid* Wolf, a more characteristic pulp cowboy hero.

The publishers and editors, always alert to sales figures, reacted with more than 140 all-western pulp magazines over the decades of the 1920s, 1930s, 1940s, and into the 1950s. Among the great popular writers who worked in these magazines were Louis L'Amour, Elmore Leonard, Erle Stanley Gardner and Robert E. Howard.

Love & Sex Pulps

The love pulps were an interesting genre. They were extremely popular in their day and the genre seems to have survived in the form of Harlequin and other "romance" paperbacks, yet they remain virtually worthless as collectors' items.

The love pulps featured the more noble romantic themes involving meaningful relationships, chaste sexual encounters, and the culmination of romantic entanglements in marriage. The sex pulps had none of this but featured casual, but usually innocent, sexual fantasy material, and they are extremely collectable today. Women read the love pulps; men the sex pulps! No surprises here.

The love pulps came in three basic packages: solo love stories, detective-theme tie-ins, and Western tie-ins (of which there were a large number). The best of the straight love pulps was *Love Story Magazine*.

Although *Love Story Magazine* had been around since 1921, it wasn't until 1929 that the magazine's sales shifted into high gear with the arrival of Daisy Bacon as editor. Within three years of Ms. Bacon taking over the editorial reigns, circulation had risen to

600,000. The magazine became so popular that Street & Smith made it a weekly and it quickly became the top newsstand seller in its field. Later on, the indefatigable Ms. Bacon would also edit *Real Love* (a first-person magazine which lasted only two years), *True Love Stories*, *Pocket Love* (collections of love stories in paperback format), and *Romantic Range*, one of the many Western tie-ins on the market. None of these magazines would approach the success of *Love Story Magazine*.

Love Story Magazine carried the following hype in its front pages as a sort of truth-in-packaging preview:

> *Love Story Magazine* has recently made its appearance. Its contents are, as the name implies, based upon the greatest thing in the World: love. *Love Story* is not just another of those sex-problem magazines which have done incalculable harm. *Love Story* is clean at heart and its stories are written around the love of one man for one woman. Civilization has been built upon this sort of love — all the great accomplishments of mankind have been inspired by good women who were greatly beloved....

The sex-exploitation pulps all featured great cover girlie art and prose visions of milk-white bosoms (usually swelling) and flashing thighs. Most of these stories did not take events "all the way," as was said in those simpler days, and the sexual tone was more suggestive than explicit. Some, however, like *Saucy Detective*, went further:

> He reached out to caress her breasts, to cup the lush mounds...
> His hands slipped lingeringly down to her rounded thighs,
> stroked her legs, [etc.].

The cover art and interior line drawings in the explicit sex pulps were a bit more daring; for example, nipples were shown (almost all the ladies in the cover art were shown in imminent danger of being stabbed just over a breast).

The four most popular sex pulps were the Culture Publications, Inc. (later Trojan) spicy titles: *Spicy Detective*, *Spicy Adventure*, *Spicy Mystery* and *Spicy Western*. Cover art by H. J. Ward was exceptional and one of the principal reasons that readers coughed up their thin dimes.

The Flyboys

Of the approximately 50 war titles, better than 40 were devoted to World War I air battles, and the air-war genre would remain popular until the realities of World War II air battles overshadowed the pulp air wars. The contents of the air-war pulps were usually summarized in the table of contents where one could get at least the gist of the story:

> "The Dead Won't Help You": The Germans were already toasting their certain victory — but they reckoned so without Jeff Carver. Get a fighting fool of a Yank ace, give him enough plane, and anything can happen.
> "We'll Drink to the Living": McNamara and Molloy, a pair of wild-flying giants who hurl their Spads around with the same hair-trigger skill and reckless abandon as their rock-sized fists, are out for vengeance and destruction.

While the prose style remained constant over the war years, the villains, who were rather ill-defined between the two World Wars, changed to our World War II enemies after the attack on Pearl Harbor:

> "Seahawks from Hell": December 7, 1941, two hate-filled warbirds batter each other while Japanese destroyers prowl the Pacific.

This piece is an example of the evolution of air wars from Spads and Fokkers to P-51s, P-38s, and B-17s.

Included in each of the air-war pulps was a section devoted to reader commentary and a non-fiction piece such as those printed in the *Sky Fighter's Caterpillar Club*. The May 1938 *Sky Fighters* non-fiction piece was hailed as "One of a series of famous parachute leaps as compiled by Lt. Jay Blaufox." This piece concerned a pair who claimed to have parachuted out of the Goodyear Blimp over downtown Chicago. The content of these "non-fiction" pieces was highly questionable at best — in all probability they were written from local movie house experience.

The writers of these action yarns were an interesting breed of cottage-industry hacks who found little difficulty in transforming an old western taken from their files into an air-war yarn. With little difficulty the cowboy was made a pilot, the old trusty mare changed into a Spad, the ranch into an aerodrome, the six-gun showdown on a dusty street became an aerial battle against an azure-blue sky, and so on until the old Western was ready to ship off to *Dare-Devil Aces.*

Perhaps the most popular air-war pulps were those that featured a series hero the likes of Terrence X O'Leary or Bill Barnes — Air Adventurer. Barnes had his own pulp magazine and would usually be able to out-maneuver and out-shoot the enemy because of his ability to develop unique prototype aircraft which could take any enemy out of the skies:

> The BF-4D is a low-wing, all-metal, two-place fighter. It is powered with the Barnes twin-diesel motor, developing 3,000 horsepower at 20,000 feet.... Drives two triple-bladed, automatic-pitch propellers which revolve in opposite directions, thus neutralizing torque....

Dusty Ayers and His Battle Aces took the air war into the next generation with such stories as "The Telsa Raider" in which the enemy has a weapon capable of "cleaning the allies out of the skies" — a mysterious "Telsa" cannon which shoots a ring of fire which envelops the doomed aircraft.

The most popular of the air-war pulps was *G-8 and His Battle Aces,* featuring a character who fought his epic battles with some of pulpdom's strangest villains.

> On silent wings of night came a weird bird of doom — and to hear its voice meant to die a madman's death! While all civilization lies sentenced to this monstrous fate, G-8 and his Battle Aces roar into the death-laden skies to stop the fiend who holds the fate of the World in his hands.

But fear not — G-8 is on the job:

> Then, with a rush, angry orange burst around the Jerry's belly, swallowing the center of the fuselage. The green ship rocked off on one tip and the nose pitched down. In a dozen seconds more it was caught in the first deadly spiral of a spin. The greasy black smoke scarred the sky as it fell.

Clearly, the villains made G-8 stories unique and accounted in great part for the long publication run of this pulp.

The Rest

The major genres: science fiction, detective, western, horror and hero pulps could not contain the imagination of the pulps. For the ladies there were the love pulps with stories of romance and marriage. Often combined with one of the major genres (as in *Ranch Romances*), the love pulps were marketed straight at the ladies, much as the Harlequin paperbacks are today.

If it's sex you're looking for, try one of dozens of titles the likes of *Saucy Movie Stories* or *Spicy Detective Stories*. The sex pulps were quite mild (considered in hindsight); sexual encounters were suggested offstage happenings.

There were pulps devoted to the railroads (*Railroad Stories*), newspapers (*Newspaper Adventure Stories*), the Civil War (*Civil War Stories*), ghosts and witches (*Ghost Stories, The Witch's Tales*), and aviation (*Army-Navy Flying Stories*). There were pulps describing war on the ground (*Over the Top*), in the air (*Flying Aces*) and at sea (*Navy Stories*). There was a pulp devoted to the Zeppelin (*Zeppelin Stories*) and dozens of straight-up adventure pulps such a *South Sea Stories*. There were pulps with nothing but spy stories (*Spy Novels Magazine*), the Foreign Legion (*Foreign Legion Adventures*), and criminal gangs (*Gang World Stories*).

Pulp editors were continually looking for untapped subject matter, of which there was very little as the number of subjects grew to the limits over the first decades of the twentieth century. Just when you thought all possible pulp bases were covered, along came *American Autopsy*.

All in all there were over 1,000 different pulp titles published over the pulp era. Judging by numbers alone, the sports pulps ranked seventh in popularity behind the detective genre, westerns, adventure pulps, love pulps, science fiction pulps, hero and aviation pulps.

Sports in the Pulps

In an article (*The Dime Novel and Its Successors*) about the demise of the dime novels, Edward LeBlanc discusses the forces which led to some new forms of popular fiction: movies, boys' and girls' series books and the pulps.

The three major genres represented in the dime novels were detective fiction, the western and sports fiction. Dime novel sports fiction can be summed as the Merriwell saga and all the rest. While the Merriwell saga extended into the pulp era in *Sport Story Magazine* (and later in *Super Sports*), this juvenile fiction was clearly at the end of its popularity. It was only the beginning of the athlete as hero, however, and this theme would be produced in the boys' series books. Series books were based on the adventures of a single character and were often referred to as "juveniles" (after their target audience).

The Stratemeyer Syndicate, as it would come to be known, was to series hardcover books what Henry Ford was to automobile production and Currier and Ives were to popular lithography. Over the post–dime novel era its books would achieve great popularity with juveniles and their parents. It is not uncommon today to find sentimental flyleaf inscriptions from relatives when one is fortunate enough to find surviving examples of these books in used-book stores.

Sports were one of the most popular subjects in the boys' series books, second to adventure/mystery subjects the likes of "The Lakewood Boys in the African Jungle." There were sports series such as the Lansing series (1912–1915): "Batter Up," "The Winning Hit," and "Fair Play" and there were sport stories within a series like the Oakdale Series (1911–1913): "Rival Pitchers of Oakdale." One of the more popular sports series, the Baseball Joe books (14 books in the period 1912–1928), was written by Stratemeyer under the pseudonym Henry Chadwick.

There would be basketball series (Basketball Series, three books, 1926–1930); hockey series (Hockey Series, three books, 1929–1931); football series (Football Stories, twelve books, 1914–1927), and sports books would appear in most of the schoolboy series (The Oakdale Series, The High School Boys Series, etc.). Through the 1940s there was only an occasional girls' book with a sports setting (*The Girls of Central High*, 1914; *Billy Bradley Winning the Trophy*, 1932), a fact which pretty much reflects the public role of girls in sports at the time.

As popular as the series books were, they were purely juvenile fiction with simply-drawn characters and plot situations and it would be up to the pulps to extend the range of sports fiction beyond the juvenile saga.

The new pulp fiction was a mass-produced hero saga aimed at a slightly more mature audience. Indeed, in some cases where adult themes such as political corruption creep into the plot, a post-adolescent audience was hoped for. Plots were pure pulp and so were the characters in these stories, although there were a few pleasant surprises such as this piece done in the style of Damon Runyon:

> I am sitting on a hard seat in the Superson Theater on 42nd Street, New York City, watching a double or maybe it is a triple feature, when on comes the newsreel and I see a very annoying picture of Felony Jones crowning Miss Sports of Miami Beach.
> —"Cutie and the Beast" by Tom Thursday, *Super Sports*.

Similarly, the *Popular Sports* piece "Freud on Cleats" by William Mayer explores the comedic possibilities of the pulp sports story with a player who tries to improve the game of football using Freudian analysis.

The workaday sports character was drawn in part from a subspecies of the detective genre—the defective detective. This detective (usually a private eye) was a protagonist with a problem, usually some physical deformity, sometimes a bad habit such as drinking booze, but always a man true to his calling. He will serve his client come broken head, betrayal, or worse. He will do what he has been paid to do, even if he hasn't been paid.

After the story of the star, the hometown hero, you will begin to see these men. There is baseball's Baldy Peterson — a hypochondriac, Mike Shannon — the ex-con, the coward, the ego-maniac, the congenital choker, the windbag, the man with the chicken wing or chicken heart, the drunk, the punchdrunk and the guy who is too old to compete anymore. When the defective hero is set into a pulp sports plot he must first overcome his personal problem and then, typically, a larger social problem into which he has been placed by virtue of his personal problem, before he can then attend to the sports problem (typically, the BIG game).

For the non-sports enthusiast or the marginal follower of sporting events, the element of a BIG game is a necessity. H. P. Lovecraft, in a January 16, 1932, letter to Robert E. Howard, spells it out: "I suppose my primary coolness towards games lies in the fact that they are only symbolically connected with any larger end." Speaking metaphorically about the Persian Wars, Lovecraft goes on: "When the pair are transferred from the battlefield to a prize ring where nothing but a purse is decided, I find my interest in the combat rapidly waning."*

The BIG game/fight/race/whatever is the most common of sports pulp lots and all the minor pulp problems come together there. Often, the BIG game has its own dramatic coin as well. Will the hero settle the score with his (unworthy) adversary? Will he throw the fight or the race? Can he come back from ... you name it? Unlike dime-novel fiction, the hero sometimes loses the BIG game, but rarely does he fail to overcome his personal conflict.

While the pulp sports yarn can be defined as the finite, two-person zero-sum game (one winner, one loser), the game theory utility-function concept applies. In short, while the pulp hero player may win (or lose) the BIG game, he may also win (or lose) some secondary plot objective (the girl, self respect, etc.).

Ultimately, the pulp sports hero would be restricted by the rules and realities of the game. He cannot, like the Merriwells, win every

---

*Lovecraft, H.P. Selected Letters 1932–1934, August Derleth and James Turner, editors, Arkham House Publishers, 1976.

game or fight. The pulp formula would have to reflect this reality to make conflict resolution believable. So the pulp formula would sometimes push the winning or losing into the background, thus humanizing the conflict. Whether or not Slugger Casey ripped the cover off the ball became less important than the circumstances of subplots that rode on his performance. Winning was not "the only thing," although often the pulp sports hero had his cake and ate it.

The first of the sports pulp stories were in the general fiction magazines like *Argosy* and *Blue Book*. While not common, they did achieve enough popularity to warrant an occasional cover story. In 1923 the first all-sport format pulp would be published by Street & Smith: *Sport Story Magazine*. Harold Hersey observes, in his autobiography *Pulpwood Editor*:

> Street & Smith, with its usual foresight in the matter of fundamental titles, has made a success of *Sport Story Magazine*, though the circulation of the sheet has never equaled that of Love/Detective/Western story titles.*

In Quentin Reynolds' history of Street & Smith (*Fiction Factory*) he describes *Sport Story Magazine*'s circulation rising "immediately" to 150,000 as not large by Street & Smith standards but "a steady circulation with few returns."† In 1928 the first single-sport pulp would be published by Fight Stories Inc., one of the Fiction House group of pulp magazines. Later, there would be single-sport pulps for basketball, baseball and football.

Sports fiction would evolve from the occasional story found in the general fiction magazines of the type published by Frank Munsey to the point where the titled format identified a guaranteed sports story each month (*Ace-High Magazine — Western, Action and Sport Stories*). An occasional sports story would find its way into the western, adventure and detective/mystery fiction pulps, and speculative sports fiction could be found occasionally in the science fiction pulps. In fact, the science fiction/fantasy sports story would prove to be the most literate as well as the most imaginative in the pulp format. Sports fiction of any sort in the hero, war, railroad,

---

*Hersey, Harold Brainerd, Pulpwood Editor, Frederick A. Stokes Company, 1937.
†Reynolds, Quentin, The Fiction Factory, or From Pulp Row to Quality Street, *Random House*, 1955.

horror/weird, and romance/love/sex pulps was a rarity. The types of sports represented covered the gamut: track, rowing, mountain climbing, tennis, baseball, as well as obscure sports like automobile polo. There was no sport, no matter how you define the activities subsumed by the word, which was not represented at some time or other in the pulps, and there were two westerns with a titled focus on the rodeo.

While the general fiction pulps were free to include sports stories of any sort, as were the general sports magazines which followed, there was a class of magazines which focused on one sport, the first of which (1928) was *Fight Stories*. This category included magazines dedicated to what are now the big television-viewing sports: baseball, boxing, basketball and football.

While the popularity of the sports pulps covers, roughly, three decades, there were three levels of durability within the span of their popularity, roughly 1923–1955.

Street & Smith's *Sport Story Magazine* was first published in 1923 and remained on the newsstand until 1943. Its 20-year run, long for any magazine, is a record for the general fiction sports pulps. There were 11 sports pulps which had a minimum 10-year life span: (*Dime Sports, Baseball Stories, Best Sports, Complete Sports, Fight Stories, Five Sports Classics, Popular Sports Magazine, Sports Novels Magazine, Sports Winners, Thrilling Football Stories* and *Thrilling Sports*). With the exception of *Dime Sports* (1931–1944), these magazines were first published in either the late 1920s or early 1930s and ran through 1949 or the early 1950s, when they ran into the brick wall of television.

At the other end of the durability scale there were a number of sports pulps which did not last more than three issues, and in some cases they were one-shot publications. Their short lives, not an unusual pulp magazine phenomenon, can be attributed to the myriad circumstances which affected all publishers. These pulps were published over the period 1927–1950, most appearing in the late 1930s and 1940s: *All-American Sports, All-Baseball Stories, All Football Stories, Basketball Stories, Big Baseball Stories, Bull's Eye Sports, Exciting Baseball, Jack Dempsey's Fight Magazine, The Life of Gene Tunney, Popular Baseball, Real Sports, Sports Action, Sports Leaders Magazine, Thrilling Baseball,* and *Variety Sports Magazine*.

The 1920s, which marked the beginning of the pulp all-sports format, were a decade of emerging interest in sports. In this period attendance at college football games doubled. Pro football attendance grew steadily and tennis would capture public interest. In 1923, the West Side Tennis Club built the first modern tennis facility in the United States with a seating capacity of 14,000. While there was little interest in golf before 1920, the country club with its 18-hole course came of age during the decade. Interestingly, attendance at baseball games over the same period failed to match population growth. Pro basketball (American Basketball League) had some success over the last half of the '20s and attendance grew through 1946 when the National Basketball Association was created.

To grasp the impact of sports over the 1920s one has only to look at the sports figures of the day: baseball's Ruth, boxing's Dempsey, tennis' Tilden, football's Grange and golf's Bobby Jones — all characters of mythic proportions. Sports interest would decline during the Depression and World War II but was kept alive in no small part by radio broadcasts of sports events (mostly baseball and boxing) and the sports pulps. Both the radio broadcast and the pulp required a certain amount of mental activity. To keep up with the action over the airwaves or on the course, pulp page required some imagination.

Every Red Sox away game, for example, was broadcast back to Boston via telegraph key. Prior to the game the radio announcer would have broadcast the lineups and warmed up his listening audience with some baseball chatter. The key began clicking out a shorthand message something like "Cronin out 5–3." The announcer would turn up the background crowd noise and then, with much enthusiasm, report "Joe Cronin slams a hard ground ball to Apling's left — Luke grabs the handle and fires the ball...." There would be long silences, more clacking of the telegraph key, and more "telegraphic re-creations" by the announcer over the long, hot summers of the 1930s and '40s.

One saw in one's mind's eye the field, the stands, the players and the action and to the extent that these were creations of tangible synaptic firings and intangible mental processes, the activity was intellectual. Not fusion physics, perhaps, but nonetheless intellectual. Television broadcasts of sporting events would bypass this process. Viewing the event was a passive yet visceral process and would ultimately play a major role in the decline of the sports pulp magazine.

Discounting the typical female roles of the era, there was little female presence in the sports pulps. The sports of the era which were generally available to women focused on "the joy of movement" and this would not be perceived as having market value by the sports pulp editors. In the professional ranks, there were women swimmers, golfers and tennis players but, like the "joy of movement" activities, they could not compete with a World Series game or a heavyweight fight, or so the editors felt.

A review of girls' series books published between 1840 and 1991 shows that girls and women appeared in fewer than ten sports stories, and these were largely of the "joy of movement" variety. There were exceptions of course: John Tunis' *American Girl* (1930), which was a fictionalized treatment of the life of tennis star Helen Wills Moody, and the earlier (1929) *Mother of a Champion*, which placed the Moody character (Florence Farley) in circumstances involving greed and corruption.

The sports pulp was a man's reading. In the December 1947 *Super Sports* pulps there appears the following ad for falsies:

> A thrilling, glamorous, bustline — instantly! ... with Outlaws ... styled in Hollywood.... Don't feel embarrassed because of a flat chest and unappealing body lines a minute longer! Follow the example of movie stars by wearing Outlaws.

This ad carries the not-too-subliminal sports pulp message for a woman who might be reading a brother's or a boyfriend's copy. Interestingly, the name of the bra was lifted from the Howard Hughes film of the same name. The Hughes-designed bra, according to Jane Russell, was never worn in the film.

Pulp ads were earthy: "False Teeth by Mail — Send No Money"; "NOW! Get amazing new comfort and relief with RUPTURE-EASER!"; and the ever present Charles Atlas ad that promised all the skinny kids a new body: "I can make YOU a new man in only 15 minutes a day."

These ads were common to all pulps, not just the sports pulps. Sports pulp ads rarely aimed a product specifically at the sports market. A rare exception is the June 1950 *Sports Fiction* ad for a souvenir autographed baseball from any of the eight National or American League teams. The price was $1.98 and the balls were undoubtedly signed by others than those whose names were shown. This was, however, probably one of the first commercials for what would evolve into the sports collectible craze.

The sports pulp itself — the physical magazine — was identical to all the other pulps. There were three sizes: the standard 7 × 10 inches, 128 pages; the bedsheet, 8½ × 11 inches, 66 pages; and the digest, 5¼ × 7¼ inches and 128 pages. Page count would vary between magazines and within the publication history of one magazine, but these were the basic dimensions. The sports pulps would publish only in the standard format until the 1950s, when the digest form became favored by *Best Sports* as part of a last-ditch survival plan.

Prices varied from a low of 10¢ to a high of 25¢, with 5¢ multiples between these two figures. Again, this was pretty much in line with the rest of the pulps except for the short-lived *Nickel Western* and *Nickel Detective*. Some of the pulps (like *12 Sports Aces*) published all fiction, but most had a balance of fiction, sports fact material, and so-called departments (short, fact-based filler material). Most of the sports pulps had the typical artwork: a glitzy, slick cover with a few interior line drawings at the front of each story. Many of the sports pulps, *Baseball Stories* for example, had newspaper-type sports-page art. The Summer 1949 *Baseball Stories* had a full-page devoted to Lou Gehrig and a full-page of Satchel Paige artwork similar to that found in the major newspapers. The accompanying text was also typical of the illustrated newspaper profile.

The sports pulp faced the same problem as the modern-day news magazine faces. It couldn't compete with the newspaper for timeliness of information, so, instead of reporting daily scores of current league standings, it sought to do material with a broader view ("All-America Candidates for 1939"), biographical pieces ("Fritz Chrisler—Pigskin Pulmotor"), opinion pieces ("Red Sox—Boom or Bust?") or the inside-story feature ("How the Yanks Make Their Stars"). All of the material was upbeat; there were no sexual or personal exposés. It was the best of all possible worlds. Except...

One would have to look long and hard for a story of the women's baseball league started by Wrigley to keep baseball alive until the men returned from World War II. There were occasional pieces. One would have to look even harder for stories of black baseball. I remember as a boy watching black pitcher Cannonball Will Jackman set down the Lynn (MA) Frasers when he was well into his fifties. It was the most exciting baseball I ever saw. Jackman was a submarine pitcher with a fastball reputed to be better than Bob Feller's in his prime. I can see him pitch in my mind's eye to this day. But don't look for black baseball in the sports pulps; you won't find it there.

The majority of sports fiction in the pulp magazines was white, male and professional. This was unfortunate; the pulps missed an opportunity to develop a focus which would have differentiated them from the newspaper coverage of the day.

The Magazines and the Stories

More than 60 general fiction pulps were published over the last half of the nineteenth century and first quarter of the twentieth. Many of them had an occasional sports story. In the 150 plus detective/mystery/crime pulps published during the pulp era (the first half of the twentieth century) there were occasional sports stories. Sports fiction was rare in the adventure, war, spicy, western hero and aviation pulps, as it was in the science fiction pulps. The all-sports pulps, which numbered 54, were just that — all sports. Most of these covered a wide range of sports, everything from archery to polo, but a few featured only one sport.

An examination of the progression of the pulp sports story from the general fiction magazines to the all-sports pulps gives some idea of the origins and evolution of a much neglected chapter of pulp-magazine history. First, then, the general fiction pulps.

The Cavalier

One of Frank Munsey's many publications of the day, *The Cavalier* (1908–1914) was nearly 400 pages of short and long fiction, poetry, and a few ads suitable for family consumption. Featured in *The Cavalier* were the long, serialized stories by H. Bedford Jones and Albert Payson Terhune, to name just a couple of familiar pulp names.

In one of the six short stories in the July 26, 1913, issue (*About That Bout*) the sport of pro wrestling is described as background to a championship match. The most interesting revelation is the hype which surrounded the match at and just after the combatants' signing of the proper papers:

> With these formalities settled, the great Mel-Ball bout was at last put before the public. And the public responded to the feast with enthusiasm. The wrestlers displayed the proper amount of animus through the papers. The newspapers were given inflammable copy by the press-agents which led the public to believe that the two contestants were being fed on raw beef, and that they had to be led by a chain and collar to keep from flying at each other's throats before the time set and agreed upon.

Surfing through the cable channels one can see recreations of these theatrics on today's "rasslin" shows and post weigh-in boxing ceremonies.

Inside the cover of the July 26, 1913, issue, Frank Munsey noted some changes in his magazines: beginning with the June number, *Munsey's Magazine*, the flagship of the Munsey Publishing House, initiated the publication of a complete book-length novel in each issue. This was an epochal event in the making of standard magazines, something distinctly new. It marked the beginning of the end of serial publication in monthly installments. It meant that when the serials then running in *Munsey's Magazine* were finished, all fiction and everything else would be complete in one issue.

Munsey said that this policy had been inaugurated in *The Argosy* and *The All-Story* about a year before (1912). The editorial was captioned in oversized print: "MUNSEY'S MAGAZINE AGAIN BLAZING A NEW PATH" and concluded with the one sentence (the only one necessary) which fully described the planned change: "The only change will be the substitution of the complete book novel for the serial story." It was dated June 2, 1913, and signed by Munsey in bold letters.

Short Stories

The June 19, 1946, issue of *Short Stories* featured the cover story "*Cop's Holiday*" by Wilbur S. Peacock, a murder mystery focused on skeet shooting. The same issue carried the department "The Shooter's Corner" by Pete Kuhlhoff. This particular column was about a gun auction the writer had recently attended. In the same issue, prolific pulp writer Hugh Cave had a white-water rafting story, "White Water Challenge." The October 10, 1946, *Short Stories* carried a cover story about running: "Miracle Mile" by Jackson V. Scholz, a *Sport Story Magazine* regular.

Guns were a popular subject in the general fiction pulps, playing a prominent part in much of the fiction and much of the department coverage as well. One had better be sure of his gun facts when writing an adventure piece; readers would spot any technical discrepancies and send off their observations to the magazine's letters section, "Camp Fire." The DuPont Powder Co. was a frequent adventure advertiser and gun ads were commonplace. The *Short Stories* column "The Shooter's Corner" was an informational editorial on old and then current firearms, often heavy on technical detail. For example: "The Ballard has unusually short lock time, and target shooters generally make it even faster by installing a heavier main spring, lightening the hammer weight and notching it to position closer to the firing pin in the cocked position."

Five-Novels Monthly

Five-Novels Monthly had a little something for everyone: love, murder, high adventure, cowboy yarns — "Every Story Complete." In the early 1930s, many of the "novels" had a strong romance theme. For example, three of the stories in the September 1933 issue are heralded thus: "Conquering Herd — A Vivid Romance of the West"; "Escape — Love and Adventure in India"; and the sports story, "Flashing Mallets — A Glamorous Story of Polo and Love." If I had to guess how many readers of *Five-Novels Monthly* had ever played a chuckker or two of polo or had ever seen a polo match, I would put the figure at none.

"Flashing Mallets" is a pot-boiler about Tommy Chapin, a down-at-the-heels guy with a yearning for Alexis Adriance, a girl whose family history can be traced in *Burke's Peerage*. Not to worry; in this dime-novel plot anything can happen. In true Alger fashion, Tommy impresses the Adriance family with an act of sportsmanship "that was the greatest I've ever seen" when he forsakes a goal to let an opponent (who also happens to be a suitor of young Alexis) recover his dropped helmet — and this despite the opponent's unsportsmanlike conduct.

Entirely predictable and totally forgettable, this is probably one of a handful at most of polo stories ever to find its way into pulpdom.

Blue Book

Blue Book was among the best of the general fiction pulps for a number of reasons, among them that it looked better than the rest. Slightly narrower, it had a more imperial look enhanced by its trimmed pages. Its covers, drawn by the likes of Herbert Morton Stoops, gave the magazine an elite look, and the fiction by pulp pros like Frederick Faust and H. Bedford-Jones made it a quality read.

The plotting in pulp sports fiction was mostly reduced to a single formula: underdog prevails, or the "Rocky" plot. The sports pulp, sometimes avoiding the "big-game" central theme, would occasionally be a good read because of style or character formation, as in the Robert Howard fight stories. This is not unusual in popular literature, as attested to by Chandler's comment about all not being lost if the last few pages of a good hard-boiled yarn had been torn out of the book. While a formula story is often predictable, however, it can be enjoyable on another level: that of the writing style.

Blue Book carried an occasional sports story and they were generally of better quality than the all-sports pulp fiction. The October 1938 "Cauliflowers Bloom in the Ring" by Edward L. English is readable from the opening sentences, "When I was young, I was foolish. I ain't young anymore," to the hero's reaction to some punishment: "I got to wondering why they built that arena on a turntable and why it kept sagging to the left." The story is formula, but interesting because of the central character's Runyonesque style, much like the Howard stories.

Most of the *Blue Book* fiction (including sports fiction) was of this higher quality. Even the ads in *Blue Book* aimed at a higher audience level. No Tijuana Bibles or nose trusses, not even an occasional Johnson Smith Co. ad for those glorious whoopee cushions or joy buzzers. The *Blue Book* ads were few (for the typical pulp format) and were dominated by correspondence schools and those Everready battery ads where the flashlight saves the day for Frank Buck and other lesser heroes.

The Popular Magazine

The turn-of-the-century general fiction pulps carried bits and pieces of sports reportage, trivia and anecdotal material as well as sports fiction. The 200-plus page *The Popular Magazine* of June 20,

1917, had a little something for everyone, including blatant racism. A trivia piece told of Senator Hoke Smith's background as a championship boxer in Atlanta, Georgia. Baseball was the subject of H. C. Witwer's "Swat the Rye," a story which spoke to the influence of booze on the game of baseball. Dave Curtis, the protagonist, is so addicted to the booze that he fails to run out what could be an inside-the-park home run in order to dig up a bottle of hootch buried under first base by the opposition. While the fiction was slapstick, the influence of booze on baseball was more like epic tragedy.

The racist material that freezes you in your seat is under a two-page headline: "Baseball — That's All." Of the five short anecdotal squibs, the following is typical:

> The Value of Education
> Education is a matter of pride in most of us, and particularly in a Southern darky. Last spring one of the major-league clubs was in training in Georgia. As the prepping season drew to a close, the darkies made themselves particularly handy and obsequious. All had hopes of a trip into the fabled North with the ball players. The night the team was to leave arrived. The trunks, traveling bags, suit cases, etc., were being hauled out. There was a scramble for the honor of superintending their disposal on the village express wagon, with one dignified old coon finally winning out, crying as he did so: "Go 'way from here, niggers! Go 'way from here. Kaint you-all see it takes an education to read de 'nitials and names on all dese here baggage.'"

The pervasive racism of the day that is encapsulated in this short piece on baseball speaks more eloquently than academic tracts.

The Popular Magazine was published by Street & Smith, 1903–1931; changed its title to *Popular Stories*, 1927, to *Popular* in 1928, and back to *Popular Magazine* in 1928. *Popular Magazine* contributors included Ralph Barbour, Edward Ellis, Upton Sinclair, Bertha Bower and Rex Beach. Its last issue was October 1931. Street & Smith got sports into many of their products but *Popular Magazine* favored sports somewhat more than most. As stated by editor Henry Harrison Lewis in the first issue (1903), the objective was:

> to publish a monthly magazine that will be read by every boy in the United States and one that will be welcomed by fathers and mothers of the boys.... We start with the belief that every boy

worth having on our list has good red blood in his veins; that he is fond of athletic sports.

Popular Magazine was known as a training ground for slick magazine writers and cover illustrators. Issues of the magazine reflected a shift to adult fiction at the time when Charles Agnew MacLean was made editor. According to Quentin Reynolds, MacLean "discovered" H. G. Wells, was responsible for Zane Grey's writing westerns, "discovered" John Buchan (whose *Thirty-Nine Steps* was first published in *Popular*), and "encouraged" a host of writers including Rex Beach, Jack London, Mary Roberts Rinehart and other notables.

Sports pulp writer Bill Fay tells a story which illustrates the need to be delicate when dealing with editors. It seems that Roland Oliphant, editor of *Popular*, had noticed Fay's sports pieces in *Sports Novels* and *Dime Sports* and asked him what he thought was the difference between these two pulps and his. Not wishing to tell Oliphant they were paying better, he opined something to the effect that *Sports Novels* and *Dime Sports* were striving for a more mature audience. He never again sold to *Popular*.

The Detective Magazines

Sports stories were rare in the pulps and when there was an occasional story with a sports involvement, the sport and the players were secondary to the crime and the perpetrators. Typically, these stories would involve illegal gambling or the fixing of a fight or race. The focus of the story, as one would expect, is on the crime and the detecting, not on details that might enliven the sports activities.

The exception to the rule is to be found in a number of issues of *Dime Detective* where bookie, Mr. Maddox, plies his trade at racetracks across the country. Mr. Maddox is one of only a handful of continuing characters in pulp sports, the others being Robert E. Howard's fighters. This is unusual, as one of the pulp writer's goals was to get (and keep) such a character in print in the hope that a long-term relationship would develop with readers.

Following is a brief review of some of the more successful detective pulps which published the occasional sports story.

Black Mask

Roughly one percent of the 2,509 stories to appear in *Black Mask* over the period 1920–1982 had a sports angle.

Sports, either as background or central-to-the-plot material, were largely missing from all pulp detective fiction. The 1920s spawned the great hard-boiled writers Carrol John Daly and Dashiell Hammett, and in the 1930s genre writers Raoul Whitfield, Paul Cain (Peter Ruric) and Raymond Chandler extended the style and influence, but there were few sports subjects in their works. The hard-boiled writers of the 1940s, Ross MacDonald, Howard Browne and others, generally avoided sports material.

William Campbell Gault's introduction in novel form of ex-L.A. Rams football pro, Brock "The Rock" Callahan, in 1955 (*Ring Around Rosa*) was the first novel-length melding of sports with the hard-boiled story.

Callahan weighed in at 220 lbs and played guard for the Rams after an All-American football career at Stanford. Gault continued to produce Callahan novels well into the 1980s. But while the Rock is *of* the sports world, he never gets involved in a basic sports story. This theme is adopted by a large number of stories to follow: a career in professional sports followed by an injury, followed by a P.I. career, but the hero never works within a sports story.

The first series to set the central character in the middle of a sports environment is the Kin Platt, Max Roper stories. Platt's P.I. Roper appears in seven novels, in each of which a different sport is central to the story. Typically, there is a murder of a sports figure and some secondary crime such as betting, fixes, dope dealing, etc. Although formulaic, the series is entertaining and innovative in its use of the sports milieu.

Stephen Dobyns' series of horseracing novels were followed by Robert Randisi's *Eye in the Ring* (1982), and Richard Rosen started Harvey Blissberg's career in *Strike Three You're Dead* (1984), the same year that Doug Hornig introduced P.I. Loren Swift in *Foul Shot*. A year later, Robert Reeves, in *Doubting Thomas*, introduced P.I. Thomas Thereon, a pro wrestling fan and racetrack regular.

Before these novels, there was rarely a sports angle in the detective pulps. Perhaps the first was a fight story by Carroll John Daly in the September 1923 *Black Mask*: "Kiss the Canvas Crowley." Boxing stories by Frederick Nebel appeared in a few issues of *Black Mask* ("Strumming Sam Malone," July 1930; "Grain to Grain," November 1926; and "With Benefit of Law," November 1927). The P.I. in "Grain to Grain," an ex-boxer, may well be the first ex-jock P.I. of the pulps.

Typical of the sports-angle stories in *Black Mask* are "Strike Three" (June 1938, by Joseph Csida), in which a baseball player is killed on the field; "Club Fighter" (December 1937, by John Lawrence); "One Fall for Murder" (a murder story with a wrestling backdrop by K. Webster, March 1946); and "Hardboot Homicide" by Fergis Truslow, in which the P.I. is an ex-jockey (November 1945). Raymond Chandler's "Guns at Cyrano's," which appeared in the January 1936 *Black Mask*, may well be the best early hardboiled fiction involving the sports world. Chandler's pre–Marlowe P.I., Ted Carmody, becomes involved with a fixed fight where the fix goes wrong, and Chandler shows that he knows his way around boxing's turf and a thing or two about boxing skills:

> The dark one, Deacon Werra, a powerful, loose-limbered Polack with bad teeth and only two cauliflower ears, had the physique but didn't know anything but rough clinching and a giant swing that started in the basement and didn't go anywhere.

Frequently, the race track was used as backdrop for a *Black Mask* story. Such was the case with James McKenna's "Caliente" in the May 1945 issue. This was McKenna's only work in *Black Mask*, a short-short piece told in the first person by boxer Scraf Douglas. The story had little to do with horseracing and nothing to do with boxing. Perhaps the strangest character in this type of story in *Black Mask*, "Strumming Sam Malone" (July 1930 by Cleve Myers) was a boxer and a singing cowboy.

Black Mask was published by Pro-Distributors, Inc. through 1940; then by Popular Publications, Inc. through July 1951. The title was changed from *Black Mask* to *Black Mask Detective* (September 1950), then to *Black Mask Detective Magazine* (July 1951). *Black Mask* is primarily of interest to the researcher looking for seminal hardboiled works of Chandler, Hammett et al., but it is also useful to the researcher interested in early treatment of sports in hard-boiled detective friction.*

---

*Hagemann, E.R., A Comprehensive Index to Black Mask, 1920–1951, Bowling Green University Popular Press, 1982.

Spicy Detective

Among the detective pulps there was a sub-genre that tested the limits of public morality at the time. *Spicy Detective* was the first of a quartet of "spicy" titles (*Adventure, Mystery* and *Western* were the others) issued by Culture Publications, Inc. between 1934 and 1942, at which time it changed its name to *Speed Detective*.

Spicy Detective's unique contribution to pulpdom was the unforgettable Dan Turner. Turner came roaring out of *Spicy Detective* with a vengeance and a surrealistic style that moved S. J. Perelman to call him "the apotheosis of all private detectives." Turner's turf was Hollywood and his work took him into "the naked lives of Hollywood's great and near great." Turner's creator, Robert Leslie Bellem, imbued Turner with a taste for booze (to the tune of a quart of Vat 69 a day), a vocabulary reminiscent of Leo Gorcey of the Dead End Kids, and the tolerance of Genghis Khan:

> I got out of my jalopy and stepped toward the closed gate of the ranch. Then this greasy-looking Max went for his knife.
>
> I walked into the dimly-lighted Chink restaurant; took a quick squint around the joint.
>
> I stiffened, copped a hinge at the guy with the gate. His map was masked from glims to chin.

Turner ran in *Speed Detective* through early 1947 when the magazine folded, but he remains one of the most memorable pulp characters.

The sex in *Spicy Detective* was quite mild, as can be seen in one of its rare sports stories by regular contributor and Lovecraft pal, E. Hoffman Price. "Death Takes the Wheel" (February 1938) is a car-racing story in which Cliff Cragin tries to keep his eyes on the track in spite of the charms of one Illona Janos:

> Illona's ventilated blouse filled out from the sudden lift of her breast. He wondered if she were olive tinted all over.

Cragin drives the Garrett Special, named after the West Coast engineer who developed a special fuel which would eliminate the need for pit stops over a 300-mile race. True to the Spicy formula, the action alternates between the excitement of the race and the excitement of Illona:

> The perfume exhaled from the white curves that peeped from her black negligee raised his blood pressure when she leaned closer...
>
> How he ever made that first curve was quite beyond him. Then a double spin. The engine coughed, almost died; blazed into fresh fury and went screaming down the back stretch. The grandstands were going crazy.

"Death Takes the Wheel" is as far as sex would ever go in a pulp sports story; suggestive adjectives leading to suggestions of offstage happenings. The sports pulps had none of this.

Detective Fiction Weekly

Detective Fiction Weekly was one of the Munsey magazines that lasted more than three decades (1924–1951) under various titles: *Flynn's, Detective Fiction Weekly, Detective Fiction*, etc.). Its forte was clearly the detective story in all of its manifestations and it would provide a cadre of some of the best popular fiction writers of the day. Writers like Erle Stanley Gardner, Frederick Faust (Max Brand) and George Harmon Coxe provided quality detective fiction on a par with *Dime Detective* and *Black Mask*. A writer's solicitation in the March 1932 *Writer's Digest* indicated that it was open to all forms of the detective story, not just the hard-boiled:

> We buy a wide variety of stories, no types are barred, but trite plots are avoided and the impersonal superdetective is not liked.

While this was certainly the case, as the private eye was not a *Detective Fiction Weekly* staple, the use of sports milieu was rare. One exception was the David Manners short story, "Tee Off for Murder," in the July 27 issue. The protagonist is not only not a superdetective, he is a golf pro, and the story is told from his point of view. An improbable tale, it recounts the story of caddy Lester Harris, who is developed into a full-fledged National Open pro under the tutelage of golf pro Amon McQuillan. Harris, at the cusp of his career, gets into a bar fight with a fellow golfer who is later found dead on the golf course. Tried, Harris is found innocent, but the fact is that the victim was indeed killed by a golf ball driven by our hero Lester Harris. The only person to know this is McQuillan, who decides to keep it to himself as he doesn't want this information to contaminate his protégé's game.

As a source of pulp era detective fiction *Detective Fiction Weekly* is considered to be underrated by today's collectors and anthologists, although that evaluation is not supported by this story.

Dime Detective

Dime Detective was a long-running (1931–1950) *Black Mask* wannabe published by Popular Publication's Harry Steeger. Over the years it was able to attract some of the best writers of detective fiction including Raymond Chandler, Carroll John Daly, Erle Stanley Gardner, Cornell Woolrich, and John MacDonald. Early on it produced what became known as "shudder" fiction, a particular brand of horror story started by Steeger to boost sales.

Steeger took inspiration for this brand of story from the Grand Guignol Theater in Paris which featured simulated acts of mutilation and torture. Later, Steeger would have pulp magazines devoted to these tales and the contents of *Dime Detective* would be modified to the conventional detective tale. At this time the magazine seemed to prefer snappy titles: "I'll Drown You in My Dreams," "Just a Corpse at Twilight," etc.

T. T. Flynn was a frequent contributor to *Dime Detective*, beginning with fiction in the first issue (November 1931) and multiple stories in each following year through 1950. Flynn's principal *Dime Detective* character was Mr. Maddox, the "smartest bookie operating." His occupation took him to racetracks all across the country from the first story, "Death Rides the Favorite" (Oct. 1938) to the last, "Build Up for Murder" (November 1950); 35 stories in all.

Joe Maddox is described as "huge and genial" and known and respected by turf fans from Long Island to the West Coast. When he requests information from a hotel clerk, "his vast, assured dignity" gets results. He drinks scotch and soda, smokes the best cigars, drives a flashy convertible, and stays in the best hotels. His involvement with fixed jockeys and horses and murder cases is an incidental product of his booking activities, and his special knowledge of the track and its denizens is always key to the solution of the crime. Maddox is always, however, on the wrong side of the law:

Maddox and his sidekick, Oscar, always had to tread softly, no matter what track they were working — for running a handbook was outside the law even if it was honest. —*Dime Detective*, Jan. 1940.

Perhaps the only series pulp detective (amateur) to operate in a sports milieu, Mr. Maddox predates other, currently popular racetrack detectives.

Detective Tales

Detective Tales was typical of the handling of sports in detective pulp magazines. In gestalt terms, the murder was the figure and the sport, the background. As such, the sport activity was not developed to the point where it would be of interest purely as a sport story.

Examples of the use of sports in these stories are as follows. In "The Long Count" by Robert Turner (Oct. 1947) the story begins after the fight referenced in the title when the boxer returns home to find his wife murdered. The story proceeds as a murder investigation and there are no further boxing scenes.

In the July 1938 story, "The Killer Strikes Out" by William B. Rainey, a baseball game is in progress as the story opens but before the first half-page is completed, the pitcher has been shot dead, and from here the story progresses as a murder investigation without further baseball material.

The June 1944 *Detective Tales* story by John J. Scanlon, "Daily-Double Trouble," is set in a racetrack but, other than the process of betting, little track or racing drama is included in this story which soon settles down to an industrial espionage story with a murder investigation.

Detective Tales, over its 18 years (1935–1953), was pure pulp. Its covers featured the most improbable crime scenes: masked villains in red, monk-like robes attacking a helpless female with a scimitar while in the foreground a tuxedo-clad gent shoots it out at close range with another monk (and this is just one cover). Another has a female ventriloquist firing a gun through her dummy's mouth, and there are midgets jumping out of mailboxes with .45 automatics. And my favorite shows a mad scientist (we can tell he's mad by the beard and thick glasses) about to smash a bottle of vile-looking chemicals on our hero's dome while his girlfriend is shooting it out with a second party and the hero is duking it out with a character in a hospital-like gown. Best yet, the hero is in a tux and his girlfriend is dressed for an evening on the town. This cover graced the February 1939 issue.

The Superhero Pulps

The most enduring of all pulp characters is the costumed hero who goes about fighting crime in all of its forms. The pulp hero pursued evil in the air (Bill Barnes), in space (Flash Gordon), at sea (Don Winslow), in the jungle (Sheena), and out in sagebrush country (Hopalong Cassidy). Most of the 50 or so pulp heroes who operated on terra-firma did so in disguise. The most notable of these were Doc Savage, the Shadow, and the Spider.

Like the heroes, the villains were larger-than-life characters: Doc Savage's John Sunlight; the Shadow's nemesis, the evil Shiwan Kahn; and the Spider's evil adversary, the evil Black Death.

There were no sports in the forefront of the superhero story. The sport story in the superhero pulp (and there are very few) serves as a setting for the hero-versus-villain goings-on, which in turn are just a platform for the superhero. Sport is gestalt ground to the superhero figure.

In the December 1936 issue of *The Whisperer* (aka James Wildcat Gordon) Gordon faces his enemies in a football milieu, in "The Football Racketers." Jerry Wade (aka The Candid Camera Kid) hunts down bad guys in the August 1940 issue of the *Detective Novels* story, "The Auto-Race Murders." The Phantom Detective (aka Richard Curtis Van Loan) fights killers in "Racehorses of Death" in the October 1941 *Phantom Detective Magazine*.

While these may not be all there is involving a sports background in the hero pulps, there are very few of these stories, certainly fewer than a half dozen or so, and in each, the sports setting is incidental to the crimes being executed by the bad guys who are eventually subdued by the invincible superhero.

Reading the Joe Maddox stories in *Dime Detective* one finds actual racetracks and nearby cities as well as typical track denizens. There is none of this verisimilitude in the superhero pulps.

Thrilling Adventures

The Standard line of pulp magazines was created by the American News Company when, upon losing its big pulp client, Street & Smith, it was left with distribution resources but nothing to distribute. An old pulp pro, Leo Margulies, took over and created the "Thrilling" group. The "thrilling" tag was a popular one in the pulp world and Margulies attached it to 16 different magazines, among them, *Thrilling Detective*, *Thrilling Mystery*, *Thrilling Ranch Stories*, *Thrilling Western*, *Thrilling Love*. Included in the pot were three sports titles: *Thrilling Sports*, *Thrilling Baseball* and *Thrilling Football Stories*.

Sports fiction was often used in the non-sports magazines, one of which was *Thrilling Adventures*. Modeled after the pulp *Adventure*, *Thrilling Adventure* catered to homebound, would-be world travelers with tales set in exotic ports of call and an editorial department entitled "The Globe Trotter" in which alleged personal adventures are recounted. Frank Gruber had mentioned in his autobiographical history of the pulp era that a lot of these writers began to believe the backgrounds they assumed when posturing as experts to add a pinch of verisimilitude to otherwise routine pulp fiction. When the pulp writer stuck to his last he could, on a good day, produce a "thrilling" story — not *War and Peace*, but solid story-telling. A case in point is Allan R. Bosworth's "Short Timer" in the July 1940 *Thrilling Adventures*.

"Short Timer" is a story of Navy short-timer Ricky Holley. Under the management and handling of Chief Gus Planck, Holley has enjoyed a perfect boxing career with a dozen wins and no defeats. This story is an excellent illustration of the utility factor in the two-person zero-sum game (which assumes that each of two parties is doing his total best to defeat his opponent).

Holley is looking forward to a civilian career in which he can make money, and so turns a deaf ear to Chief Planck who wants him to re-up. Holley finds himself in the ring with ex–Navy Chief Flash Daggett, "the best fighter the Navy ever had." The old Chief is more flash than talent but, while Holley could easily put him away, the game theory utility factor kicks in. Holley is taken with Flash's daughter, Ann, and finds himself pulling punches and eventually losing the fight.

At tale's end Holley re-ups and gives his share of the Flash Daggett purse to the old Chief so that he (Holley) and Ann can retire to the chicken farm the old Chief will buy. While the denouement is a bit hokey, the story is a good pulp example of the two-person zero-sum game gone awry, when the BIG game becomes secondary to some more desirable objective.

Louis L'Amour wrote a pair of boxing stories for the Thrilling magazines: "The Phantom Fighter" in the January 1942 *Thrilling Sports*, and "The Rounds Don't Matter" in the February 1942 *Thrilling Adventures*, plus a number of western and private eye stories for *Thrilling Ranch Stories*, *Thrilling Detective*, and *Thrilling Western*, in which the protagonist is always handy with his fists. Take, for example, his P.I. Bruce Blake in the June 1949 issue of *Thrilling Detective* ("Under the Hanging Wall"):

> A gigantic fist smashed out of somewhere, and I was knocked rolling. Lights exploded in my brain and I rolled over, getting to my knees. He turned and started toward me, and I made it to my feet, weaving. He swung low, hard and I caught the punch on my forearm and swung my right.

P.I. Blake's fight continues with embellishments worthy of a *Ring Magazine* article. L'Amour's fight prose rings true, and his and the stories of Robert E. Howard rank as some of the best examples of boxing fiction in the pulps, and compare quite favorably with most slick-paper fight fiction.

L'Amour's aptitude at writing the fight story derives from his own skill in the ring where he accumulated a 59–5 amateur record, knocking out 34. He fought under several different names.

Science Fiction

The science fiction pulp magazine provided a unique look at the world of the future. It spoke to things that could be and of unknown worlds. It was the popular literature which provided a sense of wonder. It was also flashy, semi-literate and technically flawed, but it would improve over the first five decades of the twentieth century to become sensible, literate and sound in its technical assumptions.

3. Sports in the Pulps

A page of the ads typically found in the pulps, from *Argosy*, Oct. 28, 1937.

In the few sports stories that appeared in science fiction pulps it is apparent that the sports story has great possibilities here. Not constricted by known games, it is free to experiment with games as we know them — and as we don't know them. It's just possible that the future of the short sports story may be in this genre.

Amazing Stories

The modern version of the space opera first appeared in the pages of *Amazing Stories*. While there were earlier such stories in the dime novels and in hardcover, there are also stories which could qualify in ancient Greek literature, stories involving such science fiction topics as utopian societies and moon trips. The modern science fiction story did appear in various general fiction magazines before WWI ("Science Fiction by Gaslight"), but it was Hugo Gernsback's *Amazing Stories* that would package modern science fiction in magazine format and sell it to a six-figure-sized audience on a monthly basis. He can truly be said to have created the science fiction market.

Amazing Stories' format differed from that of the pre–WWI general fiction magazines in that it was *all* science fiction. First published in April of 1926, *Amazing Stories* appeared at bedsheet-size (8½ × 11½"). Initially reprinting the fiction of H. G. Wells, Jules Verne, and Poe, it would soon attract a core of readers who would come to be the leading genre writers: Isaac Asimov, Jack Williamson, John Campbell, and Otis Albert Kline are a few such. The term "science fiction" was yet to come; the subtitle read: "The Magazine of Scientifiction" and the lead editorial was a science-based discussion of some aspect of the fiction feature headed: "Extravagant Fiction Today — Cold Fact Tomorrow." An example of this format can be seen in the November 1929 issue when editorial direction had been taken over by T. O'Connor Sloane, Ph.D., and Gernsback had gone on to create a series of "Wonder"-titled magazines in the same style, content, format and price (25¢) as *Amazing Stories*.

In the November 1929 *Amazing Stories*, the lead editorial is "Acceleration in Interplanetary Travel" and its technical prophecy is quite good:

> One of the ideas in interplanetary travel is to use a rocket-propelled vehicle — that is, a vehicle from whose stern gases will be propelled at high velocity by some explosive mixture.

3. Sports in the Pulps

Wild-eyed constructs of future and past civilizations were common in the pages of the Ziff-Davis pulp *Amazing Stories* where the imagination of the writers and artists knew no bounds. In the editorial page of the September 1940 issue, managing editor Ray Palmer admits to something only regular readers of *Amazing Stories* knew:

> Mr. Binder (writer, Eando Binder) stands before a row of four finished science-fiction paintings. He studies them for a few minutes, then points to one and says: "I think I'd like to do that story." That little scene, readers, reveals exactly how almost all our cover stories have been written in the past six months.

In that same issue of *Amazing Stories*, writer Leonard Gipson takes what appears to be a hard look at "Sports of the Future." Starting from 1900 to the then current 1940, Gipson analyzes track and field records decade by decade, then projects what records will exist in the year 2000. In some cases, specifically the track and field sports, Gipson's predictions are reasonable, given the statistical data base from which he's operating. In the one-mile run, for example, the following are Gipson's projected figures:

1900	1910	1920	1930	1940	2000
4m15s	4m14s	4m12s	4m9s	4m6s	3m55s

If Gipson had stuck with the hard-data track and field events he might have avoided contamination of his prognostications by some wide marks. In a column subtitled "Some Blanket Forecasts," Gipson offers the following predictions:

> After about 1945, football will probably be de-emphasized considerably.
>
> Baseball is on the way out and will be replaced by softball as our national sports pastime.
>
> The year 2000 will find no millionaire professional boxing champs such as the Dempseys, Tunneys and Joe Louises of today.

While Gipson's prophecy gifts were somewhat lacking he was on to something when he put science fiction and sports together. Because it provides unbounded story circumstances, the mix of sports and science fiction offers great promise for sports fiction. In fact, the unimaginable has happened — a sports science fiction story has been successfully imitated on the field.

The story was James Thurber's "You Can Look It Up," which appeared in the *Saturday Evening Post* of April 5, 1941. A favorite Casey Stengel quote, "You Can Look It Up" tells the story of Squawks Magrew, manager of a National League team, who meets Pearl du Montville in a local tavern. Pearl du Montville is a midget and Magrew reasons that given the right game circumstances, Pearl would be certain to draw a walk. Magrew inserts du Montville into the lineup with somewhat different results than occurred when Bill Veeck used midget Eddie Gaedel for the same purpose in a St. Louis Browns game ten years after Thurber's story.

The use of robot baseball players has been a somewhat common theme, appearing, for example, in one of Rod Serling's *Twilight Zone* episodes ("The Mighty Casey," 1963) and in Fred Pohl's "The Celebrated No-Hit Inning" (*Fantastic Universe*, September 1956).

The Year the Yankees Lost the Pennant by Douglas Wallop (Norton Books, 1954) is a retelling of the Faust legend with Washington Senators fan Joe Boyd cutting a deal with the devil. Wallop's story was the basis for the stage play, *Damn Yankees.*

In *The Natural* (Harcourt, Brace, 1952) Bernard Malamud makes use of Arthurian legend, with Roy Hobbs drawing his wonder bat from the heart of a tree much as King Arthur drew the sword Excalibur from a stone. Much of the film based on this novel blends fantasy and reality. Robert Redford, who plays Hobbs, patterned his character after Ted Williams. A concluding scene in which Hobbs smashes a tremendous home run, destroying the game clock high in center field, is based on the real hit by Bama Rowell of the Boston Braves. Rowell, incidently, was supposed to have received a free watch for the feat but never did ... until the Redford film was shown and the *New York Times* ran an interview with Rowell, whereupon the watch company coughed up old Bama's watch.

It Happens Every Spring by Valentine Davies (Farrar, Straus, 1949) tells the story of chemistry professor Vernon Simpson's invention of a substance which repels any object in its way. The story was the basis of the 1949 movie of the same name.

W. P. Kinsella's *Shoeless Joe* was made into the popular film *Field of Dreams*. Another of his stories, *The Iowa Baseball Confederacy* (Houghton Mifflin, 1986) tells the story of Matthew Clarke, who is struck by lightning and as a result, can recall the entire circumstances, players, games, etc., of the Iowa Baseball Confederacy — a league no one else has heard of!

One of the best pieces of short fantasy baseball writing is Harlan Ellison's "The Cheese Stands Alone," which appeared in *Amazing Stories* in 1981. The story follows middle-aged dentist Cort (we never learn his first name) to a strange store where he is shown a Big Little Book — a kids' book sold in five and dime stores in the 1930s and 1940s — which reveals to him the high point of his life: an incident he has forgotten but one which is described in glorious detail. Needless to say, it happened on a baseball diamond.

The July 1979 *Fantasy & Science Fiction* collaboration by Bill Pronzini and Barry N. Malzberg, "Prose Bowl," is the ultimate send-up of the BIG sports event. The action is described in the style of a heavyweight title fight, only in this even the contestants, Rex Sackett and Leon "The Cranker" Culp, are writers. The competition is staged in a Coliseum which seats 100,000 screaming fans, and the TriDim televised audience is estimated at 30 million. All the tension is there as the tide goes back and forth, with Sackett at first in the lead with a flurry of transition dialogue and some cat-and-mouse action, then Culp countering with more dialogue before being penalized for unacceptable phrasing, and seemingly throwing the advantage to Sackett who is threatened by an attack of writer's block. The contest ends with a winner and a loser but the contestants realize their mutual victimization in this truly BIG event. "Prose Bowl" is prima facie evidence that sports, science fiction and humor can blend well when done by writers who could, themselves, be considered Prose Bowl contestants.

The early, elemental version of the BIG story is exemplified by Frederick Brown's "Arena" (June 1944 *Astounding Science Fiction*). An armada of aliens has invaded earth and a competition is engineered by these "Outsiders" in which a human and one of the post-BEM aliens (who have retractable tentacles!) must do battle to determine which race shall survive. The contest is "equally unpleasant" for both contestants (i.e., fair):

> It is fair. The conditions are such that the accident of physical strength will not completely decide the issue. There is a barrier.

You will understand. Brainpower and courage will be more important than strength. If you die, your failure will be the end of your race.

Were Brown alive today he would undoubtedly be embarrassed by this simply-plotted tale, but it was seminal for both Brown and this particular type of sports-science fiction tale — the BIG event, a tale which undoubtedly grew out of the musings of GIs.

4

The All-Sports Pulps

The all-sports pulps, like the general fiction Munsey pulps before them, offered a sport for every possible taste. Pulps like *Sports Action* and *Complete Sports* routinely carried baseball, basketball, boxing, tennis, golf, track, football, boxing and other sports fiction in each issue and typically included a one or two sports-facts departments along with an illustrated double-page spread of sports figures and their exploits.

The all-sports pulps favored baseball and boxing over a period of time but in any single issue you could count on finding stories of boat racing, the shot-put, bowling, crew, tennis, etc. Typical of these magazines, the May-June 1939 issue of *12 Sports Aces* carried a variety of sports fiction and the cover was a composite of track, baseball, auto racing, horse racing and boxing scenes. *Sport Story Magazine*, over the years, had dozens of different sports represented; everything from horseshoe-pitching to polo. A headcount of types of sport fiction in *Sport Story Magazine* over the course of a typical year (1927) shows an amazing range. Baseball, track, boxing, hockey, horse racing, football, golf and tennis each had ten or more stories. In addition there was sports fiction in the following categories: water polo, bowling, swimming, steeple chasing, horseshoe pitching, log-birling, motorboat racing, dogsled racing, tug-o-war, canoe tilting, ice boating and handball, among others.

The emphasis was on mainstream sports, in season, but it can be seen from the range of sports covered that the editorial objective was universal appeal.

Sports Pulps: First Year of Publication

With the exception of three sports pulps published in the 1920s, the remainder were published in the 1930s (28) and the 1940s (24). The following non-fiction sports magazines were published over this period:*

1921–1924:	:	*Athletic Journal*
1922–	:	*Outdoor America*
1931–	:	*Scholastic Coach*
1936–	:	*Ski Illustrated* (later *Ski Magazine*)
1946–	:	*Sport*
1947–	:	*Golf World, Road & Track, Skiing*
1948–	:	*Hot Rod*

When *Sports Illustrated* was first published (1957) all of the sports pulps but two (*Super Sports* and *Ten-Story Sports*) were defunct and neither of these would survive into 1958. Following is the first year of publication for the sports pulps:

1923:	*Sport Story Magazine*
1927:	*The Life of Gene Tunney*
1928:	*Fight Stories*
1931:	*Dime Sports Magazine*
1933:	*The All-American Sports Magazine*
1934:	*Jack Dempsey's Fight Magazine*
1936:	*Ace Sports, Thrilling Sports, Star Sports Magazine*
1937:	*Basketball Stories, Best Sports, Blue Ribbon Sports, Champion Sports Magazine, Complete Sports, Football Stories, Knockout Magazine, Popular Sports Magazine, Sports Action, Sports Novels Magazine, Sports Winners*
1938:	*The All-American Football Magazine, Baseball Stories, Bull's Eye Sports, Real Sports, 12 Sports Aces, Variety Sports Magazine*
1939:	*Athlete, Football Action, Sports Fiction, Super Sports, Thrilling Football Stories*

*Janello, Amy and Jones, Brennon, The American Magazine, Harry N. Abrams, Inc., Publishers, N.Y., 1991.

1940:   *All-American Sports, All-Baseball Stories, All Sports Magazine*
1941:   *Exciting Football, Exciting Sports, Five Sports Classics Magazine, Popular Football*
1942:   *Sport Story Annual*
1943:   *Rodeo Romances*
1946:   *Real Sports*
1947:   *All Basketball Stories, All Football Stories, Big Book Sports, Big Sports Magazine, New Sports Magazine, Sports Short Stories*
1948:   *Big Baseball Stories, Big Basketball Stories, Fifteen Sports Stories, Sports Leaders Magazine, Ten-Story Sports*
1949:   *Exciting Baseball, Popular Baseball, Thrilling Baseball Stories*

The Dime Novels

The dime novel was mass-produced sports fiction for an American juvenile market anxious to read the exploits of larger-than-life sports heroes, one of whom would survive for decades in sports lore.

With no radio or television and limited access to sports events, kids of late 19th and early 20th century America turned to the dime novel for entertainment. There they read of the sports exploits of characters like Owen Clancy, Fred Fearnot, Jack Standfast, and the greatest of them all, Frank and Dick Merriwell.

If the Merriwells couldn't beat you with pluck (dime-novelese for guts) they would do so with superior skill. In one episode titled "Dick Merriwell's Wing," Dick Merriwell has injured his pitching arm in a mine blast set off by an archrival bent on getting Dick out of the big game.

"How in thunder are you going to pitch?" asks a teammate who is unaware of the unlimited resources of the Merriwells.

"Be a southpaw, I reckon, if I find the other wing won't stand the racket."

Damaged arm and all, Dick bunts home the winning run. This is the stuff of adolescent fantasy on the field of dreams circa 1890–1925. Chalk one up for pluck.

As for his baseball skill, Frank Merriwell developed the fearsome "double-shoot," a curve ball that broke in two different directions on its way to the plate. This pitch, by the way, was used by Frank to defeat the Boston Red Sox! While the Merriwells didn't play professional sports, they would occasionally play against pro teams while they were students at Fardale Military Academy and Yale University.

It's difficult to imagine how this predictable formula sports fiction could capture the imagination of kids of any era, but as Ron Goulart says, the dime novel era was an age of innocence and, more importantly, there was no media access to professional sports. If you were lucky enough to have town sports and a horse and carriage you could get to see the real thing.

How much influence did these "novels" have on kids of the day? Frank Acker, Brown University Merriwell scholar,* says that turn-of-the-century dime novels had a greater positive effect on millions of kids than any other influence before or since! The early dime novels were issued every two weeks in a variety of sizes and formats, ranging from pocket size to full newspaper size before the publishing house of Beadle & Adams standardized the format which was advertised as "a dollar book for a dime" (thus the name these publications carried); they ran to 100 pages.

The writers who produced these "novels" were an odd bunch who churned out stories to order at an astonishing rate. Edward L. Wheeler, for example, wrote the popular Deadwood Dick westerns without ever having been farther west than Jersey City.

William Gilbert Patten (aka Burt Standish) produced a series of dime-novel westerns under the pseudonym Wyoming Bill, a name he earned by virtue of having been a passenger on a train that passed through Wyoming. Patten's mark was not made with the western, however, but with his stories of the sports exploits of the Merriwells. The Merriwells were what every boy wanted to be. The phrase "pulling a Merriwell," meaning winning the game by some last-minute heroics, remains in the sports lexicon to this day.

Patten began the Merriwell saga in April of 1886 for Street & Smith when the magazine requested a series about a clean-cut boy who goes to military school and then on to Yale. Each of the Mer-

---

*Frank Acker, personal correspondence.

riwell stories was pretty much the same, and, after producing a Merriwell egg per week for 20 years, Patten quit and reflected on his creation:

> Did I love Merriwell? Not at first. Those early stories were more of a joke to me than anything else. But when it got so that half a million kids were reading him every week, I began to realize that I had about the biggest chance to influence the youth of this country that any man ever had.
> Yes, I loved him. And I loved him because no boy, if he followed in Merriwell's tracks, ever did anything to be ashamed of.

This prototype of the all–American boy would extend into the radio era thanks to the likes of Jack Armstrong, the all–American Boy. Jack matched Merriwell's feats on the fields of Hudson High but branched out to involvement in non-sports adventures when sports fiction outgrew the stilted writing and plotting of the dime novels. By the mid–1920s this type of printed fiction would be no more, thanks mostly to juvenile radio drama and a more sophisticated juvenile reader. In his day, however, there was no one like the Merriwells. Even in later years the success of the Merriwell phenomenon was still being pondered. Writing in *The American Mercury*, George Jean Nathan ventured that the Merriwell character was the most widely known fictional character of his day. He also noted that Street & Smith "made a fortune out of him"— perhaps Merriwell's most amazing feat.

As popular as the dime novel was (and it survived into the 1930s in reprints), the infallible hero and the stilted dialogue ensured its demise:

> That was a dandy run, Fearnot, said Captain Dick Dunn with delight, as the boys lined up again. I thought you would go over the line for sure. Another time, Dick, laughed Fred. That fellow tackled me hard. They haven't got started yet but they will give us a game before we are through. If we can score now it will mean a lot to us.

As glassy-eyed as this prose makes us, the memory of one of the dime-novel characters lives on. Edward LeBlanc* comments:

*Edward LeBlanc, "The Frank Merriwell Saga," Dime Novel Roundup, Vol. 55, No. 1, Whole No. 577, February 1986.

> Hardly a day goes by during the baseball or football season when the name of Frank Merriwell is not used by a sports columnist or sportscaster in describing a spectacular play. Recently Doug Flutie of Boston College was compared to Merriwell when his long, completed pass in the last seconds of the game turned defeat into victory.

LeBlanc goes on to tell of the use of the Merriwell name by Howard Cosell, Curt Gowdy and "many others" in similar, dramatic game-winning situations.

While the Merriwell mystique would survive (if only as an icon), dime novel fiction would give way to the more plausible neo-realism of the sports pulps.

Change was slow to come, however. The dime novelists did not disappear. In much of the prose of the early sports pulps the reader could find warmed-over dime novel hash and the "new" pulp fiction in the same issue. The January 8, 1925, issue of *Sport Story Magazine* contains several dime-novel potboilers: Ralph Paine ("The Letter of the Law"), Wallace Watson ("Brazen Victory"), a quality piece by John Tunis ("The Limelight Kid") and a humorous story by Clarence Cullen ("Xantippe for Mine") in which a high-school principal escorts some of his female teachers to New Orleans where he gets embroiled with a race horse:

> Tomorrow, ladies, with your indulgence, I shall leave you to your own devices. I have been told — it is a gossamer family tradition — that I have relatives here in New Orleans. I must devote one day to seeking them out. Ladies, pray with me that I shall not find them.

This kind of humorous aside was never to be found in the dime novels.

Even the Merriwells would survive for a while in the pulps. Gilbert Patten came out of retirement to resume the dime-novel series in *Top Notch Magazine* (1929–1930) and in *Sport Story Magazine* (1927–1928), and Merriwell stories would be ghosted under the Patten name by Warren Carleton, Joseph Ames, and J. Irving Crump.

Super Sports

Nearly 20 years pass and we are sure we've seen the last of Frank and Dick Merriwell ... but wait! Can it be? Yes, the boys are back for one last day of glory. The September 1947 issue (Vol. 6, No. 3) of *Super Sports* recounts, in "The Man Who Beat Merriwell," the inglorious end to the careers of Frank and Dick Merriwell.

Mike Rocklin has arranged a pair of charity games, matching his professional baseball and football teams against the college boys fielded by the Merriwells. The baseball game took place on Long Island and the football game was played before a sell-out Polo Grounds crowd.

The games, like all Merriwell games, were nip and tuck throughout, with neither team having a clear edge. In the end Mike Rocklin's teams would prevail in spite of Frank's impossible-to-hit double-shoot curve and the presence of both Frank and Dick performing as running backs. The final tally was: baseball, Rocklins 8, Merriwells 7; football, Rocklins 19, Merriwells 16.

It's bad enough that the Merriwells lose both a baseball and a football game in their last ever appearance but at game's end Frank proves to be that sport's anathema of a bad sport, venting his ire by slapping Rocklin's face.

All in all *Super Sports* was a rather run-of-the-mill sports pulp. A product of the Double Action Group, its fiction was routine pulp and its ad content might lead one to think it was one of the Spicy group of pulps. In a single issue of *Super Sports* the following ads can be found: "For Men Only" (Cartoons! Photos!); "Special Offer to Lovers (Three Books for $1)"; "Who Needs a Wife? When He Has Bachelor Quarters (Intimate Tales of Women!)"; "Pa Feels Like New! (After Taking a 'Romantic Product from Brazil'")"; "Love Me!" (A perfume); "Gorgeous Studio Models" (slides); "A Thrilling Glamorous Bustline Instantly" (bust pads); An ad for books with the following titles: *Six Times a Bride*, *Past Sing*, *Love on the Run* and *Men Are Molehills*; Book (*The Bathroom Reader*— Eye-opening stories for men who enjoy the spice of life); and so on.

The *Super Sports* format was a routine blend of three novelettes, two short stories and one department ("Dope from the Dugout"). With the exception of the aforementioned Merriwell piece the fiction was about average pulp, and the only reason the Merriwell piece stands out is that it is probably the last pulp story written about the boys Merriwell.

Dime-Novel Round-Up*

The Dime-Novel Round-Up reports research of the membership of the Happy Hour Brotherhood—"An organization devoted to the collecting and preservation of dime novels, story papers, and popular literature of the 19th century." There is material in most issues of some interest to the popular sports fiction researcher. The following issues are largely dedicated to the subject of dime novel sports fiction:

> July 15, 1970 (V39N7): The Anatomy of Dime Novels No. 19: "Stories of Boarding School and College Sports," by J. Edward Leithead.
> August 15, 1970 (V39N8): The Anatomy of Dime Novels No. 19: "Stories of Boarding School and College Sports (Conclusion)," by J. Edward Leithead.
> June 1976 (V45N3): "Fred Fearnot Was There," by Ross Craufurd.
> June 1978 (V47N3): "True Friends," by Steve Press, "A play for young people adapted from the Frank Merriwell stories of Bert L. Standish."
> August 1978 (V47N4): Supplement to Dime Novel Round-Up of that date: "Frank Merriwell's All-Star Opponents—Battling the Best in Baseball," by Robert McDowell (A "new" FM story).
> August 1982 (V51N4): "Frank Merriwell's Hundredth Birthday," by David Soibelman.
> February 1986 (V55N1): "The Frank Merriwell Saga," by Edward T. LeBlanc.
> August 1989 (V58N4): "The Dime Novel and Its Successors," by Edward T. LeBlanc.
> June 1993 (V62N2): "Frank Merriwell Didn't Inhale Either!," by E. M. Sanchez-Saavedira.

The All-American Sports Magazine

The All-American Sports Magazine was edited by Nat Fleischer, boxing's man-for-all-seasons, and over the first eight issues he pub-

---
*Published by J. Randolph Cox, P.O. Box 226, Dundas, MN 55019.

lished a biography of his favorite boxer — Jack Dempsey. On the back of the rear cover Fleischer hypes his "Universal Boxing Course" which carries a photo of Dempsey in boxing trunks. The July 1934 (V, No. 8) issue, which is standard pulp size and page count and sold for 15¢, included two boxing stories: "Plastered in Paris" by James P. Olm, and "The Autograph Bug" by John MacNeish; each of these was routine pulp.

Fleischer, instead of making *The All-American Sports Magazine* a fiction version of *Ring Magazine* (which he also edited), sought to cover as wide a range of sports fiction as possible, including in the aforementioned issue, a polo story ("The Spur" by Charles B. McCray) and a yachting story ("Rough on Rigging" by John Scott Douglas.

In "The Spur," it takes the Mannington players a chukker or two to prove to the reader that they are just regular guys; that is if one can find his way through the polo-ease:

> With a wondrously (can you imagine a home run or basketball hoop being so described?) deft twirling of his stick, Smith deflected the sphere to Rollins, prevented the upraised mallet of Yardley's outpost man from getting in his hit.

Similarly, it is difficult to steer a course through the salty yachting color:

> Nothing to do but veer port, and hope to pass as they cornered the yacht! Thorn split a brown curve in the wind, his bulldog face grim...

In addition to the polo, yachting and boxing, Fleischer included in this single issue a pro tennis story ("Winner Takes All" by Felix Winsten), a racing story ("A Horse and a Jockey" by Walter N. Des Marias), and a golf poem ("Dub") and baseball story ("Gallup Comes Back" by Edgar Daniel Kramer) in which Gallup's comeback rides on a Merriwell-type double-shoot pitch which defies gravity by breaking up.

This issue (V. 1, No. 8) had track and additional baseball stories and an autobiographical piece by the then-manager of the Cleveland Indians, Walter Johnson, baseball's Big Train. In "Plenty on the Ball!" Johnson writes about control, autographs, the role of newspapers and magazines in baseball, his career highlights with the Washington Senators and the future of baseball.

Filling out the issue were a sports sketch piece, "Brushing Up Your Memory," in which several athletes are sketched, along with a trivia question and an exercise program, "Taking a Slice Off the Middle" by Yale athletic trainer Major Frank Wandle, which is awkwardly folded into some preachy fiction.

The best material in the issue is Fleischer's Dempsey piece, "The Idol of Fistiana." Considering Fleischer's dominant role in boxing (editor of *Ring*, referee, judge, matchmaker, etc.), one might think *The All-American Sports Magazine* could have been the best of the boxing pulps, had he just chosen to give that impetus.

Sports Short Stories

Interstate Publishing's *Sports Short Stories* was a hurried product which ran for only a few issues at the end of the pulp era. Selling for 20¢, it was overpriced by 15¢ because of hackneyed writing and poor artwork. There were no name writers in the Interstate stable, and none of the 10 potboilers which were crammed into a 98-page count was a decent pulp yarn.

The cover art featured a waist-up view, novel in itself, but the depiction of fighter A throwing an overhand left to the left side of fighter B's face defies Euclidean geometry. The interior art was sparse, in some cases a few inches square, and generally not athletically correct, as in the depiction of a college basketball team sporting jerseys with no team names or numbers. Body motion and movement are similarly out of whack. The interior artwork of *Sports Short Stories* rates only a 1 compared to a 10 for the artwork in *Sports Novels*.

Sports Novels Magazine

Sports Novels Magazine was a Popular Publications all-sports pulp for those who wanted anything and everything on his plate, like the reader whose letter was printed in the November 1949 (V. 18, No. 3) letters column, "The Home Plate":

4. The All-Sports Pulps

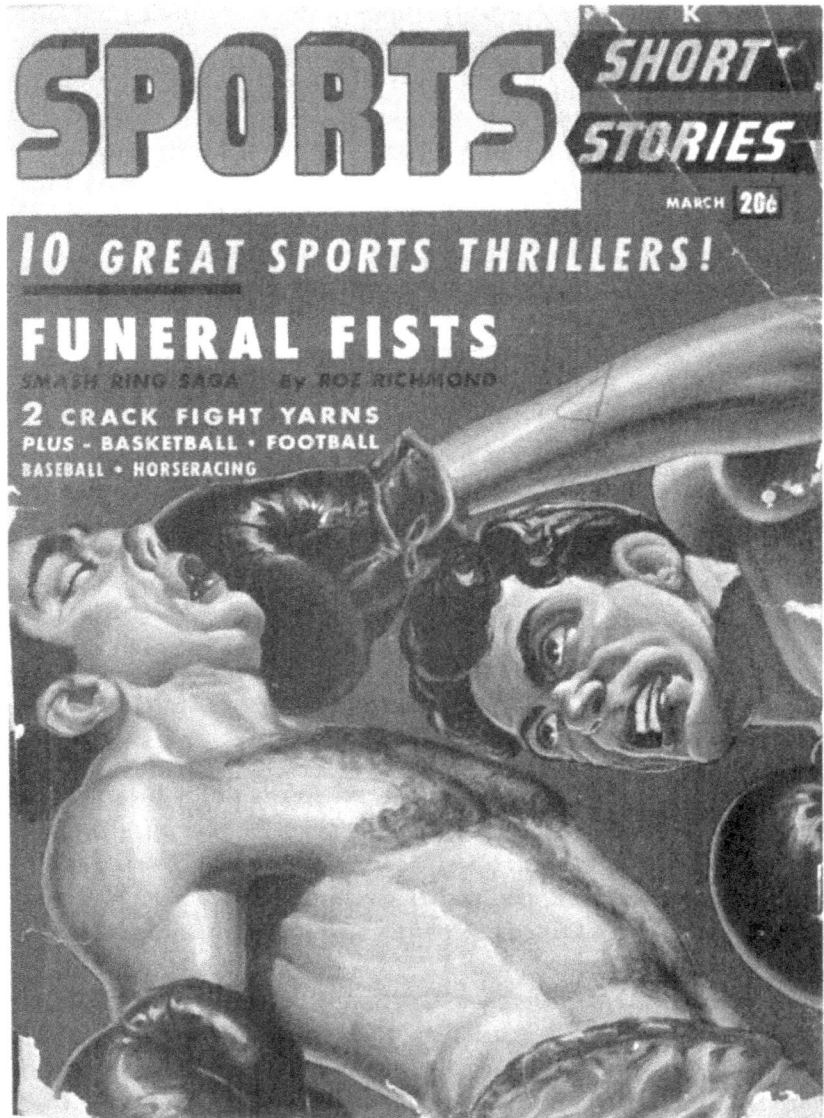

I wonder if you would listen to one reader's plea and publish more water-sports stories. Of course you sometimes print stories about swimming, but how about a real competitive team sport like water polo? It's one of the most exciting sports there is, but I know a lot of people up North never heard of it — a Palm Beach reader.

The variety of sports represented in the November 1949 issue is typical of *Sports Novels*: football (both pro and college), boxing, midget auto racing, golf, basketball and baseball. *Sports Novels* did have some of the better pulp fictioneers, including T. W. Ford, Bill Cox, John MacDonald and William Campbell Gault, and Norm Saunders did an occasional cover. The interior artwork was superior, capturing the jab, the golf swing, the football pass, all athletically correct, which can't be said for a number of pulps.

Popular felt it had to justify the 25¢ price (even for 1949) with a bold cover banner: "The BIG SPORTS Magazine — 32 More Pages." To get to the 130-page count (from the standard 128 pages) the publisher counted both sides of the front cover.

There was nothing really spectacular about the fiction. Midget auto racer is aging, too old for the sport, and so the driver's role passes on to a younger man; Jigger Donahue overcomes a 14-point deficit and drops the winning basket; a Los Angeles golfer learns something about life on the putting greens, etc. Gault's story of a pair of twins who grow from childhood into a trainer/boxer team could have filled a novel but was nevertheless the most satisfactory of all the fiction in the November 1949 issue.

Complete Sports

Complete Sports was one of several sports pulps produced by various publishers over the magazine's near-20-year run, the others being *Best Sports*, *Real Sports*, *Sports Action* and *Sports Leaders*. These magazines produced rather routine sports fiction and their roster of writers contained few names well known in either the other pulp genres or the sports world.

As for content, *Complete Sports* was partial to baseball, with more than half of each issue usually devoted to the game. It also seemed to favor boxing stories, one of which, "Fighters Are Born" (August 1940), is revealing in its handling of the female character. It seems Bill Allison has paid five dollars for a ticket to a lumber camp at Pine Creek where he hopes to find employment as a lumberjack. Lunching at a local beanery, Bill is smitten:

> A yellow-haired girl with very blue eyes, a very competent looking girl, took his order. Allison thought her eyes different from any he'd ever seen...

It so happens that every lumber camp has its fighting program and, ultimately, its own heavyweight champ. As pulp fate would have it, Allison finds himself vying for the title with Sledgehammer Selby of Cass Lake, a ranking heavyweight who is on the lam from legal problems. Allison wins the fight and his manager tells him: "You're on the way up." Referring to the aforementioned beauty, he adds: "Yeah, you can bring the twist along if you wanna." Interestingly, the lady's name is not mentioned in the entire story.

Complete Sports carried nine or ten stories per issue and an occasional department or fact feature, two of which were "The Sport-O-Quiz" (10 sports questions) and "The Complete Sports Camera," a cartoon story. In the September 1947 "Camera" the story was a two-page history of the origins of hockey. In this same issue was a short tennis story, "Net Nemesis" ("a dramatic novelette"), which shambles toward the BIG tournament where Lee Purvis is matched with Dink Avery. This writer (John Wilson) must have been a dime-novel holdover to give anyone the name Dink and to write such 23 skidoo prose as: "Pardon me, keeds. Be back in a flash with a flask, hah?"

Complete Sports now and then redeems itself. The patient reader will find some gems here and there, not necessarily in the story telling. In "Touchdown for Sale" by Theodore J. Roemer, the rare pro-football story (the bulk of pulp football fiction was collegiate) tells the story of hot-shot Wally Price, just up from the college campus:

> Price hit the dummy again, did a handspring in football togs and took a bow. Chub saw Masters' swarthy face darken.

One player mumbles, "He won't fit. He's a college lily." But Price will eventually redeem himself by kicking the winning field goal in the BIG game. He's then welcomed to participate in a post-game celebration ritual which tells us something of the state of pro football at the time (1947):

> Chub grinned and pushed open the door. A small barrel of beer stood on a bench in the middle of the floor.... Duke, remember the time I had breaking you of drinking two years ago? I thought it was bad for training. You were a good team man then. I think we'll go back to those ways. The gang will like it.

The gang did. They made a rush for the glasses stacked there.

From across the room one of the players offers a glass to Price.

Football Action

Considering the number of titles (7), pulp football was more popular than pulp baseball. *All Football Stories* ran just one issue, *Thrilling Football Stories* lasted 11 years, *Exciting Football*, *Football Action*, *Football Stories* and *Popular Football* enjoyed nine years of publication, and *All American Football Magazine* lasted five years — all between the years 1933–1950.

While professional baseball was grist for the baseball pulp mill, college football played the key role in the football pulps. Over the period 1921–1930, attendance at college football games doubled. College football weathered the Great Depression better than the pro gram, which saw several of its small franchises fail. By 1937, attendance at college football games doubled again. Knute Rockne, Amos Alonzo Stagg and Pop Warner became household names.

Professional football would thrive for a while but would face the problem of declining attendance. In 1949 the Los Angeles Rams drew 205,109 fans to their home games. In 1950, when all home games were televised, attendance fell to 110,162. While pro football would recover from this temporary blip in the public attention span, the sport pulps would not.

Like boxing, football came to America as a lower-class sport played in working-class neighborhoods. Over the first half of the twentieth century it gradually gained respectability and would ultimately become popular both as a college game and as professional entertainment. Between 1921 and 1930 attendance at college football games doubled and professional football began its growth to the billion-dollar industry it is today, thanks to Red Grange and his Chicago Bears touring around the nascent professional league at the front-end of sport's Golden Age.

Football fiction could be found in the general fiction pulps in the 1930s and by the late 1930s and 1940s there were all-football pulp magazines on the market.

4. The All-Sports Pulps

The college game not only meant a lot to the players, the student body, and the college itself; it often had wider consequences, and this theme is explored by Judson Philips in a three-part story, "Off-Side," in consecutive issues of *Argosy*, November–December 1935. The story, as told through the eyes of reporter/political lackey Tom Carey, follows the role played by the state college's football team in the re-election campaign of Jim Markle.

Carey pitches a plan which will ingratiate Markle with the football fraternity:

> Big Jim poured himself a stiff shot of rye from the bottle he'd unpacked from his bag. His eyes were narrowed in a bright, shrewd look. The more I think about this stunt, Carey, the better I like it. When I looked at that crowd out there, realized how keen they are about the game and that there are thousands more like them ... he took a big swallow and smacked his lips. If I can help bring a championship to State it'll pack more votes in the ballot boxes than a thousand promises. It's too bad I'm not an alumnus. That'd make it perfect. But I'll adopt State as my alma mater.

An interesting slant about this story is that, unlike most pulp football fiction, the story focus is outside the game itself; the team and its players are only significant to the story as a function of a politician's ambition.

Football Action came on the market in the Fall of 1939 with "Three Line-Smashing Novelets of College Football." They were pretty lame. The first, "Swivel-Hipped Yokel," was the standard yokel (the equivalent of baseball's busher or rube) yarn, written by Mark Adam:

> Shucks, I ain't nobody—I'm jus' Luke Woods. I come down from the farm lands to get an education an' play football for Crandall.

The second "line-smasher" is "The Triple-Threat Phoney" by Gilbert K. Griffiths:

> Yellow Belly Jim Halliday has the football skills but lacks the guts ... until... With a silent prayer as the ball came back, he toed the pigskin with a superhuman kick. The ball rose, headed straight for the goalposts—but it seemed for a moment that it would fall short...

Have no fear, dear reader, the ball is wafted by a sympathetic breeze neatly through the uprights and all is well with Jim Halliday.

The third "line-smasher," "Anchors Aweigh!" is a navy buddy story, but midshipmen Ingalls and Dinsmore could easily be confused with the brothers Merriwell:

> I'm going to gamble — I can't pass with my right hand, but I used to throw a fair southpaw pass in high school. We'll try it on Number Nine.

In addition to these three featured pieces there are "Six Grid Short Stories," one by sports pulp regular Bill Cox ("Work Horse and Glory"), and a fair short story by crime writer Richard Sale ("Mudder") in which the principal character takes on football as a body of knowledge to be studied scientifically. In addition to his work for the pulps Sale worked as a screenwriter for Paramount and Twentieth Century–Fox and later as a television writer-producer-director. The bulk of his detective fiction can be found in *Super Detective* and *Detective Fiction Weekly*, with a few stories in *Black Mask*. There is no sports material in Sale's post-pulp work.

The non-fiction material in *Football Action* is bylined as "Three Hard-Hitting Football Features"; the first, "Heads Up!," explores the theme that "Raw brawn and wholesale brute force no longer win football games." It employs some homespun aphorisms: "The good quarterback is as circumspect as an Indiana banker making a loan." Eddie Dooley wrote this piece. A second item, "Staging the Gridiron Shows," is an insider's look at the college publicity agent's job. At the time Tim Cohane wrote the piece he was doing that job for Fordham, but perhaps comparing his job to planning for war is a bit over the top:

> Football, like war, is planned ahead. Long before the big guns of the grid powers begin firing in early October, a host of diplomats are busy arranging the terms of war, deciding who the actual combatants are to be, and where the battle is to be fought. Competent generals have prepared their pigskin fodder for the fray.

In addition to the foregoing there is a complete college football schedule (eight pages) for the 1939 season.

The science-fiction-cum-sports tale was found mostly in the

science-fiction magazines; only rarely did this type of story appear in one of the sports pulps. The exception is in a 1951 issue of *Football Action*: the sf/sports potboiler, "Revolt of the Robot Eleven."

Rodeo Romances

Sports fiction was not to be found in the nearly 200 western fiction magazines — unless you consider rodeo a sport. Never popular east of the Mississippi after the 1930s and '40s, the rodeo remains a cowboy institution in some quarters of America's West, and an occasional film such as *The Lusty Men* or *Junior Bonner* reminds the rest of us that rodeo events have not gone the way of the dodo. *8 Seconds* (the time a rodeo bullrider is required to hang on) is a documentary of the life of Lane Frost, a real-life rider who was killed on the job.

The rodeo was an occasional setting for one of Frank Gruber's seven western plots (the Union Pacific story, the ranch story, the empire story, the revenge story, Custer's Last Stand, the outlaw story, and the marshal's story), and there was one western pulp dedicated exclusively to rodeo fact and fiction: *Rodeo Romances* (A Thrilling Publication).

Rodeo Romances typically carried one long and one short story, four short-shorts, and four departments covering current rodeo events and historical or first-person fact pieces. The fiction was straight-up cowboy fare with a strong romance flavor. Many of the writers for *Rodeo Romance* were female and there were a few male regulars including Zorro-creator Johnson McCulley and Joe Archibald.

With an obligatory romance woven into the plot by writers familiar to readers of western pulps (Johnson McCulley), *Rodeo Romances* was one pulp which required some specific knowledge on the reader's part:

> Willoughby was riding with blunted spurs and a supple back. He rode out of a series of buck jumps and gave the colt its head.
>
> Wild Fire took a spur whipping for three seconds, straightened out of the circle, and began to fence-corner.

If you couldn't make any sense out of this you probably shouldn't be writing for, or reading, *Rodeo Romances*.

The department "Thrills in Rodeo" was bylined by Foghorn Clancy, billed by *Rodeo Romances* as "America's Most Famous Rodeo Expert." Judging from the names on letters to the editor, I suspect that *Rodeo Romances*' readers were almost exclusively female. The fiction in *Rodeo Romances* was more romance than rodeo, but the rodeo information/news departments provided coverage as good as possible for a quarterly magazine. A typical news item in Foghorn's "In the Arena" department heralded post–World War II "News of Rodeo Folks":

> Among the many rodeo cowboys recently returned from overseas duty and receiving discharges were Tom Mix, Jim Eskew, from the South Pacific area, Jack Kennedy from the European area and Bob Matthews from the China-Burma area. All three were formerly with the JE Ranch Rodeo, and Matthews, in September 1944, helped to stage the first rodeo ever staged in India.—*Rodeo Romances*, March 1946

Not a popular sport subject outside of the single rodeo-titled pulp, rodeo was only featured in one rodeo story in *Sport Story Magazine* over more than a dozen years, and this may have been the only one to appear in any of the non-rodeo titled sports pulps.

The rodeo itself was an opportunity for women to participate in tough, competitive sport, and, as noted earlier, the rodeo pulp often featured stories by, and articles about, women. The autobiographical piece "Born to Ride" in the April 1947 *Rodeo Romances* traces the career of Vera McGinnis:

> It was one hotel room after another, with no home of our own except for a few winter months and then we were busy practicing training horses and planning for the next season.
>
> During those years in the saddle, I won many championships, bucking contests, steer riding, Roman races, relay and flat races.
>
> The largest and perhaps the most gratifying, however, were the two international ones I won at the Wembley exhibition in London in 1924. There I won the relay and the trick riding. And from that time until I returned, I tasted defeat only once in any trick riding contest.

The *Rodeo Romances* magazine was one of the off-size pulps measuring 6¾" × 9¼" instead of the standard pulp size, 7" × 10".

Argosy ran the longest-single rodeo story ever: its six-part series titled "Rodeo," by author Arthur Hawthorne Carhart. The series started with a cover story in the November 9, 1935, *Argosy* and ran over the next five consecutive issues. "Rodeo" is a comeback story, as Hi Lowe (yes, that's his name) tries to overcome some personal devils and get back in the saddle again.

Rodeo is still alive and well in Canada, the Calgary Stampede being the year's big event. The *Canadian Rodeo News*, which is published 12 times a year, covers rodeo events across Canada much as *Rodeo Romances* had done for the U.S. in its heyday.

Basketball Stories

The two basketball titles lasted one issue each: *Basketball Stories* (Winter 1937–38) and *All Basketball Stories* (Winter 1947–48). The 1937 date coincides with the emergence of the first college basketball hero, Hank Luisetti, and by the time *All Basketball Stories* came along, college basketball was beginning to draw the kind of crowds that would eventually make it one of the two college sports to consistently turn a profit. In 1947, however, basketball was still very much small time. National college champs, Holy Cross, didn't have a gym of their own and the game was not giant-dominated as it is today.

Basketball Stories (*Fact and Fiction Basketball Stories*) provided 128 pulp pages of college basketball with "Five Big Basketball Novelets," "Three Fast-Moving Basketball Features" and "Three Short Stories of Modern Basketball." The "Features" were the fact pieces.

Among the fiction writers were some familiar pulp names: Nelson Bond and Bill Cox. Bond's story, "Gawky for Guard," is a clumsy hayseed potboiler about one Dan Carter who would develop into "the flashiest, hottest hoopster in the Central Conference" at little Crawford College. "Gawky for Guard" is full of pulp clichés and some interesting historic stuff such as two-handed set shots and game scores in the 20s, not to mention some pulp heroics:

> And the ball. It struck the backboard glancingly; teetered, hit the outside rim of the basket, and then, as a tomblike silence engulfed the open-mouth spectators, it fell backward through the hoop.

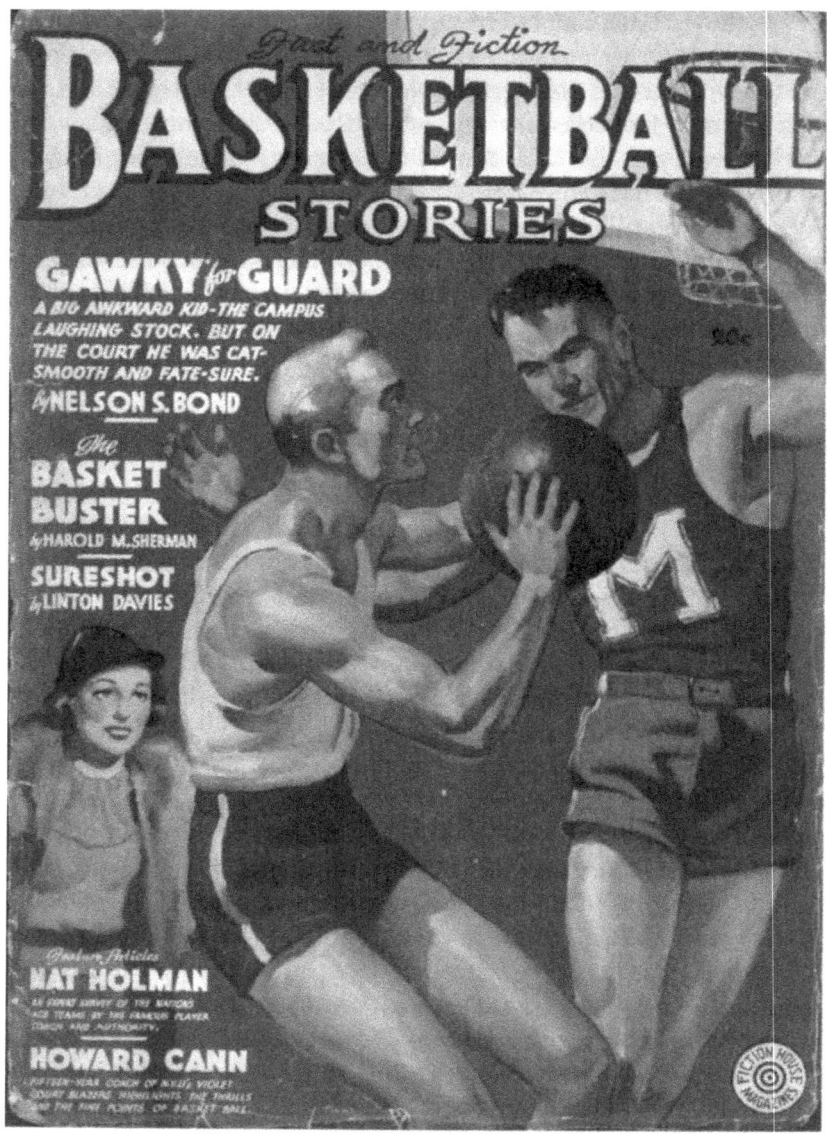

Bill Box's story, "Razzle-Dazzle Racketeer," tells the story of Denver University coach Tip Colson, who is more interested in the point spread than his team's play. He's ultimately uncovered for the cad he is and is "allowed to resign and leave town."

More than any other sport, the basketball pulp reveals a game no longer played; even the punishment for gambling is a thing of the past. Today, the FBI would be in on any college game gambling scam. The fact pieces are of historic interest, too. "New Rules, New Thrills" by "Specialists" explains the new game rules, such as two Free-Throws for an intentional foul, and the "Court Parade of '38" by CCNY basketball coach and game pioneer Nat Holman reviews the national college teams.

And be sure that Frank Merriwell still lives, at least in the heart and pen of Linton Davies, writer of "Sureshot," in which sharpshooter Lefty Lash injures an arm but manages, with arm in sling, to win the day for Taylor. Only in pulpland!

Big Book Sports

Everything about *Big Book Sports* was second rate, except for the price (25¢), which tops out sports pulp prices. The writing was second rate and the cover and interior art were equally bad, but its second issue (V1, No. 2, Winter 1947–48) did something that few all-sports pulps did: it featured basketball on and between the covers. Basketball, never as popular as baseball, football or boxing, was rarely treated as a cover story. Of the seven fiction pieces (there were no fact pieces), three were basketball stories: "Brimstone Basketeer" by Robert Turner, "Hang Tough, Hoopster!" by John Wilson, and "Five Men Don't Make a Team" by Ernest Hamilton. The lead story, "Brimstone Basketeer," is a pulpish drama of competing coal town interests and biases, played out on a basketball court. "Hang Tough, Hoopster!" is a story of a tough bunch of kids (the Roundhouse Gang) who play an indoor-football style of basketball and are rejected by the more polished teams ... until coach Lanny Warren whips them into shape and civilizes them sufficiently to win the league title before he goes off to coach college basketball. "Five Men Don't Make a Team" has guard Steve Tappan thinking his teammates (Dolphins) are all in on a fix. He's mistaken.

There was nothing very big about *Big Book Sports*. On the cover, in an attempt to distinguish itself from the standard pulp page count of 127 pages, its announcement of "130 Pages" in block letters belies the fact that included in this count are both sides of the front cover and the first full-page ad.

Champion Sports Magazine

Champion Sports Magazine offered 144 pages of sports fact and fiction (11 pieces on average) for a mere 15¢. In addition to better-than-average writers like Nelson Bond, Joe Archibald and Jack Kofoed, *Champion Sports* used some of the better cover artists. In

the case of the January 1938 issue, it used the best. Rafael M. de Soto's rendering of Murray Murdock is top-quality sports pulp art. Murdock, called the Lou Gehrig of Hockey for his uninterrupted string of 600 games played for the New York Rangers, is the subject of a tribute by Jack Kofoed in the same issue: "Hockey's Iron Man," in which Kofoed details the factors which made this remarkable record possible.

Champion Sports did its best to offer up something for everyone. The aforementioned issue has boxing ("Punch Parade" by Alex Rossoff and "Ring Tyrant" by Joe Archibald), football ("Victory Waterloo" by W.H. Temple), track ("Suicide Sprint" by Jeffrey Strictland), auto racing ("Jalopy Inferno" by Kent Sagendorph), hockey ("Ice Hog" by Robert C. Blackman, and Jack Kofoed's fact piece), basketball ("The Hero Maker" by Charles Marquis Warren), a skiing story ("Sky Shooter" by Ralph Powers), a skiing instruction piece ("Ups and Downs of Skiing" by Cliff Howe), and a novelty piece ("Grandfather Sampsons" by William J. McNulty) describing the athletic feats of the 40-plus age group, such as Bill Tilden:

> Among the racqueteers, Bill Tilden, former amateur and pro champ of the courts, at 48, is still able to cope with about 95 per cent of the world's tennis players successfully.

Champion Sports Magazine was published by Periodical House, Inc., along with a slew of other pulp magazines: *Ace Sports, Western Aces, Western Trails, Sure-Fire Western, Ten Detective Aces, Red Seal Western, Secret Agent X, Flying Aces, Love Fiction Monthly, Ten-Story Love, Secrets, Movie Merry-Go-Round* and *Reel Humor*.

Jack Dempsey's Fight Magazine

The first issue of *Jack Dempsey's Fight Magazine* (May 1934) was an impressive one, featuring a right to the jaw by cover artist E. K. Bergey, an editorial by Dempsey himself, a training piece by Philadelphia Jack O'Brien (aka Joseph F. Hagan), fact pieces about Frank Gotch and Max Baer, and a Robert E. Howard fight story featuring Sailor Costigan ("The Slugger's Game"). Jack Dempsey is listed as editor and his first editorial hypes both the magazine and the fight game:

> This business of editing a real ring magazine gives me something of the old thrill I used to feel when I was smashing my way through to a crack at the title. The thing I want to do in this magazine of mine is to pass on to you in story form the raw, thrilling action, the humor, the drama and struggle that is part and parcel of the sport of throwing leather.

Wm. Kofoed had been the idea man behind *Fight Stories* and was the creator/publisher of *Jack Dempsey's Fight Magazine*. Fiction and fact pieces in both magazines are the best the pulps had to offer. One of the pieces in the first issue, "I Saw 'Em Fight," was a first-hand account of the Dempsey-Willard fight by "The Ringsider," told in graphic, ring-style prose:

> He led once more ... and that was the moment Jack went into action. He ducked under the Willard lead and smashed a devitalizing right to the heart. It had dynamite back of it, that punch did. With almost the same motion Jack whipped a left to the chin. The instant it landed, a glow of exultation burned in his heart. Under the terrific impact of leather and bone he felt the collapse of the giant.

What the Ringsider could have added to that last sentence was something about the impact of wrapped hands soaked in plaster of Paris and hardened to rock-like consistency. This allegation was a strong one, although, to my knowledge, never admitted by Dempsey.

Jack Dempsey's Fight Magazine was premiere sports pulp material. A nice balance of short fiction (3), one novelette ("The Gold-Brick Kid" by Franklin Martin), three fact stories, one editorial and four departments: "The Mat" (wrestling fact), "With the Leather Pushers" (boxer profiles), "Training for Health, Strength and the Ring" by O'Brien, and a letters section.

The letters section, "The Turnstile," opened in the first issue with good wishes from boxers Gene Tunney and Tommy Loughran, and a letter from British fight fan Jack Hare extolling the virtues of the English boxer Joe Beckett.

Gene Tunney: The Fighting Marine

The Gene Tunney pulp was a one-shot biographical study as "told by his old friend Ed Van Every." Bylined "The Fighting Marine and the Great Dempsey-Tunney Fight," the story is told in six parts over 29 pages: Part 1, The Boy; Part 2, The Man; Part 3, The Fighting Marine; Part 4, The Pugilist; Part 5, The Challenger; and Part 6, The Champion.

Selling for 25¢, *Gene Tunney: The Fighting Marine* is not done in standard pulp format. There are no ads, editorials or departments, but the cover (a drawing of a smiling Tunney from the shoulders up) and the pulp paper are familiar pulp earmarks. The biography is pure puff: "In purpose, courage and condition Gene Tunney cannot easily be excelled — therefore he is a champion. And because he happens to be a champion with ideals he is going to be the best influence the prize ring has ever known."

Fight Stories

For most of the nineteenth century boxing was an outlaw sport performed in defiance of public mores in locations kept secret by boxing insiders. While boxing was as old as the gladiatorial games of Caesar's Rome, the nineteenth century practitioner was an outlaw — although a much-admired one. The boxing scene in the film *Far and Away* is based on Harry Hill's New York saloon where boxing "exhibitions" (which were legal in New York) were held.

Gene Tunney had his first match in such a setting. He talks of this bout in his autobiography, *Arms for the Living*:

> The first public bout I ever fought was an amateur. Club smokers were the amateurs of the day when and where youngsters got their first chance to show what they had — a few to progress and become professionals, others to become useful tinsmiths, shipping clerks, or policemen. It was largely an affair of parish and church. Boxing was fostered to keep boys off the streets and out of evil company during the era of the gangs of New York.

Oddly, it was the American Expeditionary Forces that resulted in the public acceptance of boxing. Army, Navy and Marine divisions stationed in France during World War I held intradivisional bouts during the war and as the war ended, interdivisional bouts were arranged. Of these latter, Gene Tunney commented:

> Battles for A.E.F. titles were staged in a gala extravaganza in Paris. Virtually every man in the A.E.F. (two million) partici-

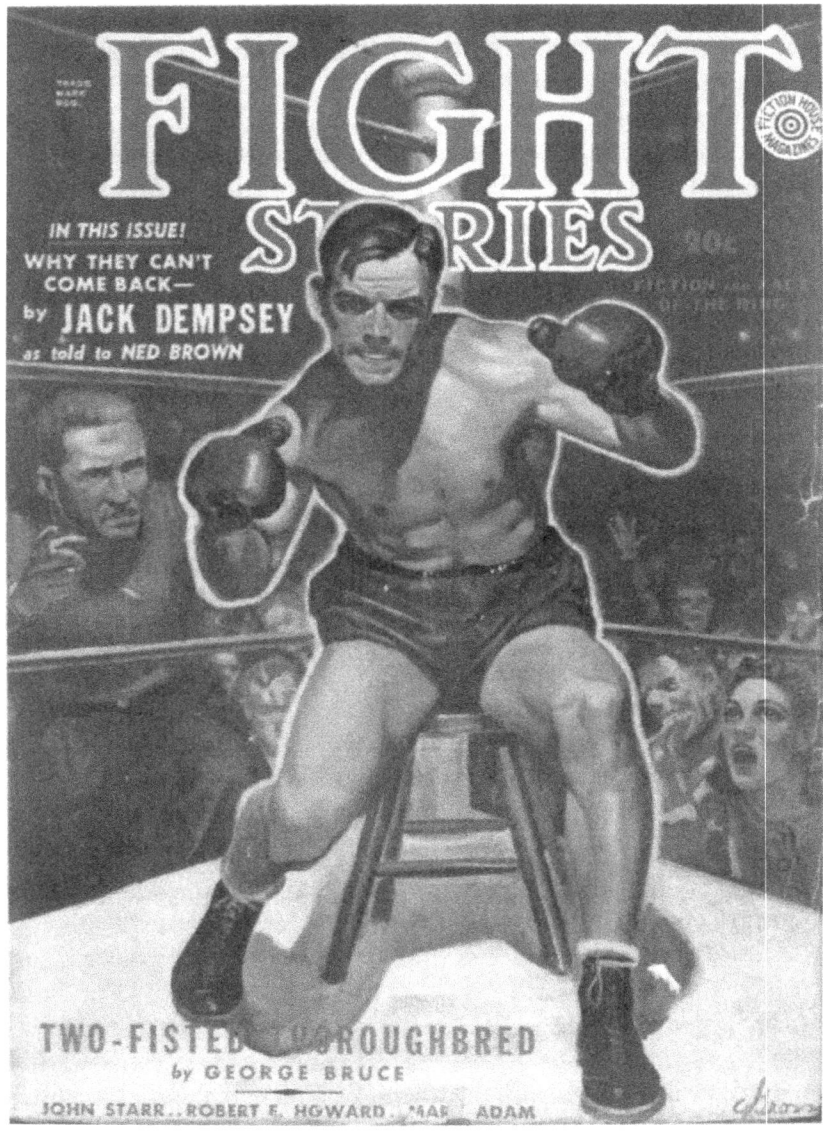

pated in the tournament either as a contestant or spectator — not to mention bettor.

Shortly after the war Tunney's career and the future of boxing would be assured when promoter Tex Rickard's skills were producing million-dollar gates. Since that day interest in boxing has not diminished. In fact, the non-fiction rehashing of old matches in the pulps can still be found in a number of boxing magazines today. It is probably the only surviving sports magazine retro-fiction.

Baseball and boxing were the two sports which provided the most material for the sports pulps and *Fight Stories* (subtitled *Fiction and Fact of the Ring*) was one of the few sports pulps to provide a single-sport treatment of the world of professional boxing.

When *Fight Stories* was first published in June of 1928, Gene Tunney was heavyweight champion of the world. When it ceased publication 20-odd years later, Rocky Marciano had the heavyweight title. Over this span of time, Joe Louis dominated the boxing world in and out of the ring. He could take out an opponent with one, sudden, unexpected, six-inch punch. It was mainly this knockout power which gave the sport and its fiction a unique excitement. The second longest-running fight pulp took its title from the punch: *Knockout Magazine*. Unfortunately it published only eight issues between 1937 and 1938. *The Life of Gene Tunney* was a one-issue special and *Jack Dempsey's Fight Magazine* lasted only a few issues in 1934. But *Jack Dempsey's All-Sport Magazine*, a bedsheet-sized, pulp-like magazine ran for about a half dozen issues in the late 1930s. This magazine almost qualifies as a pulp except for the fact that it contained no fiction. In all other respects it was pure pulp.

In 1928, Bill Kofoed talked Fiction House into starting a boxing magazine, similar in some ways to *Ring*, but one which would include some typical pulp fiction. The magazine, *Fight Stories*, would be subtitled "Fiction and Fact of the Ring."

Fight Stories did a good job on three fronts. First, its fiction was equaled by few writers of the day and it managed to publish some of the boxing stories of Robert E. Howard. Howard's "Stand Up and Slug" (Summer 1940) was a typical slam-bang Sailor Costigan yarn. Costigan's "I can lick any waterfront punk again" is reminiscent of the "I can lick any man in the house" boast of John L. Sullivan. Howard's prose reflects his knowledge of the sport and is tinged with a bit of the humor found in his Breckenridge Elkins westerns:

> I forgot to say our weights was 190 for me, 193 for him. In addition, he was six feet three, or just three inches taller'n me

> and me musta had a reach of anyways fifteen fathoms. When we was still so far apart I didn't think he could reach me with a pole when — bam! his right licked out to my chin.

Reading *Fight Stories* fiction today, it holds up fairly well. Most of the fight fiction was set in the professional ring; some lesser number of fights were in military encampments and fewer still in carnivals, where such as Ted Roscoe's Carnival Kid fought two-rounders with anyone willing to take a chance on winning $50.

Jack Kofoed's retrofights and profiles were among the best nonfiction. His "The Ten Greatest Fights of All Time" (Winter 1951) could well be read in today's *Ring Magazine*. Among the ten fights he selects is the Lavigne-Walcott lightweight title fight in which Lavigne suffers a brutal beating but manages to win:

> No man ever took a more frightful beating in the ring. His nose was broken, his eyes nearly closed, his mouth cut badly, and his left ear was nearly torn off.

Kofoed tells these stories in dramatic style, leaving out none of the brutality. There is something about the one-on-one nature of boxing which lends itself to the art of storytelling.

A similar form of this storytelling is the "as by" piece, and the Summer 1940 "Why They Can't Come Back" by Jack Dempsey as told to Ned Brown, is a prime example:

> There's hardly an ex-ring man alive who wouldn't hock his soul to step into that magic square again and push a pair of gloves on his mitts. And yet most of us are wise enough nowadays to know it's no use. The human body is geared for a few years of perfection, and once a man has passed his peak, then it's better to say goodbye to the ring.

In addition to the regular interior artwork (usually a title-page line drawing) *Fight Stories* occasionally had a full-page profile typical of the sports pages or a two-page Ripley-type segment, "Ringside Review," which related obscure boxing trivia: "George Washington was amateur boxing champion of Virginia. He defeated five opponents in a series of contests sponsored by one Cyril Geddings to win the title … 1748."

4. The All-Sports Pulps 91

Fight Stories ads were a cut above average for the pulps. Ads for the complete works of Shakespeare and an ad by a lawyer: "Patents and Trade Marks ... Protect your most valuable assets..." in various issues indicate that advertisers assumed a more adult audience.

Knockout Magazine

Perhaps the most dramatic moment in sports, the knockout has long been the boxer's badge of manhood. A boxer's ring record is recorded and reported in wins, losses and knockouts. Hence the editorial idea behind *Knockout Magazine*, first published in January-February of 1937 and surviving through June-July 1938.

The initial issue of *Knockout* contained "A Dedication" by the unnamed editors, calling for a "clean" sport and also for a commission to cleanly administer it. Boxing has always had a problem with criminal influence, if not control, and the dedication was replete with pleas for cleansing.

Interestingly, most of the *Knockout* stories have strong elements of crime, typical of which is Roger Torrey's "The Bad Boy and the Butcher," in which the Boy's manager dopes him and bets against him and, if this were not enough, tries, unsuccessfully, to repeat the process in a later rematch. Similarly, the lead story, "Gloves for a Ghost" by William O'Sullivan, is replete with dirty deals as well as the common racism of the day. Dave Kettery is the fighter and one of his two handlers is Sambo Mullins, who speaks in Stepin-Fetchitese: "Yassah, Mistah Barsh."

In spite of these faults, *Knockout* was one of the better sports pulps. It provided one long piece and five short fiction pieces, all a click better than the run-of-the-mill sports pulp story, and it was well-illustrated with a great action cover by Charles De Feo and interior art by John Flemming Gould. With a title like *Knockout* we know beforehand that there will be no decisions, controversial or otherwise, in its fiction; all fights end in decisive knockouts.

In addition to the fiction, *Knockout* provided three fact pieces: "Three-Cornered Dynamite" by William Jerome, "Knockout's Fistic Gallery," and "The Neutral Corner." "Knockout's Fistic Gallery" was a boxer profile with a pen-and-ink drawing of the boxer. The first issue featured Tony Canzoneri, a tough lightweight. The art

work by Jon Blummer shows Canzoneri in a typical, posed boxing stance. "The Neutral Corner" was a readers' letters department, and to stir up the fight crowd, Jerome's "Three-Cornered Dynamite" goes into 11 pages of Joe Louis ring history, starting with what has to be a unique opening sentence:

> Picking the winners of prizefights is often less desirable than picking your nose, because in the latter case you have something to show when you're finished.

In this piece, essentially a Joe Louis ring biography, writer Jerome reviews the entire heavyweight picture from Schmeling to Maxie Baer to Jimmy Braddock and concludes:

> We imagine that Louis, for years to come, will be the biggest shot in the fight game.

All-Baseball Stories

Published in October of 1947, *All-Baseball Stories* was one of a half-dozen or so sports pulps to be in and out of business with one issue. True to pulp fashion, the table of contents lists the book-length novel as "great," the horsehide novelette as "crack" and the five short stories as "exciting."

The cover, which promises "Seven Big Diamond Thrillers," headlines the book-length novel: "Hit Away, Has Been!" by Roe Richmond, which is a routine comeback story capped off by the BIG game:

> The season narrowed down to one final series in Boston that would decide the American League entry for the World Series.

A unique feature of the piece is the fact that the writer uses actual team names and ball parks but slightly-disguised player names. The ace pitcher for Cleveland is Bob Fellows (Bob Feller), the Detroit Tigers' big hitter is Hank Greenhurst (Hank Greenberg), the Red Sox pitcher is Dave Farrin (Dave Ferris), etc.

One of the short stories, "Iron Man in the Mask" by Theodore J. Roemer, is a comeback story with a Rocky twist. Kerry Martin is out of baseball (Class D) because of an injury incurred in a slide. His doctor fears he may not be able to throw again. Martin gets himself into sandlot baseball and ultimately works his way back into the Class D championship (the BIG game). With a "big-time scout" in the stands it would appear that Martin's Class D days are over.

Unfortunately, minor league baseball was rarely covered in the sports pulps and this was an area where these magazines could have competed with the newspaper sports page. A rare minor league piece in *Popular Sports* (Summer 1949), "Class C Baseball Can Have Its Thrills, Too!," reviews some of the players and a recent game.

The short story, "Curves Crazy" by Gene D. Robinson, in *All Baseball Stories*, is a rare sports pulp tale involving a girls' baseball team, the Hawks, who are engaged (unknowingly) by Forrest Darwin to play his Gobblers:

> They trotted onto the field. The Gobblers meekly gave way. The apple whizzed about peppily. Millie batted grounders, a tall girl flies. The crowd stopped wise-cracking, cheered. These gals could play ball.

The Gobblers, a town team of sorts, are reluctant to play the girls until they discover their won-lost percentage (.745) against male teams. The game is played in front of a big crowd and the denouement is pure pulp of the era. A male pinch-hitter is sent in for one of the girls and it's his home run which wins the game. The pitcher's response:

> Anyhow it took a man to beat us, he muttered, dismally.

If this were not enough, the coach of the girls' team hooks the manager of the Gobblers:

> Say, how come you never tried a matrimonial bureau — with your looks?

Baseball Stories

Of the six baseball pulps, only two lasted for more than a few issues. *All-Baseball Stories* had one issue (10/1947), *Big Baseball Stories* had three in 1948, *Popular Baseball* had fewer than a dozen during 1949–1950. The successes, *Baseball Stories* (1938–1953) and *Exciting Baseball* (1941–1950) had relatively long runs, but all of these magazines ran into the television wall at about the same time.

The period encompassed by these magazines (1938–1953) was dominated on the baseball diamond by the New York Yankees, who

won 11 World Series, dominating the American League and the game itself. Four times over this period the Brooklyn Dodgers were the Yankees' adversaries. These two teams had more of an influence on the pulp baseball story than any writer's imagination. Their games did not want for excitement, and the task for the writer was to capture this real-world excitement on the printed page. Judson Philips was already a regular *Argosy* contributor when he became a sports

reporter and a fight manager, and he once qualified for the National Amateur golf tournament. He would draw on this background when writing his sports fiction for *Argosy* and occasionally had a cover story. His cover story in the October 5, 1935, *Argosy*, "Big League Bandit," is about a familiar character in baseball's early days — the tramp player. The tramp was a player who knocked around the league, going from one team to another when he was free of his personal devils — usually booze. Philips' tramp is a tramp both in and out of baseball:

> Right away I spotted him for a panhandler. Florida was lousy with 'em that spring. He wore a ragged, dirty suit, he hadn't shaved for several days and he had a checkered cap pulled down over his face — a face that hadn't seen much Florida sunshine. He had a tiny stub of a cigarette between his lips, so short that it seemed as though it would burn him any second. Somehow I knew he had picked up a butt where someone had dropped it.

As it turns out in the world of pulp baseball, the tramp displays superior pitching skills, wins the BIG game and at story's end is on his way again.

Baseball Stories was the first all-baseball sports pulp. First published in 1938, it included the usual mix of fact and fiction; in fact, its full title was *Fact and Fiction Baseball Stories*. A typical issue included the following: a book-length novel of the diamond, two action-packed novelets, three stand-out features and a short story. The fact pieces were done by writer Jimmy Powers, often with illustrations by artists Mario De Marco and Walter Galli. A unique piece in the Spring 1952 issue entitled "Better Than a Hit" attempted to identify words peculiar to baseball and phrases used by players, broadcasters, fans, etc. The final alphabetized list contained hundreds of words and phrases not to be found in Fowler: a quail-high hit, a coffin-corner triple, a Texas leaguer, and a foozler. Some of the colorful announcer talk is quoted. The following is attributed to Jim Britt, a Boston Braves announcer:

> If he had ever connected with that one the ball would have gone over the fence, over the Charles River, over the fields, past Harvard College, through the woods and right up to grandmother's front door.

The complete list compiled by Walter Putney contained hundreds

4. The All-Sports Pulps

of words either unique to baseball or which had a unique meaning when used in a baseball context, such as the Alphonse-Gaston single.

Since more than 40 years have passed since this list was compiled, it could surely stand updating with such current terms as bonus baby, franchise player, a biting curve and a play which is worthy of the weekly highlights.

Burgess Leonard, a frequent *Baseball Stories* contributor, tells a comeback story in the Summer 1949 issue ("The Last Pitch of Hap Andrews"). Hap Andrews has been banished from baseball for 10 years and is making a comeback of sorts as a relief pitcher. It seems that the gambler who had been key to Hap's banishment has made a deathbed statement clearing Hap, so here he was, back with the Hawks. The story leads to the BIG game where Hap wins the day and the series:

> Hap stretched. He reached far back. He reached back into dead years. He blasted the ball, shoulder-high, right over the middle. And Red Willis, shocked, simply missed it.

The sports pulps presented a steady diet of this type of story for its male audience. The All-American Girls' Professional Baseball League had completed six seasons when this issue of *Baseball Stories* was published and it was a surprise to see a brief, half-page tribute to the league, as women's baseball had been ignored by all of the sports pulps.

The piece, titled "A New Headline Sport!," chronicles the history of the league starting with P. K. Wrigley, Jr.'s creation of it just to keep the game alive during the war years. While the piece is complimentary, it goes too far (a pulp habit), suggesting that "it now threatens to run men's baseball a close race at the box office."

The piece lists the modifications made to accommodate the game to women (changes in pitcher-home plate and base separation distances and ball size) and the eight teams which were owned by the cities they represented: Racine and Kenosha, Wisconsin; Grand Rapids and Muskegon, Michigan; Fort Wayne and South Bend, Indiana; and Peoria and Rockford, Illinois.

In a face piece in the same issue (Summer 1949), Doc McGee picks the Boston Red Sox to finish first in the American League. The New York Yankees were predicted to finish fifth. The Yankees finished first and proceeded to beat Brooklyn in the World Series four games to one.

McGee and sports writer Jimmy Powers were frequent contributors of such prognostications, fact pieces, player and team profiles. In the Spring 1954 *Baseball Stories*, McGee picks the Yankees and Dodgers to win their respective leagues. He got the Dodgers but Cleveland, which he picked to finish fourth, came in first in the American League but lost the Series to the Dodgers in four straight games.

If there were any doubts about the target audience of *Baseball Stories* one had only to look at the ads for pipes, body building, judo training, the Rupture-Easer ("over 700,000 Grateful Users"), and the book *What Men Don't Know About Women*.

The postwar prosperity would make both the radio and the live ball game available to the pulp reader and if the other factors leading to its demise weren't enough, televised baseball would finish off *Baseball Stories* by 1954. In retrospect, it's surprising that it lasted that long.

A few words about women in sports fiction. First, when women figured into a story the sport was not one of the big three: baseball, basketball, football. Typically the sports action was a sidebar to a mystery theme. This fiction was found in the girls' series books* and depicted girls involved in gymnastics, track and field, and crew. In these stories winning or losing was not central to the story. Sports fiction in these books told the reader that the sole benefits from sports participation were those resulting from physical activity.

Popular Sports

Popular Sports Magazine produced some of the better sports fiction. Using sports writers like Jack Kofoed and Jackson Scholz, and pulp pros like Robert Leslie Bellem and Robert Sidney Browen, it produced more literate material than some of the lesser magazines like *Complete Sports*.

The non-fiction material published in *Popular Sports* was also of superior quality. Jack Kofoed (a regular contributor to *Sport Story Magazine* and *Fight Stories*) had a long-running newspaper-like column, "The Whirl of Sports," in which topical sports material and some nostalgia subjects were covered over several pages. The column

---

*University of Minnesota Libraries, Girl's Series Books 1840–1991, A Checklist of Titles Published, *Children's Literature Research Collections, Minneapolis, Minnesota.*

was bylined "By Jack Kofoed — Famous Sports Commentator" and a typical menu covered: "Looking Back at the Heroes of 1925," "What's Your Favorite Superstition?" "Class C Baseball Can Have Its Thrills Too!" "The Saga of White-Headed Bob, Prize Fighter" (A brief story of Ned Baldwin taken from the London *Morning Herald* in 1923), "Lou Gehrig Was One of Baseball's Finest," "Here's What Made Golfer Johnny Farrell Blush," and a human interest story about baseball pitcher Charlie DeBedts, "When We Know the Answer We'll Pick More Winners."

Sports writer Cap Fanning produced a "Sports Preview" segment in which the past of a league, player, or team was appraised and its future assessed. The column was alternately used to hype forthcoming fiction in *Popular Sports* and "companion magazines" which were listed on the magazine's title page: *Thrilling Sports, Everyday Astrology, Popular Western, Thrilling Mystery, Thrilling Detective, Thrilling Adventure, Thrilling Love, The Phantom Detective, The Lone Eagle, Sky Fighters, Popular Detective, Thrilling Ranch Stories, Detective Novels Magazine, Thrilling Wonder Stories, G-Men, West, Masked Rider, Western Magazine, Range Riders Western, Startling Stories, Strange Stories, Texas Rangers, Popular Love, Thrilling Spy Stories, Rio Kid Western, Black Book Detective Magazine, Captain Future, Thrilling Football Stories, The Ghost, Air War, Exciting Western, Exciting Detective* and *The Masked Detective*.

The letters segment, common enough in the science fiction magazines, was a rarity in the sports pulps and the few reader letters published in *Popular Sports* looked suspiciously contrived: "Dear Cap Fanning. I am an inveterate reader of *Popular Sports* Magazine and its companions *Thrilling Sports* and *Exciting Sports*" starts one, and it continues with a sports trivia question which the old Cap easily fields. Cap's sign-off reads:

> Well, that's that for the nonce, as someone once said. See you next time and don't forget to write your sports problems to us at Suite 1400, 10 East 40th St., N.Y. 16, N.Y. Thank you and so long for now... Cap Fanning

Other non-fiction material included "From the Annals of Sport" by Simpson M. Ritter, a look at some obscure sports data:

> You may not be surprised to learn that Kelly Pool was neither invented by a man named Kelly nor is it of Irish origin. Its

inventor, Celestus Mulvaney, was of Irish origin but invented the game in 1893 in Chicago. The first games were played in that city at the Hannah and Hoggs Billiard Hall on Madison St.

Occasional baseball statistics were published without editorial fanfare, such as an incomplete listing of major and minor league batting averages in the Fall 1940 issue, and on occasion a brief (half-page) sport history lesson was provided, as in the Summer 1949 "Baseball as She Was" which looks at the origins of baseball in the middle 1800s.

The most highly prized (by readers) non-fiction material was the interview with a prominent sports figure, as when Jack Kofoed interviewed Max Schmeling's manager, Joe Jacobs (Summer 1940). This was an area in which the sports pulp could compete with the daily newspaper's sports page. Another is the ghosted or "as by" story in which the sports figure speaks in his own voice, as in the Jack Dempsey piece, "Sports for a Living." This piece has an editorial note: "No one is better qualified to write to young men about the advantages of professional sport than he," and is by-lined "Especially Written for *Popular Sports*." In it Dempsey goes through several sports assessing their potential for providing an income: "I haven't heard advisers of the young tell the boys of our nation to look for success in this field." Dempsey is cautiously optimistic for the future of baseball, tennis, wrestling and boxing if the young man has some talent and ambition. He sees (this is 1940) pro football growing, perhaps a minor league. He sees the "average wrestler keeping his overhead down, driving from town to town where he lives in moderate-priced motels. As a whole I would say the wrestler is usually in better financial condition when he quits than any other athlete, with the exception of the major league ball players."

Dempsey states flatly: "Golf isn't a huge money maker and will never be" but he sees some potential for basketball: "Basketball at the moment is not a productive field in a professional sense. It was once — and it will be again."

He sees some potential for making money in skiing but says of skating: "Skating? You can't make any money at that!" Overall, though, Dempsey is optimistic: "The doors of sport are wide open for those who are geared for it. Why not come in and see what it has to offer?"

This piece was probably written by Jack Kofoed and based on some few words in a phone conversation with Dempsey. In any event, this type of material featuring the big sports name was done better by *Popular Sports* than perhaps any other sports pulp with the possible exception of *Sport Story Magazine*.

5

Street & Smith's Sport Story Magazine

> Subscribe today!
> If you are a full-blooded sport fan who demands a top-notch magazine with plenty on the ball, you want SPORT STORY MAGAZINE.—Street & Smith ad in *Sport Story Magazine*

In 1855, Amos Williamson sold the *New York Weekly Dispatch* to "two ambitious employees" (according to Quentin Reynolds in *The Fiction Factory*): Francis Smith and Francis Street. The circulation at the time was a barely respectable 18,000. Over the period 1855–1909 the firm would grow into an empire, with 36 weekly publications, 29 paperback books, five magazines and a handful of cloth-bound books. In the late 1800s the popularity of dime-novel western and detective characters would send circulation numbers to regions undreamed of by Street and Smith.

Street & Smith led the way in the pulp era. They were first with a pulp western (*Western Story Magazine*, 1919), first with a love pulp (*Love Story Magazine*, 1921), first with a super-hero pulp (*The Shadow*, 1931), and in 1923 they produced the first sports pulp: *Sport Story Magazine*.

Throughout the publishing history of Street & Smith sports fact and fiction always played a role. From the Frank Merriwell dime novels to the baseball and football yearbooks of the 1940s, the Smiths, from Francis (died in 1887) to son Ormond (died in 1933) to his son Gerald (died in 1955) always put out one or more sports publications. In the late 1940s, Gerald was one of the investors behind the All-American Football Conference.

Sport Story Magazine was the best of all the Street & Smith sports publications for three reasons, the last of which is the product of the first two. First and foremost, it took sports fiction out of the stereotypical Frank Merriwell shackles and made it palatable to current tastes. It did for sports fiction what *Wild West Weekly* had done for western fiction. Secondly, it provided the widest imaginable sports menu. In 1927, for example, nearly 40 different sports were covered. Lastly, in terms of total material, it had no peer among the more than 50 sports pulps which came along in the wake of *Sport Story Magazine*.

Following is a yearly summary of the contents of *Sport Story Magazine*, starting with 1923, its first year of publication, and ending with 1943 when only five issues were published.

Story Count By Type of Sport, 1923–1943

The following table represents a count of the types of sports in all of the sports fiction printed over the calendar years 1923–1943, the year in which the magazine ceased publication.

One note about the count. Each story in each issue was tallied as "a story." That is, a four-part baseball story over four consecutive months would be totaled as four baseball stories for that year. The rationale for this is page count. The purpose is to see what sports were represented most in *Sport Story Magazine*. These were presumably reflective of America's tastes for the real thing, and the best indication of that is presumed to be page count. One baseball story over four issues totaling approximately 20 or more pages was counted as four pieces of baseball fiction. A count of this kind gives a true picture of the sports-types balance both in individual issues and in the totals.

Story Count May 1923–July 1943

Sport	Stories	Rank
Baseball	478	1
Boxing	363	2

Sport	Stories	Rank
Track	281	3
Football	259	4
Hockey	164	5
Basketball	156	6
Tennis	117	7
Wrestling	11	8
Golf	97	9
Car racing	76	10
Rowing (crew)	49	11
Swimming	49	12
Polo	46	13
Handball	26	14
Bicycle racing	24	15
Lacrosse	22	16
Ski jumping	11	17

These, the top-ranking sports by volume, show some yearly variations but baseball was always number one except for three years (1930, 1931, 1938) when boxing headed the count. Just about every imaginable sport was included at some time in one or more of the *Sport Story* issues: canoe tilting, bowling, yacht racing, tug-of-war, horseshoe pitching, ice-boating, dog sledding, steeplechase, snowshoe racing, water polo, bullfighting, etc. There was no sport which was not at some time grist for Street & Smith's *Sport Story Magazine*'s fiction mill.

Sport Story Magazine, 1923–1943

The First Year: 1923

The first issue of *Sport Story Magazine* sold for 15¢ and contained a mix of sports fiction. The date was September 8, 1923, and the range of sports indicated the editor's desire to appeal to the polo and tennis set as well as the boxing and horse race crowd.

The October 22 issue contained fiction by two classes of writers: the prominent sports figure (Francis Ouimet) and the pulp magazine writer (Octavus Roy Cohen). Ouimet was the first American golfer to draw a gallery of more than a few hundred. In 1913, more than 3,000 people watched Ouimet (an amateur) upset Great Britain's two leading pros in the United States Open. Cohen, a frequent contributor to the pulp magazines, was a prolific detective novelist whose most famous creation was the detective Jim Hanvey. His more than 50 novels span the period 1917–1955.

The sports editorial "From the Bleachers," a feature which would continue throughout the life of the magazine, was first introduced in the December 8 issue. Arthur Grahame, using the house name Handley Cross, would write this "department" through the September 1, 1938, issue.

Another pulp writer, Tom Curry, contributed his first of many sports fiction pieces with a December 22 water-polo story.

The Second Year: 1924

The year 1924 would bring to *Sport Story Magazine* an amazing mix of writers including Paul Gallico; Ernest Haycox, perhaps America's greatest western writer; Gilbert Patten, a survivor of the dime-novel era; John Tunis, the finest writer of boys' sports fiction; Raoul Whitfield, an accomplished hard-boiled detective fiction writer; and Damon Runyon of *Guys and Dolls* fame.

March 22, 1924, marked the first "The Announcer" column — a calendar of then-current sports events. The February 22 issue contained a verse piece by James E. Hungerford — the first entry of this kind. Bill Tilden, one of America's premier tennis players, would get in trouble with the United States Lawn Tennis Association for the work he contributed to three issues of this year's *Sport Story Magazine*. The USLTA would claim that Tilden's writing amounted to profiting from the sport of tennis, which they felt was unacceptable. A compromise was reached whereby Tilden could write about tennis, but not about current tournaments. Tilden generally ignored the dictates of the USLTA and would later (1928) be suspended from the Davis Cup team.

Two writers of hard-boiled detective fiction, Carroll John Daly and Harold de Polo, would have their first sports fiction in the April 8, 1924 *Sport Story Magazine*. Daly is generally credited with having written the first hard-boiled piece, "The False Burton Combs" (December 1922 *Black Mask Magazine*).

The piece by John Tunis ("The Iron Duke") was the first of three he would publish in *Sport Story Magazine*. The title and story of this magazine piece would form the basis for his first novel, published by Harcourt Brace in 1938. *Iron Duke* (a track story) won an award as the best juvenile book of the year (1938). The Tunis sports books were known for dealing with the hard issues. Class and race issues were treated realistically enough that the *New York Times* obit referred to Tunis as the man who "helped educate a whole generation of Americans."

The piece by Damon Runyon ("The Law of the Lightning," a track story) which appeared in the August 8 issue, is the only work of Runyon's ever to be published in any pulp magazine.

Paul Gallico was one of the so-called "Gee Whiz" sports reporters of the 1920s, a group of men including Grantland Rice and Heywood Broun, whose enthusiasm for sports was exceeded only by their worship of the legendary sports heroes of the 1920s. Gallico, in fact, wrote a book about these bigger-than-life characters (*The Golden People*).

When Ernest Haycox died in 1950, the Western Writers of America named their best-writer award the Ernie in his honor; it was later renamed the Spur. Haycox's western, *The Stage to Lordburg* (later made into the film *Stagecoach*) is credited with elevating the western to the status of literature. Haycox contributed a track story, "The Skeeter," to the December 8 issue.

The Third Year: 1925

The man who is generally hailed as the premier writer of boys' books, John Tunis, contributed "The Iron Duke," a track story, to the May 8 issue of *Sport Story Magazine*. In 1938 the story would be published in hardcover by Harcourt Brace. Tunis would write two more fiction pieces for *Sport Story*: "The Limelight Kid," a football story in the January 8 issue, and "Match Point," a tennis story in the March 22 issue. This was the only fiction Tunis produced for the magazine. In the March 1, 1931, issue of the magazine he would write an op ed piece, "Who Owns Football?" (subtitled "A Sensible Discussion").

Familiar pulp writers Tom Curry, Carroll John Daly, Octavis Roy Cohn, Harold de Polo, and Raoul Whitfield dominate the pages of *Sport Story*. Whitfield had 18 stories in the 1925 issues. There were a few non-fiction innovations: "How He Became a Ballplayer" is a reader segment; Handley Cross (Arthur Graham) introduced the segment "Making Champions of the Future"; and the era's most prominent track star, Charlie Paddock, had a six-part autobiographical series entitled "The Glory of the Game."

The magazine's price was still 15¢ per copy and the page count averaged 135.

Sport Story Magazine: Fiction Count for Jan.–Dec. 1925

Baseball	47	Swimming	5
Boxing	35	Golf	4
Track	24	Yacht racing	3
Football	22	Boating	2
Basketball	16	Handball	2
Horse racing	15	Pole vaulting	2
Rowing	15	Auto polo	2
Car racing	14	Roller polo	1
Tennis	11	Water polo	1
Hockey	10	Polo	1
Airplane racing	5		

1 each: steeplechase, water hockey, snowshoeing, skiing, wrestling, fishing, and hunting.

The Fourth Year: 1926

The dime novelist Gilbert Patten was still writing sports fiction for *Sport Story* and managed to maintain his status as the magazine's best-paid writer. His May 8 piece, "The Rockspur Athletic Club," earned him $620. Two other pieces in this issue earned $100 each, and the other pieces earned anything from a low of $50 to a high of $75.

The pulp writers predominated. Raoul Whitfield wrote under his own name and the pen name Stuart Osborne when he had more than one piece in a single issue, as in the June 22 issue.

The 1926 issues have a number of fact pieces: baseball (3), track (2), high jump and pole vaulting (1), swimming (1), soccer (1), high school football (1), football (1) and basketball (1).

The per issue price (15¢) and average page count (135) remained unchanged. The gradual addition of non-fiction pieces and departments was noticeable.

Sport Story Magazine: Fiction Count for Jan.–Dec. 1926

Baseball	42	Boating	8
Track	30	Rowing	6
Boxing	29	Handball	4
Car racing	19	Water polo	3
Horse racing	16	Polo	3
Basketball	14	Wrestling	2
Football	14	Soccer	2
Tennis	10	Aquaplaning	1
Hockey	10	Fishing	1

1 each: bowling, rodeo, hammer throwing, shot put, trap shooting, lacrosse, skulling, airplane racing, bicycle racing, handball, ice boating, and ice relay.

The Fifth Year: 1927

Gilbert Patten continued to contribute Burt Standish fiction in the April 8 and 22 and the May 8 issues. Others to use the Burt Standish name in 1927 were Warren E. Carleton, Joseph B. Ames and J. Irving Crump.

There were non-fiction articles in January (hockey and speed skating), February (lacrosse) and March (baseball), and a Handley Cross interview piece featuring Knute Rockne (October 8).

Pulp writers were prominent: Raoul Whitfield had 15 stories published between January 22 and December 22; Tom Curry, six; and Paul Chadwick had his first *Sport Story* entry in the July 22 issue. While baseball and track fiction prevailed, the variety of sports (37) guaranteed a wide audience.

The most prominent sports event of 1927 had to be the "Fight of the Century" between Tunney and Dempsey at Soldier Field in Chicago, with attendance exceeding 104,000. Tunney's defeat of Dempsey and his subsequent (1928) retirement after a knockout victory over Australian Tom Heeney signaled a waning of public interest in the sport of boxing. The size of the gate (more than $2.5 million) would pique the interest of organized crime, however.

Fiction Count for 1927

Baseball	34	Basketball	8
Track	27	Swimming	5
Boxing	16	Water polo	5
Hockey	16	Skiing	4
Horse racing	14	Canoeing	4
Football	14	Rowing	4
Golf	11	Wrestling	3
Tennis	9	Handball	3
Car racing	9		

Dogsled racing, soccer, motorboat racing, airplane racing   2

Diving, sailboat racing, javelin throwing, fencing, log-birling, shot putting, pole vaulting, yacht racing, horseshoe pitching, steeple chasing, tug-of-war, ice boating, lacrosse, bowling, canoe tilting   1

Sport fact articles generally preceded the sport in season, with baseball, boxing and football dominating. Gilbert Patten kept the Merriwell saga going with 4 two-part series, two dealing with Frank and "summer sports," one with college sports, and one baseball series. Raoul Whitfield again was the sportsman for all seasons, with 10 stories covering hockey, airplane racing, basketball, hockey, swimming, canoe tilting, baseball and car racing. Tom Curry contributed a pair of water polo stories and a football piece.

The Sixth Year: 1928

Gilbert Patten and the Frank Merriwell saga continued with a two-part polo story, "Frank Merriwell's Polo Team" (March); two two-part baseball stories, "Frank Merriwell and the Ivory Hunters" (June) and "Frank Merriwell and the Gamma Gang" (September).

Most of the fact pieces were about baseball/football teams and/or characters, the lengthiest of which was a six-part "Track Memoirs" series by Charlie Paddock. Paddock also wrote "A Word to Young Athletes" in the July 22 issue. There were interviews with Paul Warner (Aug. 22), Walter Johnson (June 22) and "Pop" Warner (November 2)* and several lesser sports characters.

*With Vol XXI, No. 3 issue of Sport Story the numbering of issues changed from identifying monthly issues as either 8 or 22 to First Month and Second Month.

In 1928, John Tunis published, in book form, *$port$: Heroics and Hysterics*, a polemic citing the negative influence of money on sports in general.

Tom Curry had four water polo stories and Raoul Whitfield again provided a diversified menu with baseball, airplane racing and boxing fiction.

Fiction Count for 1928 (No October Issues)

Baseball	29	Car racing	8
Track	27	Tennis	7
Boxing	18	Wrestling	7
Horse racing	14	Airplane racing	7
Football	14	Golf	6
Hockey	10	Pole Vault	5
Basketball	9		

Swimming, soccer, polo, bicycle racing, water polo   4

Javelin, lacrosse, motorboat racing, skiing   2

Dog racing, motorcycle racing, iceboating, dogsledding, broad-jumping, fencing, high jump, hurdling, canoe tilting, discus throwing, sailboat racing, shotput, handball.

1929: The Seventh Year

Page count (in the 130s) and price (15¢; $3 yearly subscription) remained the same over the first seven years of publication.

Perhaps the highlight of the year was the so-called "missing Frank Merriwell" story.* It is called missing because it was not catalogued in Eddie LeBlanc's "Dime Novel Bibliography." The story, "Frank Merriwell and the Mystery Ship," was written by J. Irving Crump as told by John Samson. It appeared in two parts (October First and Second).

One of the few articles by a woman appeared in the Second July issue: "Women in Athletics" by Ada Taylor Sackett.

*Dime Novel Roundup, Publication No. 157140, ISSN 0012-2874, Vol. 64, No. 4, August 1995, Whole No. 634.

Pulp writers Raoul Whitfield and Tom Curry were regular contributors and Arthur Burks made his entry into the sports fiction market with a boxing story in February ("The Odyssey of Oily Sing") and followed it with a second boxing story in March ("Taking Santiago"). Burks (1898–1974) was a prolific detective and adventure fiction writer in addition to being a regular contributor to *Weird Tales*. His service as a marine in both World Wars and his life experiences as an adventurer and world traveler (often lacking in pulp writers) lent a certain reality to his fiction.

Of the 38 different sports represented over the year, the most popular remained baseball (26 stories) and boxing (23). Seasonal fact articles (hockey in February, baseball in June, etc.) were now appearing regularly, as were interviews with athletes and coaches.

Regular departments continued: "The Announcer" and "From the Bleachers." A short-lived "club" made its debut in the October 22 issue: Hare and Hounds Club.

Fiction Count for 1929

Baseball	26	Pole vault	5
Boxing	23	Wrestling	5
Hockey	23	Rowing	5
Track	23	Soccer	4
Football	15	Swimming	4
Tennis	13	Polo	4
Horse racing	12	Diving	3
Basketball	10	Skiing	3
Airplane racing	10	Handball	3
Car racing	9	Boating	2
Golf	8	Bicycle racing	2

Bowling, mountain climbing, bobsledding, squash, dogsled racing, hurdles, broadjumping, shotput, fencing, hammer throwing, archery, canoe racing, javelin throwing, surfboat racing, discus throwing, steeplechase   1

The Eighth Year: 1930

Some prominent boxing names appeared as non-fiction writers: Billy Papke, Tommy Burns, Jim Corbett, Jack Johnson (undoubtedly ghosted in each case). In the April 22 issue there was only one fiction piece; the remainder of the issue was dedicated to college sports at Missouri, Harvard, Georgia, Yale, West Point, Princeton, Virginia, South Carolina, Johns Hopkins, McGill, Chicago, Annapolis and Dartmouth. Bill Tilden had a four-part fiction series starting in May. Arthur Graham (under the Handley Cross pseudonym) wrote a non-fiction piece, "These Girls," subtitled: "An Article on Girls in Athletics."

Thirty-five different sports were covered in 1930 and boxing and baseball shared the top two spots. There were monthly fact articles on in-season sports.

Raoul Whitfield continued to contribute to *Sport Story Magazine* but this year would be his last. Whitfield began writing for *Sport Story* in 1924, before he began his work in *Black Mask*. Over the period 1926–1934 Whitfield contributed nearly 100 stories to *Black Mask* in addition to producing three novels in the *Black Mask* style: *Green Ice* (1930), *Death in a Bowl* (1931), and *The Virgin Kills* (1932) and a collection of aviation stories ("Silver Wings," 1930) based on his World War I experiences. Whitfield's health forced a slowdown and finally a cessation of any writing by 1934. He died in 1945.

Major League baseball was becoming fan-friendly in 1930, a date which marks the end of the "dead-ball" era. By 1930 teams were scoring 3.5 more runs than in 1915 and the number of home runs increased from 384 in 1915 to 1,565 in 1930. At the same time interest in collegiate sports was increasing, as reflected in the fact that only one college stadium had a capacity for 70,000 fans in 1920 and by 1930 there were seven. In individual sports (boxing, golf, tennis, etc.) it was said, after Bobby Jones won the American Amateur title and several golf titles in Europe, that the age of the amateur had passed.

Fiction Count for 1930

Boxing	26	Horse racing	10
Baseball	22	Golf	9
Hockey	20	Car racing	8
Track	20	Polo	8
Football	19	Skiing	7
Basketball	10	Swimming	6

Soccer	6	Lacrosse	3
Rowing	4	Glider flying	2
Handball	4	Motorboat racing	2
Airplane racing	4	Diving	2
Tennis	4	Water polo	2

Wrestling, bullfighting, bowling, bicycle racing, fencing, tobogganing, snowshoe racing, broadjumping, hurdling, high jumping, decathlon, hammer throwing, javelin throwing

The Ninth Year: 1931

While the cover and subscription prices remained the same (15¢ and $3) the variety of stories was at a new low (23) and format changes were introduced. Boxing, again, was the most frequent fiction subject. Content typically consisted of one or two novelettes (or one serial), seven or so short stories and three fact sections: Features, Departments and Miscellany. Feature writers included Jack Kofoed (under his own name and as Ned Hazlitt), John Tunis, Jim Thorpe (Joe Burton), and Connie Mack (Edgar Wolfe). In addition to the recently increased non-fiction material, the Miscellany included as many as 15 fillers, among them puzzles by Walter Gibson (June and July). Interestingly, the Maxwell Grant house name is used for a December filler: "Is Wrestling on the Level?" Arthur Mann wrote the piece.

Familiar pulp names show among the writers: stories by T. W. Ford, a Robert E. Howard Kid Allison story ("Man with the Mystery Mitts," October) and Arthur Burks ("One-Punch Palooka," November) were included.

In July, another feature was added to the mix: a Physical Improvement Course, the first installment of which was "How to Promote Growth and Increase Height." In the same month a "feature serial" (a lengthy biographical piece about Jack Dempsey) was added. Some new directions—all toward less fiction and experimentation with formatting and greatly expanded filler material— marked this issue.

Tom Curry had a wrestling story in January and this would be his last sports fiction for *Sport Story Magazine*. While writing sports fiction, Curry was also doing his bit to fill up the detective and adventure pulps. Over the period 1926–1933 he produced 38 stories for *Black Mask*. All of this was a prelude to his work in the western genre. In 1936 (the 100th anniversary of the founding of the Texas Rangers) he started the *Texas Ranger* pulp and would contribute most of the stories, alternating with Leslie Scott, both of them using the Jackson Cole house name. Curry wrote 36 Rio Kid pulp stories from 1938 to 1950, and would continue to write westerns into the 1960s for digest magazines such as *Zane Grey Western*, using the Rohmer Grey pseudonym. In a conversation I had with Mr. Curry (March 23, 1975), he claimed to have written for almost 400 different pulp magazines.

Fiction Count for 1931

Boxing	30	Golf	4
Baseball	28	Motorcycle racing	2
Wrestling	15	Dog racing	2
Basketball	9	Rodeo	1
Track	9	Soccer	1
Football	8	Bicycle racing	1
Car racing	8	Lacrosse	1
Hockey	7	Steeplechase	1
Boat racing	6	Canoe racing	1
Rowing	4	Harness racing	1
Tennis	4	Airplane racing	1

The Tenth Year: 1932

For the second consecutive month the number of fiction stories was in the twenties (24) and the new non-fiction emphasis continued. T. W. Ford had a variety of fiction in all but three of this year's issues and Arthur Burks appeared in seven issues with boxing fiction (one, a three-parter, "The Golden Glover"). The dime-novel standby house name, Burt Standish, appeared three times: once by W. E. Carleton (baseball), once by Dabney Horton (baseball) and once by Jackson Scholz (basketball). None of these stories featured either of the Merriwells.

The feature fiction in February was "Doubling for Dynamite" by Walter Gibson (Tom Lewis wrote and Lon Murray rewrote).

Shadow Magazine editor John Nanovic wrote a piece in January about the "possibilities" of pro basketball. It was an optimistic piece but did not foresee the level to which pro basketball would expand. A milestone for *Sport Story Magazine* was a three-part fiction piece by Frederick Faust (as Max Brand) in October: "Thunderbolt," a football story.

Sport Story readers were not ready yet for physical conditioning and the Physical Improvement Course disappeared after the June issue.

While women athletes were becoming more prominent (Babe Didrickson was named woman athlete of the year in 1930), the pulp sports story still included women only as secondary characters and little non-fiction material about the woman athlete could be found.

Fiction Count for 1932

Baseball	32	Swimming	3
Boxing	31	Skiing	2
Track	20	Canoe racing	2
Football	13	Motorboat racing	2
Wrestling	13	Soccer	2
Hockey	8	Bicycle racing	2
Car racing	8	Horse racing	1
Basketball	6	Dog sledding	1
Rowing	5	Bobsledding	1
Tennis	4	Hurdling	1
Pole vaulting	4	Javeline	1
Airplane racing	3		

The Eleventh Year: 1933

Only 23 varieties of sport fiction were published in this calendar year. All-genre pulp writers like Leslie McFarlane were major contributors to the fiction content. Robert J. Hogan (of *G-8 and His Battle Aces* fame) had a bobsled story and Arthur Burks another boxing story. The Burt Standish house name was used frequently by Dabney Horton ("The Basketeers"), Robert Bryan ("Brick and Boots on the Border," "Tough Guy Halloran," "Big League Thinkin'," "The Missing Battery," and "King Cotton"), Arthur Mann ("Watch Your

Foot"), and David Garth ("Pinch Thinking," "The Bigger They Come" and "Hoops My Dear").

A three-part life story of Strangler Lewis was begun in the July 10 issue. Other non-fiction material included a "How to Play Basketball" piece by Nat Holman and autobiographical pieces about Bill Dickey and Herb Pennock by Arthur Mann. A minor format change: the Locker Room byline became more aggressive on November 25, changing from "Where readers and editor meet" to "Readers tell the editor where to get off."

Fiction Count for 1933

Baseball	28	Rowing	2
Track	25	Marathon	2
Boxing	22	Lacrosse	2
Football	20	Polo	2
Wrestling	20	Handball	1
Basketball	11	Bicycle racing	1
Tennis	9	Bobsled racing	1
Hockey	8	Handball	1
Golf	3	Shotput	1
Swimming	3	Steeplechase	1
Car racing	2	Canoe racing	1
Soccer	2		

The Twelfth Year: 1934

The Burt Standish house name was still being used liberally: fiction by Warren Carlton (football), Dabney Horton (track), Arthur Mann (baseball), and Robert Bryan (boxing and baseball). T. W. Ford was doing more than his share to fill *Sport Story*, with boxing, tennis, hockey, football and baseball fiction under his own name, and using the Eric Rober house name when he had more than two works in a single issue.

"As Told to" fact stories of Nat Holman, Bill Terry, Carl Hubbell, Mel Ott, Joe Cronin and Jimmie Foxx and biographies of Bill Tilden and Lou Little made up much of the non-fiction, non-editorial material. In addition there was biographical material about Max Baer and "How to" pieces by Bill Terry (baseball) and Nat Holman (basketball). The December issue instituted a verse segment.

Before first cracking the Street & Smith pulp magazines (and this year marks his entry into the *Sport Story* market), Leslie McFarlane got some useful advice from fellow pulpster A. E. Apple. He was told to pick up the tempo of his work — to make it more brisk and "surprise yourself by the twists and turns of the story." McFarlane says he sold everything he sent to Street & Smith after taking Apple's advice. Apple's most successful pulp writing featured the Mr. Chang character in a successful series which was reprinted in *Best Detective Magazine* shortly after his suicide.

Fiction Count for 1934

Baseball	32	Car racing	3
Football	28	Soccer	2
Boxing	17	Rowing	2
Track	16	Handball	2
Wrestling	14	High jump	2
Tennis	10	Shotput	2
Basketball	10	Pole vault	2
Hockey	8	Ski jump	1
Golf	3	Rodeo	1
Boating	3	Marathon	1
Swimming	3	Canoe racing	1
Bicycle racing	3		

The Thirteenth Year: 1935

The typical 1935 issue included a serial or two, one complete novelette, three or four short stories, and a number of non-fiction departments and fillers in addition to a feature non-fiction article. The latter focused largely on baseball and boxing figures. In 1935 these included Mickey Cochrane, Leo Durocher, Pepper Martin, Dizzy Dean, Christy Mathewson, Jim Jeffries, Frank Frish, Max Schmeling and Jim Thorpe.

Leslie McFarlane increased his *Sport Story* production with hockey, basketball, lacrosse and boxing fiction and T. W. Ford had track, hockey, football, tennis and boxing fiction under his own name and the Eric Rober house name when he had two pieces in a single issue.

Again, the Burt Standish house name was used by Robert Bryan (hockey and baseball) and Arthur Mann (baseball and wrestling), all of it sans Merriwells. Arthur Mann continued to produce the bulk of *Sport Story*'s non-fiction and T. W. Ford continued to produce prodigious amounts of material for the western pulp magazines while maintaining his role as the principal *Sports Story* fiction writer.

The newsstand price (15¢) and yearly subscription rate ($3) remained constant.

Fiction Count for 1935

Baseball	34	Wrestling	8
Football	22	Tennis	7
Boxing	17	Golf	6
Track	17	Polo	5
Basketball	13	Lacrosse	3
Hockey	8	Rowing	3

Swimming, ski jumping, shotput, marathon, bicycle racing, car racing, handball   2

Soccer, tug-of-war, softball, heel-toe walking, snowshoe racing, high jumping, canoe racing, hurdles   1

The Fourteenth Year: 1936

T. W. Ford continued as the leading fiction producer with football, boxing (2), track (2), tennis, and rowing entries under his own name and the Eric Rober house name. Leslie McFarlane's fiction count increased with two hockey stories, three boxing stories and a four-part baseball serial.

The Burt Standish house name was used 11 times. Some house names and writers who used them are:

House Name	Writer
Eric Rober	T. W. Ford
Bruce Dunn	Arthur Mann
Royal Hall	Jackson Scholz, Robert Bryan, Dabney Horton

House Name	Writer
Handley Cross	Arthur Grahame
Jack Volney	Jackson Scholz
Burt Standish	Arthur Mann, T. W. Ford, Robert Bryan, Jackson Scholz
Philip Deere	Robert Bryan, Franklin Miller

Arthur Mann ghosted four fact pieces (Mickey Cochrane, Charley Derringer, Charley Grimm and Tommy Bridges) and produced a number of other fact pieces about Jimmy Braddock, Jim Thorpe, Paavo Nurmi and others. Other fact material appeared on world series baseball and Olympic sports.

With the second September issue, the price of a single issue went to 10¢ and the cost of a yearly subscription to $2 in an apparent concession to the burden the Great Depression continued to place upon every man's pocketbook.

Fiction Count for 1936

Baseball	35	Wrestling	5
Boxing	26	Polo	5
Football	21	Rowing	4
Track	21	Swimming	4
Tennis	13	Lacrosse	4
Basketball	12	Bicycle racing	3
Hockey	11	Ski jumping	2
Golf	6		

Bobsled racing, pole vaulting, hammer throwing, hurdles, discus throwing, canoe racing, high jumping, marathon, car racing, handball   1

The Fifteenth Year: 1937

Leslie McFarlane continued to increase his varied sports fiction output with four-part hockey and three-part boxing stories and a number of hockey stories. T. W. Ford remained the big producer with five boxing, four football, three- and four-part football and tennis fiction as well as one-shot stories with football, track, tennis and other sports themes. Five different boxing stories appeared this year by T. W. Ford or under the Rober house name.

This was a banner year for the Burt Standish nom-de-plume: there were 15 different stories by diverse hands: Robert Bryan (hockey, baseball, polo), Arthur Mann (boxing, baseball), and Jackson Scholz (baseball, broad jump, golf, shotput, tug-of-war). As usual, the non-fiction materials covered a variety of sports: Princeton and Northwestern football, America's Cup, Notre Dame football, the Detroit Red Wings, the Stanley Cup, and then-prominent sports figures such as Arthur Donovan, Harry Greb, Dizzy Dean, Hans Wagner, Miller Huggins, Chuck Dressen, and Joe Cronin.

The non-fiction writing was shared about evenly by Arthur Mann, Stanley Frank and Arthur Grahame (writing as Handley Cross). Magazine subscription prices remained at 10¢/copy, $2/year.

Fiction Count for 1937

Baseball	33	Tennis	11
Boxing	28	Golf	11
Football	19	Hockey	10
Track	18	Wrestling	7
Basketball	13	Rowing	4

Swimming, polo, ski jumping   3

Shotput, handball, lacrosse, tug-of-war, water polo   2

Snowshoe racing, speed racing, steeplechase, pole vaulting, marathon, javelin throwing, broad jumping, canoe racing, walking, softball, car racing, bicycle racing   1

The Sixteenth Year: 1938

T. W. Ford again was the leading fiction contributor with hockey, basketball, tennis, boxing, swimming, baseball, track and other stories under his own name and as Rober. Leslie McFarlane continued to contribute but with diminished production (about a half-dozen stories of hockey, bob-sled racing and boxing).

There were 11 stories under the Burt Standish byline with

Robert N. Bryan (football, boxing, track), and Arthur Mann (boxing, track, hockey) doing the writing.

Arthur Graham (as Handley Cross) did the bulk of the non-fiction writing, which covered a wide range of material in 1938. Athletic figures covered in the Feature Article section included: Grover Cleveland Alexander (3 parts), Max Baer, "Slingin'" Sammy Baugh, Bill Brown (N.Y. State boxing commissioner), Bill De Correvont (schoolboy athlete), Leo Durocher, Gertrude Ederle, Tony Galento, Joe Gordon, Frank Gotch, Hank Greenberg, Willis Jones (press agent), Bill Klem, Walter Johnson (2 parts), William Johnson (tennis, 2 parts), Hank Luosetti, Kid McCoy, Joe Medwick, "Ducky" Pond (football coach), Knute Rockne (2 parts), Casey Stengel, Tommy Tonypander (boxer), Earl Walsh (college football scout), and Robert Suppke (college football coach).

Non-fiction dominated this year's *Sport Story Magazine* and boxing, for the first time, scored the greatest yearly fiction count. This was the first year that *Sport Story* spelled "basketball" as a single word.

A new feature in this year's *Sport Story* by Walter Inglis examined how boxers of different decades would perform against one another. This year's matchups included Jimmy Braddock versus Tom Sharkey, Max Schmeling versus James Corbett, Mickey Walker versus Philadelphia Jack O'Brien, Gene Tunney versus Jim Jeffries, Joe Louis versus Bob Fitzsimmons and Jack Dempsey versus John L. Sullivan.

Street & Smith managed to maintain the 10¢/copy and $2/yearly subscription prices.

Fiction Count for 1938

Boxing	28	Hockey	9
Baseball	23	Golf	9
Football	15	Tennis	8
Track	14	Rowing	4
Basketball	10	Polo	4
Wrestling	9	Bowling	4

Swimming, softball, bicycle racing, soccer, pole vaulting, ski jumping, marathon   2

Water polo, handball, bobsled racing, discus throwing, walking, shot put, diving, hurdles, board jumping   1

5. *Street & Smith's Sport Story Magazine*

The Seventeenth Year: 1939

Some dramatic changes occurred in 1939. In September, the magazine went from two issues a month to monthly publication and the format and style of the magazine took on a more modern look identical to that of its short-lived companion magazine, *Athlete*. With this month's issue of *Sport Story* the amount and variety of fiction was reduced.

Arthur Graham produced most of the non-fiction in this calendar year with pieces on the following: George Sisler, the Stanley Cup, the Willard-Johnson fight, Tom Sharkey, the Jack Dempsey–Tom Gibbons fight, Curley Lambeau and the Green Bay Packers, the McLarin–Canzoneri fight, Lou Nova, the 1938 World Series, Red Rolfe, Napoleon Lajoie, girls' basketball, and a piece suggesting that softball might challenge baseball as America's number one sport.

The new format gave cover art credit. H. W. Scott did the October and November covers. This was about the time he was being eased out of his job as the *Wild West Weekly* interior artist by Larry Bjorklund. While the western pulp fans expressed displeasure with Scott's work in the 1930s, by the early 1940s his star had risen in the world of magazine illustrators. *Life* magazine ran a two-part spread on Scott in its June 29, 1942, issue, calling him the "world's most prolific illustrator." Other covers were by International News Photo Inc. (August), Modest Stein (September), and Carlton Reed (December).

Leslie McFarlane had a new high for fiction production with four-part hockey and boxing stories and a number of single pieces. T. W. Ford was again a big fiction producer, with boxing, crew, baseball, tennis, and football stories. Jack Kofoed had a boxing story in the July issue and a football story in the November issue. The Burt Standish house name was used seven times (sans the Merriwells), all but once by Robert N. Bryan.

Another first for 1939 was in the first March issue: a girls' basketball story ("Hoop Lesson" by Jackson V. Scholz) in addition to the aforementioned non-fiction feature article by Arthur Graham (as Handley Cross) about girls' basketball: "Six Girls and a Basket." Prior to 1939 there was no girls' fiction and only sparse mention of girls' sports in the nonfiction. While *Sport Story*'s awakening to girls' sports was an interesting departure, there were no women writing about sports for either gender. As women's sports were strictly intramural, the school and college competition common to men's sports was not present to give their games the zip necessary to attract newspaper and magazine reportage.

In August of 1939 Street & Smith published the first issue of *Athlete*, a magazine identical in format and content to *Sport Story Magazine*. It was published as a monthly and sold for 15¢ a copy through to the January 1940 copy which sold at 15¢. The last issue of *Athlete* appeared in April 1940. It is not clear what the publishers intended with *Athlete*, as it must have competed directly with *Sport Story* sales.

Fiction Count for 1939

Baseball	29	Basketball	7
Boxing	22	Tennis	5
Football	12	Wrestling	4
Hockey	9		

Golf, lacrosse, polo, skiing   3

Swimming, car racing, rowing, handball, motorcycle racing   2

Marathon, diving, speedboat racing, softball, bicycle racing, water polo, aquaplaning, dogsled racing   1

The Eighteenth Year: 1940

The amount and variety of fiction and non-fiction was significantly reduced, with the page count under 100 for the first time (July issue) and staying under 100 from the September issue forward to 1943 (the last year of publication), when page count surged over the 100 mark for a few issues in what would be seen as a death throe.

Along with its new look, the dime-novel house name Burt Standish was no longer an industry staple. In this reduced market T. W. Ford would have only a pair of stories and Leslie McFarlane only one three-part hockey story. Pulp regular Bill Cox broke into *Sport Story Magazine* with a boxing story in the August issue. Arthur Mann had more fiction than fact pieces; among the latter were an Eddie Shore three-parter, pieces on coaches Ray Garrott and Steve Owen, a two-parter on John L. Sullivan, a three-parter on Glenn Cunningham and a one-shot piece on Clarence deMar.

Nine of the 1940 covers were designed by H. W. Scott, and shadow-cover artist Graves Gladney did the December cover, his first sports cover.

Fiction Count for 1940

Baseball	18	Rowing	3
Boxing	16	Swimming	2
Football	7	Horse racing	1
Track	5	Tennis	1
Hockey	4	Golf	1
Basketball	3	Ski jumping	1
Wrestling	3	Pole vaulting	1

The Nineteenth Year: 1941

Some of the *Sport Story* issues now had as few as four works of fiction and the variety of sports was again reduced to twelve (from an earlier average in the high thirties). These issues were the last hurrah for T. W. Ford (a rowing story), Jackson Scholz (track), Leslie McFarlane (hockey), Jack Kofoed (tennis) and Bill Cox (boxing, baseball and football). These men would go on to write for other sports pulps (however briefly) and the paperbacks, one of the several threats to the pulps.

Arthur Mann did the lion's share of fiction and non-fiction material and A. Leslie Ross and H. W. Scott, with five and six covers respectively, provided the cover art. Both Ross and Scott did western cover art and art for the *Avenger* pulp. Ross also worked in the comics in the 1930s and would go on to do paperback cover art for Popular Library, Bantam and Signet westerns. Scott did western comic and pulp art and in 1951 provided the cover art for Luke Short's (Fred Glidden) ten-cent Dell paperback, *Trumpets West*.

The magazine was still publishing monthly at 10¢ per copy and a $1 yearly subscription rate.

Fiction Count for 1941

Baseball	14	Boxing	9
Football	9	Track	4

Hockey	3	Golf	1
Basketball	2	Swimming	1
Rowing	2	Car racing	1
Wrestling	1		

The Twentieth Year: 1942

While 12 issues would be published in 1942 it was clear that the end was in sight. Only 10 sports were represented in these 12 issues and page count diminished to under 100 per issue. Arthur Mann provided the bulk of the fiction and nonfiction and A. Leslie Ross did all but one of the covers (the October cover was by Modest Stein). Street and Smith's comic line, initiated in 1940, overshadowed the *Sport Story* pulp.

The one-shot annual, *Sport Story Annual*, was published this year with reprinted material from earlier issues by some of the more notable writers: Damon Runyon, Bob Considine and Paul Gallico.

Fiction Count for 1942

Baseball	22	Golf	4
Boxing	14	Wrestling	3
Football	7	Hockey	2
Basketball	5	Horse racing	1
Track	5	Swimming	1

The Twenty-first and Last Year: 1943

This, the last year of publication, saw issues in January, February, March, May and July. Arthur Mann provided the bulk of the fiction and non-fiction. The mythic fights (by William Inglis) were briefly revived: McGovern–McLarnin and Kid McCoy–Tony Galento were the two match-ups. Non-fiction material was provided for Billy Southworth, Beau Jack, Barney Ross and Yankee Buddy Hassett.

Oddly, the May and July newsstand prices went from 10 to 15¢.

Fiction Count for 1943

Baseball	8	Hockey	4
Basketball	5	Track	3

Football   2   Tennis   1
Boxing   2

Sources

Curry, Tom. Interview, March 23, 1975.
Farley, G.M. "Tom Curry—A Biography," *The Zane Grey Collector*, 1975.
Reilly, John M., ed. *Twentieth-Century Crime and Mystery Writers*, St. Martin's Press, 1980.
Reynolds, Quentin. *The Fiction Factory*, Street & Smith Publications, Inc., 1965.
Schreuders, Piet. *The Book of Paperbacks*, London: Virgin Books, 1981.
Syracuse University Library. Various Street & Smith *Sport Story Magazine* materials.
Whitfield, Raoul. *Green Ice*, Gregg Press, 1980. Introduction by Pete Hamill.

Street & Smith Bibliography

Reynolds, Quentin, *The Fiction Factory–or from Pulp Row to Quality Street*. Street & Smith Publications, Inc., 1955.

A history of the Street & Smith publishing empire from 1855 to 1955.

A cautionary note based on a letter to the writer dated April 20, 1976: "I want to warn you about quoting anything from *Fiction Factory*. It was a disgrace to call it a history of S&S and the title was an insult. The writing assignment was given originally to John O'Hara, but when he found there was no one left in the business who could tell him anything, he backed out. The company was then made up of a bunch of Princeton graduates (Gerald Smith, the adopted son, was a Princeton man) who were playing publishing fashion magazines.... Quentin Reynolds was then 'at a low ebb,' not having won a law suit, and he took the job much to his regret. When he learned that there was no one in the company from whom he could learn anything, he farmed a great deal of the book out. For the most part, these people ran around interviewing all the wrong writers and editors who had never sold anything to S&S..."—Daisy Bacon

Bacon, Daisy, "The Golden Age of the Iron Maiden," in *The Roundup* (Official Organ-Western Writers of America), Vol. XXIII, No. 4, April 1975.

Daisy Bacon, editor of *Love Story, Detective Story*, and *Romantic Range*, looks back at the characters employed by Street & Smith in the declining pulp days. The title of the piece refers to the *Fiction Factory*'s elevator, which did Trojan service on Thursdays (payday).

Dime Novel Roundup: Vol. 30, No. 3, Whole No. 354: "The Merriwells—After *Tip Top*," by J. Edward Leithead and Gerald J. McIntosh, March 10, 1962.

Follows the career of the Merriwells in *Tip-Top Semi-Monthly* starting March 10, 1915. First of a series of three articles.

Vol. 30, No. 4, Whole No. 355: "The Merriwells — After *Tip Top*," by J. Edward Leithead and Gerald J. McIntosh, April 15, 1962.

Follows the career of the Merriwells through "Dick Merriwell's Counterstroke" in the Feb. 25, 1916, *Wide Awake Magazine*. Second of a series of three articles.

Vol. 30, No. 5, Whole No. 356: "The Merriwells — After *Tip Top*," by J. Edward Leithead and Gerald J. McIntosh, May 15, 1962.

Follows the career of the Merriwells in three pulp magazines: *Sport Story Magazine*, *Top Notch Magazine*, and *Super Sport Magazine* (September 1947).

Vol. 64, No. 4, Whole No. 634: "Uncollected Merriwell," August 1955.

Reveals author of Merriwell stories in the *Tip Top Semi-Monthly* and *Wide Awake Magazine* (John H. Whitson), the 1927–1928 *Sport Story Magazine* (Gilbert Patten, Warren E. Carleton, Joseph B. Ames, and J. Irving Crump), and the last Merriwell story in *Sports Story Magazine*, "The Mystery Ship" (October 1929) (by J. Irving Crump under the house name: John Samson).

The Pulp Writers

Writers of sports pulp fiction had two things in common; they had to know how to craft a formula story about one or more of 20-odd sports, which meant they had to have at least some rudimentary knowledge of their subject; and if they were writing factual material about sports, they had to know somewhat more about the subject. As with all pulp fiction, the story was the thing. And even in the fact pieces, as in life, one could freely render opinions without a full plate of information.

The second thing the writers shared was their sex; they were all male. Yes, there may have been a female writer here or there, but for all practical purposes the sports pulp was of, by and for males. The writers were males, the principals in their fiction were male, and the readers were (with the exception of those who subscribed to *Rodeo Romances*—a pulp editor's attempt to round up a larger readership by merging genres) male. *Rodeo Romances*' ploy to expand readership was used in other than the sports genre: *Rangeland Romances*, *Detective Romances*, and *Love Adventures* were other titles that followed suit.

Most of the sports pulp writers were professional pulpsters who could crank out credible text at the drop of a hat, and did so to put meat and potatoes on the table. There were a few amateurs in the business but the typical freelancer came to the sports pulps (the first of which was published in 1923) from the dime novels of the Frank and Dick Merriwell era or from a background in the general fiction pulp magazines of a later era. Writing was serious business and they had honed their skills accordingly so that they could produce words at a prodigious rate:

> Gilbert Patten, famed author of the Merriwell weeklies, wrote more than twenty-thousand words every week for nearly twenty years — an average of over a million a year. When he wanted a vacation he dictated two or more yarns ahead of time in the sagas of Frank and Dick Merriwell. Pacing the floor he tossed off wordage with the ease of a man spading up dirt and throwing it over his shoulder — to use a rather unhappy simile! [Harold Hersey in *Pulpwood Editor*].

A second category of pulp writers came to the sports pulps from newspapers. They were sports reporters who either switched full-time to the sports pulps or supplemented their typically meager newspaper salary by moonlighting in the sports pulps. Those who came to stay usually produced such material as celebrity interviews or various department fillers, typical of which was *Sport Story Magazine*'s "From the Bleachers," an early example which provided commentary on the American and Olympic sports scenes. It would change style and content over the years but remained essentially in the form of a column similar to those found in the sports pages of metropolitan newspapers.

A third category of writers was the sports figures themselves. Many times articles carried the sports figure's byline but they were ghosted by a staff writer. In some few cases they were written by the sports figures themselves. One example is the tennis stories of Bill Tilden.

A final, significantly less populated, category in sports pulp fiction is the writer who did not come to the genre from either the dime novels or the pulps, but started his writing in the sports pulps. The prime example is John Tunis. Most of these writers started and ended their careers in one issue. Tunis would grow into the best writer of boys' sport fiction America has ever produced.

Looking at writers from each of these four categories, one can see that while their product was a common one — a short story built about a sports theme — it varied in content and quality, both between and within these four categories.

These, then, were the men who filled the pages of the sports pulps from the 1920s through the 1950s. They were mostly cottage-industry professionals who could produce fiction on demand. On a good day they could turn a good tale. Some of this body of work is readable, but little, if any, is notable.

In addition to this cadre of writers there was a second group who produced the fast pieces. These men were affiliated with the sports news business and their sports pulp work is virtually indistinguishable from newspaper material of the day.

Some examples: In the summer 1940 *Fight Stories*, an issue which contains a Robert E. Howard Costigan story, there is a "Why They Can't Come Back" story, bylined "by Jack Dempsey as told to Ned Brown." These as-told-to stories were common fare in most of the sports pulps. The Summer 1949 *Baseball Stories* has three pieces belonging to this category: "Red Sox — Boom or Bust" by Doc McGee, "The Bat-Man" by Glen W. Pfeil, and "Satchel Paige" by Bill Ricketts.

While some of the sports pulps eschewed fact material — *Complete Sports* and *Ace Sports* for example — some loaded up. *All-American Football Magazine*, for example, in addition to a fiction piece by Bill Cox, had four "hard-hitting football features" including the schedules for all college football teams for 1939.

Jack Kofoed was a frequent contributor of sports fact material. "The Ten Greatest Fights of All Time" in the Winter 1941-42 *Fight Stories*, "The Black Scot" in the January 1931 *Sport Story Magazine*, and "The Whirl of Sports" in the Summer 1949 *Popular Sports* are typical of Kofoed's work.

Popular sports writer Jimmy Powers was a frequent contributor of biographies of the baseball greats to *Baseball Stories*, typical of which are "The Daffiest Dodger?" in the Summer 1952 issue and "The Flying Dutchman" in the Spring 1952 issue. Another popular sports reporter, Tim Cohane, in the 1939 *Football Action* ("Staging the Gridiron Show"), discusses the complexities of scheduling, scouting, public relations, etc., and compares the staging of a college football game to making a four-star movie. At the time Cohane wrote this piece he was Fordham's publicist.

Staff writers usually produced the cheap, starchy filler material — the so-called departments. Departments included the following: "Warming the Bench with the Editor," "Who-Dun-It," "Skull Practice," "Sportsword Puzzle," "Big Moments in Sport," "Trainer and Coach," "Locker Room," "From the Bleachers." The departments were copies of similar material found in the sports pages of the day.

A typical department was "Dope from the Dugout" in *Sports Fiction*, which also included a 12-question sports quiz, commentary on sports lingo in "Sportpourri" and five additional short pieces devoted to sports trivia.

The staff writers would, as required, turn out sports fiction but their principal job was to generate the sports quiz, the crossword puzzle, the opinion short and the reader's letters columns, when they were not doing the ghosted or "as by" pieces bylined under a major sports name. Some of the sports pulps didn't do any "as by" material (*Complete Sports*, *Super Sports*, *12 Sports Aces* are examples). Among those that did, *Sport Story* carried the most. Just about every major sports figure (and many lesser sports figures) of the day were represented in the pages of *Sport Story* over its publishing life. In a few, rare, cases, the sports figure did the actual writing, and in one case (Bill Tilden) it got him into a jam (see the 1924 summary of *Sport Story*).

While the "name" sports writers were doing the "story-behind-the-story" pieces, it was left to the staff writers to crank out whatever the editor needed to fill the page count. Most of the staff writers were lesser-known, captive (i.e., full-time) employees who doubled in spades, doing fact, fiction, and department pieces for their magazines. *Sport Story*'s Arthur Mann comes to mind. In the year-by-year review of that pulp, some of these men and their work appear frequently.

While some of the fact material in the sports pulps may be of interest to today's sports researcher, not much else is, unless one were writing a biography. Even in this case the material would be peripheral at best, as the sports writers made their name in the newspaper sports pages and the better pulp writers such as Howard made their reputations in other genres. Of all the men who wrote for the sports pulps there was but one who would make sports fiction something more than pulp. That man was John Tunis.

The Pulp Writers

Dime novel writers did not go quietly into oblivion. However, the forces that killed off the dime novel would provide new opportunities. In an article, "The Dime Novel and Its Successors," Edward

LeBlanc attributes the demise of the dime novel to three influences: movies, the pulp magazines, and boys' and girls' series books. Those dime novelists who could retool their skills would find ample markets for their work in both the series books and the pulps.

The series books prospered thanks to men like Edward Stratemeyer, who was hired by Gilbert Patten in 1893 to write for the Street & Smith paper *Good News*. One of the firm's partners, Ormond Smith, asked Stratemeyer if he would be interested in developing a project based on a strong central character and a circle of friends, and thus was born the Frank Merriwell series. This basic theme would serve Stratemeyer well when he began mass-producing hardcover books.

Stratemeyer often outlined a story himself but used hired writers to complete the book. At one time he had as many as 20 writers in his employ.

Sports figured heavily in the boys' series books published by Stratemeyer, second only to the mystery/adventure titles. There were sports series such as the Lansing series (1912–1915): "Batter Up," "The Winning Hit," and "Fair Play." There were sports themes within non-sports series such as the Oakdale Series (1911–1913): "Rival Pitchers of Oakdale." Among the most popular series, the Baseball Joe books (14 books over the 1912–1928 period) were written by Stratemeyer under the pseudonym Henry Chadwick. Baseball Joe Matson was the first professional athlete in a series book.

There were basketball series (Basketball Series: three books over 1929–1930), hockey series (Hockey Series: three books over 1929–1931), football series (Football Stories: twelve books over 1914–1927), and sports books would appear with regularity in most of the non-sports series.

Over the life span of the series books there was only an occasional girls' series book with a sports theme. *The Girls of Central High* (1914) and *Billy Bradley Winning the Trophy* (1932) are two rare examples. Mystery/adventure titles dominated the girls' series books.

As popular as the series books were during the 1920s, 1930s and 1940s, their juvenile audience would grow into the more adult pulp market. While the pulps took over the mass readership once dominated by the series books, however, series books continue to be produced today, although sports themes are rare. The Stratemeyer Syndicate continued into the 1970s.

It was the professional pulp fictioneer, the man who turned out reams of prose on demand but was only an occasional contributor to the sports pulps, who is most representative of the contributors to these magazines. Such a writer is Hugh Cave. Cave published hundreds of stories in more than 100 different pulp magazines.* He produced this material over the pulp decades (1920s–1950s) and is still writing today. He wrote adventure, horror, mystery, detective, fantasy, western, romance, and just a pair of sports stories ("The Big If" in *Super Sports*, 10–41, and "White Water Challenge" in *Short Stories*, 10–46) for the pulps. In addition to his pulp work, Cave wrote a number of books and was a frequent contributor to the slick magazines. During World War II Cave produced a number of military books for the navy. Like most pulp fictioneers, his background included world travel, but unlike most pulp fictioneers, he ran a 541-acre coffee plantation in Jamaica and investigated voodoo lore in remote sections of Haiti.

A recent biography (*Pulp Man's Odyssey*) and personal reminiscences of the pulp era ("Magazines I Remember") detail his life and writing. I received the following letter from Cave dated 14 March, 1997:

> As far as sports stories, I don't believe I did more than a handful. One that I have is "In This Corner — Death," from the June 1938 *Double Detective*. It's a boxing story and I'll be using it in my third Fedogan & Bremer collection, if they do a third. Another sports story that I have a copy of is "Education of a Killer," coming up soon in a German anthology called *Frank Nowatze Verlag*. That's a boxing story too, or at least it's about a kid boxer. It first appeared in *Double Detective*, 9-'38.

Cave goes on to say he had a sports story, "The Big If," in the 10-'41 *Super Sports*, and that among the 63 stories he did for *Detective Fiction Weekly*, he's sure some are sports yarns. Cave can't be sure, as he lost his entire inventory in a fire some years ago and has been rebuilding it since with the help of friends and collectors.

Three of the great pulp writers who also did only occasional

---

*Pulp Vault, #12, 13, Doug Ellis, editor.

work in the sports genre were Frederick Faust, Johnston McCulley, and Robert Leslie Bellem.

Faust came to the sports story from the western, in which genre he wrote under 17 different pseudonyms, the most popular of which is Max Brand. Faust wrote the big western; the scope was big and so were the characters — people like Destry, who was played on film by Tom Mix, Audie Murphy and Jimmy Stewart. A legend from the beginning of his writing career, Faust was asked by Street & Smith editor Robert H. Davis to sit down at the typewriter and crank out some prose. Davis was Munsey's chief executive and would routinely throw prospective writers into a room and give them a few hours to show their stuff. When Davis called Faust back to his office he took what he had written (which was published unchanged by the way) and told Faust his work was pretty good. He asked Faust where he learned to write. Faust pointed to the room he had just exited and said, "Down the hall."

Faust's stories number in the hundreds and he can be identified with more than 70 films released over a period of 40 years. Some of his work is still in print, mainly those westerns under the Max Brand pseudonym. Faust was killed in World War II while working as a war correspondent covering the Italian campaign. His only sports story was "Thunderbolt," published in three parts in *Sport Story Magazine* (October 25, November 10 and November 25 of 1932). "Thunderbolt" is a character study of college back Joe Cochrane, aka Thunderbolt, so-called because "once he gets started, everything in his way melts like ice in a caldron." While Thunderbolt has all of the physical equipment to play the game (at 200 pounds he can kick, run and pass) he lacks, apparently, the courage to hit the line: "he won't ram the ball over the goal line — every time he sees a solid wall in front of him he stops so soft a five-year-old kid could have thrown him on his back."

It seems that Thunderbolt has a secret life which is accidentally discovered by the narrator-coach Lew Marvin when he spots the Thunderbolt driving a horse-drawn buggy. The Thunderbolt is attacked by union teamsters for scabbing and, to the surprise of coach Marvin, promptly dukes out four of them in a vicious street brawl. The story goes on to reveal that Thunderbolt not only has a secret working life but also has a secret family which his moonlighting supports.

All in all, "Thunderbolt" is a quality sports yarn. Why Faust produced only this one sports yarn is a bit of a mystery, but perhaps the unprecedented success of his work in the western genre consumed all of his writing time. Faust descriptions of details of football play, however, show the same understanding that is evident in Robert Howard's fight scenes.

Another pulp writer to come to the sports story from the western, Johnston McCulley created one of the great fictional characters of all time — Zorro. Zorro would make his mark in all of the pop-culture venues: books, comics, movies, radio, television, and Zorro premiums galore. Like Faust, McCulley wrote under a number of pseudonyms, turning out books, plays and pulp stories of "The Robin Hood of California," aka Zorro, for several of the Munsey magazines from 1919 through the 1940s.

Born in Ottawa, Illinois, McCulley worked first as a newspaper reporter before launching his fiction career with the masked Zorro character. He produced large quantities of fiction for various pulp magazines including the *Argosy* magazines, *Detective Story Magazine*, and *West*. His Zorro character ranks with Burroughs' Tarzan in popular culture saturation. McCulley died in California on November 28, 1958. While much has been written about the Zorro character and McCulley's work in the western pulp magazines, little is known about one of his few forays into the pulp sport genre.

McCulley wrote "Duel in the Arena" for the April 1947 *Rodeo Romances*. It tells the story of champion rodeo rider Larry Parks, who will face a man-killing horse in the Mesa Springs Rodeo and also coach his girl, Betty Darte, in the women's events. McCulley's story is pure pulp. Betty Darte is disqualified from her event, but when the judges discover that her behavior was the result of saving a child's life, she is requalified. And the mankiller horse is pulp as well: "Mankiller had been kept in a special, high corral, and now half a dozen ropes were holding him as the great horse squealed his rage and tried to fight." This is basic pulp stuff, with none of the technical detail or rodeo language that one finds in the *Rodeo Romances* fiction produced by more knowledgeable hands — Walker Tompkins, for example.

Walker A. Tompkins sold his first western novel at age 21 to *Wild West Weekly* and for the following 25 years wrote for the western pulps under his own name and house names Philip F. Deere and

Jackson Cole. In his story "Tiger of the Tanbark" (August 1948 *Rodeo Romances*) one requires a cowboy dictionary to determine the protagonist's occupation (he is described as a "mere cavvy wrangler," which I took to mean working cowboy). The story revolves about the town of Haverfork, its fifth annual rodeo, and our working cowboy, Rex Donovan, who is up against the "blustering daredevil," Rowdy Rockwall. Tompkins gives the pulp an injection of drama when a new competitor shows up: the Tiger of the Tanbark, a silver-masked dude reputed to be a target of the law. The Tiger's outfit is further embellished with tigerskin vest and chaps, making this yarn a pulp fan's dream, a blending of the ordinary with the superhero story.

Tompkins earned his reputation as a western fictioneer in *Wild West Weekly* where he created characters similar to *Rodeo Romances'* El Tigre, Tejano.

Robert Leslie Bellem's great pulp creation was private eye Dan Turner. Turner was generally in the employ of one of Hollywood's movie studios, bailing out a wayward star. Like most of the hard-boiled dicks of the pulps, Turner had a taste for the grape (to the tune of a quart of Vat 69 a day). Unlike most in the genre he spoke in a pre–PC patois which sounded like a blend of Leo Gorcey and Rocky Graziano: "I walked into the dimly lighted Chink restaurant and took a quick squint at the joint. Using this mirror, I glommed a gander at the ginzo who was looking at me." Turner resolved his problems with women — whom he referred to as dolls, morsels, wrens, cupcakes, frails, quails, and she-males — with his fists: "I never trust dames so I popped her on the dimple."

Turner debuted in the June 1934 issue of *Spicy Detective* and appeared in *Speed Detective* and, later, his very own pulp, *Dan Turner — Hollywood Detective*, where he would survive until 1950. Bellem's work in the sports pulps showed none of this macho-bravado. A typical Bellem sports story, "Rebel of the Turf" (*Popular Sports*, Summer 1940), is a long-winded (80 pages) racing story with a Santa Anita background and none of the wise-guy stuff.

As is the case with Faust, Bellem's work is still being published and, again as with Faust, his work can be found in university collections. Faust and Bellem were unique creations of the pulp era.

Some of the peripatetic pulp fictioneers managed to find a solid market in the sports pulps. One can hardly pick up a sports pulp which does not have a Bill Cox story. I got a note from Cox some years ago when Stallone's *Rocky* was first shown, an event which caused Bill to reflect on the sports pulps:

> When I began in *Dime Sports* there were more than fifty sports pulps being published plus a story in *Collier's*, *Blue Book*, and *Argosy*, and occasionally in *Adventure*. That was my bag at the beginning since I believe that television has overdone the sports field, but sports films are coming back, why not in print?

Cox added a postscript to these comments:

> Bill Fay's widow said the other evening: "I've just seen *Rocky*. You and Willy and Bill Holder wrote that story thirty times each in the pulps."

Bill Fay's "Fighting Man" was heralded by *Fight Stories* as "the best fight story in ten years":

> *Fight Stories*, which gave its readers the great stories of the ring by America's outstanding fight story writers — Paul Gallico, Eddie Orcutt, Jack Kofoed, Charles Francis Coe ... gives you the first book-length novel of William Fay. Former Golden Gloves star, New York sports-writer and generally acclaimed as today's standout story teller of the ring.... Creator of the Merry Meatball, Willie Longo, Frankie the Fruitcake, Bill Fay knows at first hand the inside stories of the squared circle....

Fay's character, like Rocky, was a heavyweight. The heavyweight division has, in life as in fiction, generated the greatest fan interest from the days of John L. Sullivan, and both fact and fiction material in the sports fiction pulps reflect this fascination with the big guys, as well as with the underdog.

When *Football Action* was first published (Fall 1939), Bill Cox was there with a football story and a Rocky character whom the coach is forced to play for various plot purposes and upon whom the outcome of the game must and will turn. The story, "Work-Horse and Glory," is summarized in the title tease: "It was a screwy setup. Coach Jobey Walsh had orders to play an untried, bench-hotting jayvee in the keystone slot.... He also had orders to win the game."

Reading these pulp stories after reading a dime-novel Frank

Merriwell yarn, it's apparent that while the stories are rather simple-minded, the narrative and the dialogue are now more representative of reality: Cox's narrative — "Traveling low always, his head down, he would ram the runner. He wouldn't bother to tackle. He just rammed them with that bullet head of his and there they were." And Cox's dialogue — "You'll play Chick Corey tomorrow or you won't have a job next year." In each case, the voice is active, to the point, and terse in the style of the new (hard-boiled) detective fiction published in the pulp *Black Mask* (to which Cox was a contributor). Gone is the stilted dime-novelese of the Frank Merriwell era.

While the outcome of these stories is generally predictable, the neorealism of the narrative and dialogue was sufficient to carry the reader of the day. Roger Torrey, another *Black Mask* regular (50 stories over 1933–1942) tells a gritty story in the first issue of *Knockout Magazine* (January–February 1939), "The Boy and the Butcher." The boy, Charlie Collins, is trying to get a grubstake to start a life with his girlfriend, Rosie. Charlie's manager has different goals. Setting up the kid after betting the store on the Butcher. Six months and four fights after losing to the Butcher, the kid turns the tables on his manager who had planned to repeat the circumstances of the first fight.

Torrey's first "Boy and the Butcher" line is classic *Black Mask* third-person, terse and tough:

> He was a little the worse for wear and he didn't look overly bright, but the left hand had the flashing precision of a crack fencer's foil and the right was a fistful of dynamite.

In the pulpzine *Pulp Vault* #8,* Cox talks about a story of his in *Football Stories*:

> This is a novelette, about 14,000 words by my estimate. The magazine sports — please excuse that — a cover by George Gross showing two players in a collision against an orange background that just yells "Autumn." Gross could do exciting paintings even when there were no scantily clad damsels around, and what's more amazing, Fiction House let him. The illustration for the story is all on-field action above the title, with portraits of the

---

*Pulp Vault *is published by Tattered Pages Press, 6942 North Oleander, Chicago, IL 60631; editor, Doug Ellis.

principal characters at the bottom of the page. It looks like it may have been drawn by Joe Doolin.

This same issue of *Football Stories* (Fall 1940) is reviewed in the August 1990 issue of *Echoes*. Cox's story is given a cover blurb:

> The kid from Texas was a social flop but on swank eastern U's tradition-hallowed gridiron he had what it takes; red blood ... cuts ... and a hell-for-leather touchdown gallop.

In this piece written by Hank Reinhardt and Jerry Page there is also mention of a Jack Wiggin story, "The Ashcan Eleven": "Slated for the cellar, the breather boys knocked 'welcome' off the conference doormat." Other football stories discussed are also greeted with satisfaction by both Page and Reinhardt.

The writer of this piece, Jerry Page, reviews one of the Cox boxing stories in *Action Stories* under a pen name, Joel Reevel. The story is "In There, the White Lights Glaring":

> Gentle reader, here is one hell of a story. It's knowledgeable about boxing and carnivals and, oh so wise about men. For once Cox doesn't feel the need to toss in a love plot or a mystery. The story telling is linear, straight-ahead yarn spinning at its best. There aren't many surprises but there's a lot of satisfaction.

Bill Cox wrote his first sports story for *American Boy*—on a bet. The year was 1934. He later tried again and again to publish in *American Boy*, with negative results. The editor suggested that Cox try the pulps. Cox then wrote a track story ("Legs") which was purchased by *Dime Sports* editor Alden Norton, and from then on Cox was "a Harry Steeger slave at from a penny up to three cents a word during the next many years until the genre died beneath the weight of television." Cox's next market was *Blue Book* where he says editor Donald Kennicot "long provided me with cakes and ale." When Cox had more than one story in *Blue Book* it was under the byline Joel Reeve.

Of *his* pulp writing, Cox has fond memories:

> It was a busy time, a good time, almost the best of times. There was always money, always enough leisure. The natural story

teller had only to keep up with the media, read the classics and sit at his typewriter. It was a great life but I did not heed the warning of Syd Sanders after the war when he prophesized the demise of the pulps and urged me to concentrate on the slick paper books. Little did he know that they too were doomed.

Similarly, Cox has only good memories of pulp editors:

Harry Steeger, Michael Tilden, Harry Widmer, Dorothy McIlwraith of *Short Stories* ... they were fine editors who became friends. One could visit New York, lay out a batch of story ideas, return home, write them and sell them all. [*Echoes* #20, August 1985]*

William Campbell Gault was a regular pulp writer at the end of the pulp era, contributing nine stories to *Black Mask* between 1946 and 1950 and three to *Dime Detective* between 1947 and 1952, when the pulp markets were on their last legs. After the pulps Gault was a regular in the mystery/detective digest magazines (*Ellery Queen Mystery Magazine, The Saint*, etc.) before launching his career as a mystery/detective novelist. He wrote about two dozen of these and won the Edgar (The Mystery Writers of America Edgar Allan Poe Award) for *Don't Cry for Me* in 1953. In addition, he produced about two dozen juvenile sports novels for Dodd Mead between 1952 and 1978. Arguably his best novel was *The Canvass Coffin*.

Gault favored the boxing story and wrote a few for *Sports Novels Magazine*, typical of which is "Say It with Punches!," which tells the story of twin brothers, one the fighter, the other the manager, who go from Golden Gloves to tank town prelims, to main events, to a shot at the title.

The so-called hero pulps were, and remain, the most popular of all of the pulp magazines. Characters the likes of the Shadow, Doc Savage, Wu Fang (a super villain) and G-8 generate the most collector interest, fetch the highest prices and are the most likely to become grist for the Hollywood mill. It is an interesting paradox that while sports fiction is de facto hero fiction, one finds few sports stories written by the hero pulp writers, and less than a handful of sports themes in the hero pulps. One of the Whisperer stories comes

---

*Echoes *is published by Fading Shadows, Inc., 504 E. Morris St., Seymour, Texas, 76380; editor, Tom Johnson.*

to mind as an exception ("The Football Racketeers"), and that is basically a gangster story.

The other exception to this rule is Robert Sidney Bowen. Bowen, a prolific pulp writer, turned out hero fiction for three air/war pulps (*Dusty Ayers and His Battle Birds*, the captain Danger series in *Air War*, and *The Lone Eagle*) and ghosted other hero pulp material including some *Phantom Detective* fiction. Bowen's fiction had the credibility that comes with experience:

> Sweeping out over Boston Harbor, and past the tip of Cape Cod, he throttled a bit and slid down toward open water far below. Ten minutes of that and he started climbing up again in ever-widening circles.
>
> As he reached twenty thousand feet there was a muffled clicking in the earphones. He knew instantly that it was some small sea station speaking on a wavelength that overlapped his own. With his free hand he turned on full reception power, set the directional finder, and slowly manipulated the tuning dial ["Crimson Doom"].

One can search long and hard in other air-war pulps and not find a reference to the use of a direction finder. Bowen wrote about 20 baseball books — juveniles, over the period 1948–1950 (all published by the Lothrop Lee & Shepard) and was an occasional producer of tennis and baseball fiction for *Popular Sports Magazine* during the 1940s.

Another prolific pulpster, Joe Archibald, had some success in the boys' juvenile market. Over the period 1955–1974 Archibald wrote for this market after the sports pulp market had collapsed. Like Bowen, Archibald was a prolific writer, producing prodigious amounts of fiction for *Detective Book Magazine*, *Secret Agent X*, *Thrilling Detective*, *10-Story Detective*, *Phantom Detective*, *The Lone Eagle*, *Popular Detective* and *Ten Detective Aces*.

Some of the great western fictioneers started their writing careers in the sports pulps. Louis L'Amour's material in the pulp magazines approached the 200 mark, and most of these were westerns. All of his cowpoke heroes were good with their fists, as were his pulp detectives. L'Amour's P.I. Kip Morgan was an ex-boxer (as was L'Amour) trying to make it in the gumshoe trade.

L'Amour's admiration of the fighting man comes from his "yondering" years when he knocked about the world, working a variety of trades which would guarantee his personal fighting skills, including fighting professionally. L'Amour is reputed to have had about 50 professional fights and to have won most of them.

He was known as a man's man and his work in the sports pulps reflects his admiration for the brutal sports. His second pulp sale, "Gloves for a Tiger" (*Thrilling Adventures*, January 1938), was a story of professional boxing. He wrote "The Rounds Don't Count" for *Thrilling Adventures* (February 1942), "Fighters Don't Dive" for *Popular Sports* (Summer 1946), "Right Hand Crazy" for *Popular Sports* (1947), "Take It the Hard Way" for *Exciting Sports* (December 1948), and his last pulp boxing story would be "Fighters Should Be Hungry" in the February 1949 *Popular Sports*.

In addition to his fight stories in the sports pulps, L'Amour wrote two football stories and two rodeo stories. His football titles, which reflect his passion for power-based sports, are "Backfield Battering Ram" (*Popular Football*, Winter 1947) and "Moran of the Tigers" (*Thrilling Football*, Winter 1949). His rodeo stories are "Rowdy Rides to Glory" (*Rodeo Romances*, April 1949), and "The Ghost Maker" (*Rodeo Romances*, Spring 1950). Before his death I had a letter from L'Amour in which he stated: "I believe I learned more about writing from the pulps than any other publication or publications. Their demand was for a no-nonsense type of writing, and if one made a living at it there was no time for sitting about twiddling the thumbs." L'Amour's stature as one of America's greatest and most popular western authors is due in some small part to his use of the sports pulps as a training ground.

The same might as well be said of Ernest Haycox. Haycox's first big hit, the film *Stagecoach*, was based on a short story, "Stage to Lordsburg." The Western Writers of America have consistently ranked Haycox as one of the two truly great practitioners of the art of writing western fiction. When he died in 1950, the Western Writers of America named the award for the best fiction of the year the "Ernie" in his honor. (It would later be renamed "The Spur.")

Looking through the musty pages of the December 8, 1924, *Sport Story Magazine* one finds a sample of Haycox's early writing in the sports genre, "The Skeeter," a rather simple-minded tale about a skinny sprinter who ran like a duck. But it was in these magazines that Haycox did his own sprinting toward his eventual world status in the westerns.

6. The Pulp Writers   145

Writing as Judson Phillips, Hugh Pentacost produced a considerable amount of sports fiction over the decade of the 1930s and a pseudo-scholarly work with Robert Wood, Jr., entitled *Hold 'Em Girls: The Intelligent Woman's Guide to Men and Football* in 1936. Best known for his detective fiction, Pentacost's interest in sports dated to childhood. In a biographical piece in the October 5, 1935 *Argosy*, "The Men Who Make Argosy," Pentacost says: "I have always been keenly interested in sports of all kinds; in my schooldays I played football and baseball and I have since settled down to being a frenzied golfer."

Pentacost wrote baseball, hockey and football fiction for *Argosy*, *Detective Fiction Weekly* and *Dime Sports Magazine*. He also was author of the "Fan Forum" for *Dime Sports*. "Fan Forum" consisted of "anecdotes-gossip-inside news of the world of sports." A look back at these op-ed pieces from the vantage point of today reveals his limitations as seer. In the September 1936 "Fan Forum" Pentacost evaluates Joe DiMaggio's prospects: "Despite his tremendous build-up it is doubtful if DiMaggio will ever take his place along with the half dozen greatest outfielders of modern times" (among whom he counts Ross Young), and he goes on to say: "I can think of a dozen outfielders I would rather see play."

In his biographical piece Pentacost says that in addition to his participation in sports in his youth and golf in his later years, he had worked as a sports writer and at one time had managed a fighter.

Audrey Parente's piece, "Forgotten on Park Avenue" in the aforementioned #8 *Pulp Vault*, provides some information about Phillips' Park Avenue Hunt Club and says he admits to having "stolen" the basic idea for the series from Edgar Wallace's *Four Just Men* (apparently self-published in 1905 but later featured in short stories in Street & Smith's detective magazine).

John D. MacDonald, author of the Travis McGee series, started his writing at the tail-end of the pulp era but had two stories published in *Mystery Book Magazine*, a magazine which reversed the typical trend of going from pulp size (7" × 10") to digest size 5¼" × 7¼"). It started out digest-sized in 1945 and converted to pulp size in 1947.

One of MacDonald's *Mystery Book Magazine* stories is about as well-crafted as fiction got in the pulps. "Dead on the Pin" (Summer 1950) is told from the point-of-view of Joe Desmond, manager of the Wonderland Bowling Alley. Joe hires an odd-job type and then discovers the man's great talent. About the time this talent is about to be demonstrated, the FBI moves in to cut the effort short. MacDonald had a good feel for the game of bowling and "Dead on the Pin" blends the sport and mystery themes to perfection.

MacDonald's boxing story in the December 1947 *Super Sports* was also as good a piece of fiction as one will find in the pulp mags. MacDonald uses the terse first-person style to advantage in describing the dark underside of the world of boxing as the story moves toward the BIG fight. "Big John Fights Again" is a story reminiscent of *The Harder They Fall* and *Requiem for a Heavyweight*, told from the reporter's point of view and with a bit of a twist — the fighter is black. Not wanting to fight, Big John tells the reporter he's afraid of what might happen to him. The reporter naively responds: "That's nonsense; people don't do that." Big John responds: "Maybe not to white folks," and proceeds to enlighten the reporter on some hard facts about prejudice.

Another writer to get in on the tail end of the pulp era, Michael Avalone, known as "The Fastest Typewriter in the East," and father of the Ed Noon P.I. series, did his first writing for the sports pulp *Baseball Stories* (Fall 1950), a story titled "Aw, Let the Kid Hit." In between his 38 Ed Noon stories, 10 historical novels, 35 general fiction novels, 20 movie serializations, Avalone managed to write a number of baseball stories for *Ten-Story Sports*, *Baseball Stories*, and *Super Sports*. When asked about his writing for so many different markets, Avalone responded:

> A professional writer should be able to write anything from the Bible to a garden seed catalogue and everything in between.

Avalone was not above reworking some of the old sports clichés, however. In the Spring 1952 *Baseball Stories*, Avalone's story "One More Miracle!" does just that, as the title-page teaser indicates:

> The great Biff Baxter came to Sloan Hospital to restore a smile to Danny Montgomery's pinched face; to put some color in hollow cheeks; to infuse some of his wonderful team spirit into a dying boy. But he did his job too well. Blow-hard Baxter had promised too much; more than his failing bat could deliver ... and it meant quick death for the kid if loud-mouth couldn't produce One More Miracle.

Avalone's papers are collected in Boston University's Mugar Library. At the bottom of a sheet listing his sports story sales Avalone made this notation: "Pulp magazines disappeared after 1957 and so did sports fiction."

Steve Fisher was one of the prominent mystery fiction writers of the pulp era who learned his craft in the pulps. His best-known novel, *I Wake Up Screaming* (which deals with a sports promoter accused of murdering a female film star) was done on film with Betty Grable and Victor Mature (1942) and is considered an example of early film noir. In addition to his mystery-detective fiction in the pulps, Fisher was a contributor to the sports pulps. Typical of his work in this field "Winner Take Death" in the September 1936 *Dime Sports Magazine*. Fisher does an excellent job of telling a crime story against a boxing backdrop and his action is pretty-good pulp:

> The albino struck the first blow. It stung Bill's chest and he recoiled, swung out instinctively. Bronson leaped away, and as Bill followed him, he plastered a light one-two into his face. It was neatly executed and made Bronson look good. What the crowd didn't know was that the punches had no sting. Bill didn't back down from them. His right suddenly shot out, caught Bronson in the stomach. The fighter with the cotton hair bent, his face contorted. Bill cracked at the even jaw of the champion. Fisher's career in the pulp was sandwiched between a hitch in the U.S. Navy (which he joined in 1928 after running away from a California military academy) and a later career as a Hollywood screenwriter from the 1940s to the 1960s.

Raoul Whitfield's *Death in a Bowl* was one of the seminal hard-boiled private-eye novels and the first of the genre to feature a Jewish P.I. Whitfield's detective fiction skills were developed in the premier hard-boiled pulp of the day, *Black Mask*, starting with "Ten Hours" in the December 1926 issue and ending with "Death on Fifth Avenue" in the February 1934 issue. Whitfield's first pulp work was in the March 8, 1924, issue of *Sport Story Magazine*: "Flashing Towers," an airplane racing story. Through the 1920s Whitfield would be a frequent *Sport Story* contributor, writing fiction in a variety of sports settings under his own name and using the penname Stewart Osborne when he had more than one story in a single issue.

Jackson Scholz was pure pulp stories writer, starting with his first track story, "A Matter of Temperament," in the October 22,

1924 *Sport Story Magazine*. One of his last stories was in the Spring 1950 issue of *Popular Baseball*, "Umpire Bait." In between, as far as I know, he produced sports fiction exclusively, mainly in *Sport Story Magazine* where his total output numbered in the dozens. Scholz wrote exclusively for Street & Smith until the 1943 end was in sight, often contributing more than one piece per issue. When this happened he wrote under one of three house names: Burt Standish, Jack Volney and Royal Hall.

Scholz's sports fiction can be found in *Short Stories, Popular Baseball* and *Dime Sports* as well as dozens of issues of *Sport Story Magazine*. He wrote a variety of sports stories but favored track and field.

Arthur Mann wrote exclusively in the sports pulps and, for years, exclusively for *Sport Story Magazine*. Later, he submitted his material to other sports pulps when a pulp sports writer could no longer depend on just one market.

Robert E. Howard (1906–1936) — of Conan the Barbarian fame — was one of the better pulp sports fictioneers and his work would have achieved greater popularity had he lived beyond 1936 when the pulp sports fiction magazines were, except for *Sports Story Magazine*, virtually non-existent. Of the 50-odd sports pulps, only four were available as markets for Howard's work in the early 1930s (*Sports Story, Fight Stories, Dime Sports* and *Jack Dempsey's Fight Magazine*), and of these four, only two would survive beyond 1934. In spite of the limited market for his boxing stories, however, Howard's interest in "the manly art" was deep enough and his marketing ingenuity clever enough to assure the publication of most of his stories.

Howard's interest in boxing dates back to his elementary school days in Cross Cut, Texas, when he wrestled and sparred with his friends. In *Dark Valley Destiny*, the de Camp biography of Howard, a childhood friend, Austin Newton, recalled the circumstances of their sparring, noting that they didn't have boxing gloves. Pictures of Howard and friends in sparring postures confirms his early interest in boxing; de Camp says that "aside from buying books and attending movies, his main amusements were walking in the woods and boxing with his friend Tyson" (Lindsey Tyson). While rooming with Tyson at Howard Payne College, Howard became an avid reader of a *Saturday Evening Post* series of boxing articles — a series which, given Howard's imagination and writing skills, led him to produce fight fiction for magazines as diverse as *Ghost Stories* and *Argosy All-Story Weekly*.

In a letter to Wilfred B. Talman in 1931 (*The Second Book of Robert E. Howard*), Howard says: "My tastes are simple; I like prize fights, football games, horseraces and beer." Howard's writing would reflect his "taste" for the fights. *Fight Stories* published 27 of his boxing stories (about one-half after his death), and he would have three fight stories published in *Sport Story Magazine* (1931), three in *Jack Dempsey's Fight Magazine* (1934) and one in *Dime Sports* (1936).

Howard also published fight stories in *Action Stories* (1931–1937), *Argosy All-Story Weekly* (1929), *Ghost Stories* (1929), and *Magic Carpet Magazine* (1934). In the June 1929 issue of *The Ring*, Howard wrote a non-fiction piece about the death of George "The Kid" Lavigne, a rough-and-tumble turn-of-the-century fighter who won the lightweight title for America is 1896. Lavigne's fights took place over the period 1895–1899, and in one bout he delivered a knockout punch to a fighter named Andy Bowen who later died from its effects. Lavigne's style had none of the scientific touches. It was all brutal assault, and this had a special appeal for Howard. His fighters were dynamite punchers. Sailor Steve Costigan was such a puncher.

E. Hoffman Price, reviewing Howard's Breckinridge Elkins Bear Creek westerns, talks about Howard's "impossible-hokum dialogue." The Elkins yarns are similar in style and content to Howard's fight stories; all are humorous, tongue-in-cheek, tall tales which de Camp compares to the Keystone Cop school of visual humor. But make no mistake about it, Howard's fight stories are among the best of pulp sports fiction. First, they meet the criteria for all pulp fiction — they tell an interesting story with style. Howard's fight stories are set in exotic locales and told with a flourish that keeps the reader interested. His knowledge of boxing allowed him to write fight scenes that ring true. Often going over three pages, his fight descriptions reveal an understanding of both defensive and offensive ring tactics. If this were not enough, Howard also understood the politics of boxing. In "Fist and Fang" (*Fight Stories*, May 1930), Howard writes of a fighter "sent back to Frisco to pad his k.o. record and keep in trim by toppling hand-and-eggers."

Most of the Sailor Steve Costigan stories were written for *Fight Stories* and *Action Stories*. With few markets available for his fight stories, Howard would soon have a surfeit of fight fiction which never saw publication in his lifetime. Howard researcher Glen Lord collected these stories in *The Incredible Adventures of Dennis Dorgan*. Dorgan (also a sailor) often found himself in strange and exotic ports of call; a circumstance which made his adventures suitable for sale to *Magic Carpet Magazine* ("The Alleys of Singapore," Jan. 1934, written under Howard's Patrick Ervin pseudonym). While these stories all wind up in epic ring battles (in one case in medieval armor), the Costigan–Dorgan stories are told with a light, comedic touch, using the first-person patois of the principals.

Howard's fight fiction pulls no punches, as can be seen in the following excerpt from "The Mandarin Ruby" (from *The Incredible Adventures of Dennis Dorgan*):

> It was a rough night for a sailor, even for Dennis Dorgan, Able Seaman. In the fourth he knocked my head back so far betweenst my shoulders I could count the freckles on my own spine. In the fifth he throwed me through the ropes and one of his pals busted a bottle over my head as I clumb back in the ring. It was the bottle which made me lose my temper.... I stuck my left mauler up to the elbow in his hairy belly and then cracked a meat-axe right on his ear whilst he was trying to get back his wind.

All of Howard's Costigan-Dorgan fights are in the style of the fighter he most admired: Kid Lavigne. The following action is as described in "Stand Up and Slug" (*Fight Stories*, Summer 1940):

> I battered him back across the ring, and he rallied and smashed over a sledge-hammer left hook that rocked me to my heels and made the blood splatter, but I bored right in with a sizzling left hook under his heart. He gasped, his knees buckled, then he steadied hisself and shot over his left just as I crashed him with a right. Bam! Something exploded in my head, and then I heard the referee counting. To my chagrin, I found I was on the canvas, but Roach was there too.

Although he wrote entertaining westerns and fight stories, Howard's post–pulp era reputation is based on his *Weird Tales* work; mainly his tales of Conan. Most of Howard's *Weird Tales* colleagues wrote this kind of story almost exclusively, if we can subsume various adventure, oriental, ghost and horror fiction within this specialized genre. Some of the *Weird Tales* crowd took a turn at the western on occasion (Joseph Payne Brennan produced 17 westerns before making his first *Weird Tales* sale in 1952) but few wrote sports fiction.

Manly Wade Wellman, who taught creative writing at the University of North Carolina after his *Weird Tales* career, had a small non-fiction piece on boxing in the September 23, 1933, *Argosy*, a story about George Taylor, a 16-year-old member of James Figg's boxing academy circa 1733. For the most part, though, the *Weird Tales* writers had little interest in sports fact or fiction.

One exception is Carl Jacobi's improbable blend of golf and warlike aliens. "The Player at Yellow Silence" (*Galaxy*, June 1970) tells an alien invasion story against a futuristic golf course (Yellow Silence) with 1,325-yard holes, time warp and magnetic grass traps, electronic clubs and robotic caddies. This story was included in a book of Jacobi's short stories, *Disclosures in Scarlet* (Arkham House, 1972). A second exception is Arthur Burks' boxing stories in *Sport Story Magazine*, which undoubtedly derive from experiences related to his 12 years in the Marine Corps. "Gloves for a Ghost" (*Fight Stories*, Spring, 1940), for example, is typical boxing fare, in a Marine Corps context and with a *Weird Tales* type setting (the Dominican Republic). This issue of *Fight Stories* lists the story on its cover page under the name Tom O'Neill while the contents page lists the story as by Arthur J. Burks. Unfortunately, none of these stories are collected in Burks' Arkham House short-story collection (*Black Medicine*, 1966) which consists of 16 *Weird Tales* stories set in the Dominican Republic.

A lesser-known Howard fighter, Kid Allison, was drawn in the Kid Lavigne image and appeared in about 10 pulp stories, three of which were published in *Sport Story Magazine* in 1931. Allison was a popular character name of Howard's, showing up in weird fiction (James Allison) and westerns (Steve Allison aka the Sonora Kid) as well as in the aforementioned fight stories. The name probably derives from one of the old West's killers, Clay Allison, a man who once cut off the head of a victim, impaled it on a pike, and rode 29 miles with the impaled head to his favorite saloon. On another occasion Allison had what seemed to be a casual breakfast with an unsuspecting victim before, just as casually, blowing the man's brains out when the meal had been finished. Allison commented to bystanders that he didn't want to send a man to hell on an empty stomach.

Howard's fighters were men capable of delivering and absorbing unrelenting punishment, men like "The Iron Man" (one of Howard's straight-up boxing stories sans hokum dialogue and bravado style —*Fight Stories*, June 1930). Howard once said that when writing the Conan stories he found himself on the side of the barbarian. Howard's fighters were just that —fighters, not boxers. There's a lot of Conan in all of them.

Necronomican Press (P.O. Box 1304, West Warwick, RI 02893) reprinted all of the Robert E. Howard fight stories with the exception of those published in *The Incredible Adventures of Dennis Dorgan* and *The Iron Man*, in eight separate paperback issues averaging about six stories per issue.

Howard's fight stories published in pulp magazines include the following Steve Costigan stories:

Action Stories

    The TNT Punch (January 1931)
    Blow the Chinks Down (October 1931)
    Breed of Battle (November 1931)
    Dark Shanghai (January 1932)

Fight Stories

    The Pit of the Serpent (July 1929)
    The Bull Dog Breed (February 1930)
    Sailor's Grudge (March 1930)
    Fist and Fang (May 1930)
    Winner Take All (July 1930)
    Waterfront Fists (September 1930)
    Champ of the Forecastle (November 1930)
    Alleys of Peril (January 1931)
    Texas Fists (May 1931)
    Circus Fists (December 1931)
    Vikings of the Gloves (February 1932)
    Night of Battle (March 1932)
    Manila Manslaughter (Fall 1937)
    You Got to Kill a Bulldog (Winter 1937–38)

6. The Pulp Writers

Costogan Versus Kid Camera (Spring 1938)
Champ of the Seven Seas (June–July 1938)
Cannibal Fists (Winter 1938–39)
Shanghaied Mitts (Summer 1939)
Sucker (Winter 1939–1940)
Stand Up and Slug! (Summer 1940)
"...Includin' the Scandinavian!" (Fall 1940)
Leather Lightning (Winter 1940)
The Waterfront Wallop (Fall 1941)
Sampson Had a Soft Spot (Spring 1942)
Slugger Bait (Summer 1942)
Shore Leave for a Slugger (Fall 1942)

Jack Dempsey's Fight Magazine

The Slugger's Game (May 1934)
General Ironfist (June 1934)
Sluggers of the Beach (January 1934)

The only Dennis Dorgan story to be published in the pulps was "Alleys of Darkness" in the January 1934 *The Magic Carpet Magazine.*

Non-series boxing stories in the pulp magazines include the following:

Iron Jaw (*Dime Sports Magazine*, April 1936)
The Iron Man (*Fight Stories*, June 1930)
The Apparition in the Prize Ring (*Ghost Stories*, April 1929).

Howard's Kid Allison stories were all published in *Sport Story Magazine* in 1931: "College Socks" (September 25), "Man with the Mystery Mitts" (October 25) and "The Good Knight" (December 25).

John Tunis did what no one before him in sports fiction had done; he expanded the sports story to include the nasty things found in other facets of life—things like racism. In "All-American" the pivotal issue is whether or not the team will decide to accept an interdivisional bowl game. The Miami-based high school team has one stipulation: Ned LeRoy, the left end, can't come. He's black. The team and the community must face this issue.

In "Keystone Kids," a story about the Brooklyn Dodgers, anti–Semitism is spreading and the target is rookie catcher Jocko

Klein. While many of the boys' books of the era included overt racist remarks, Tunis didn't just avoid this reality, he took it on head first, and he did it with other moral issues as well. In *Buddy and the Old Pro*, an Eddie Stanky-type coach tries to show Buddy how to gain advantage by less-than-honest means.

While these stories were groundbreaking, Tunis' most popular series would address what Bobby Knight now tells his team: something to the effect that you're not playing against "them," you're playing against yourself. The John Tunis Roy Tucker trilogy is about a boy, growing into manhood, fighting his own demons.

John Tunis wrote the three Roy Tucker books over the period 1940–1946. Tucker starts his baseball career with the Brooklyn Dodgers (*The Kid from Tomkinsville*), plays against the Cleveland Indians in a World Series (*World Series*), and makes a comeback when nearing the age of 40 after having suffered serious injuries in World War II (*The Kid Comes Back*). The *New York Times* said that the Tunis books had "prose which has the good hard smack of ash against leather," and a survey of some 50,000 boys in 1949 revealed John Tunis as their most popular author.

The Kid from Tomkinsville (1940) follows Roy Tucker from a Connecticut farm to Dodger Stadium where he starts his career as a pitcher, and concludes at the end of the regular season. Over the season, Tucker encounters the expected rookie problems and one problem not expected — a pitching arm injury which forces him to convert to an outfield position. Throughout the story Tucker is counseled by an older member of the staff, one Dave Leonard. Leonard informs him early on that courage is the secret ingredient in baseball as in life. Later, when the Kid has lost his arm, Leonard tells him that "Only the game fish swim upstream."

When Tunis wrote these books he informed the reader that the characters he wrote about were "drawn from real life." A lot of kids grew up wondering who some of these Dodgers were. Who was Gabby Gus, Red Evans, Razzle Dazzle Nugent? Who was the Kid himself? Popular belief at the time was that he was Pete Reiser. The secret identity of these characters can be found in a box of materials at Boston University's Mugar Library.

The second book in the series, *World Series* (1941), takes the Dodgers and the Kid through the Series with the Cleveland Indians, and the final book, *The Kid Comes Back* (1946), follows the Kid to the end of his career, at which time he becomes the Dave Leonard type of character he met as a rookie in *The Kid from Tomkinsville*.

John Tunis was born in 1889 in circumstances which can reasonably be called privileged. Graduating from Harvard, he worked briefly in a cotton mill in Newburyport, Massachusetts. Later, after a stint in World War I, he married and settled down in Rowayton, Connecticut.

In 1938 he wrote his first sports book, *Iron Duke*. Based on a May 8, 1924 *Sport Story Magazine* piece of the same title, it was voted the best juvenile of the year. Tunis was now, officially, a writer, at the age of 49. He had a lifelong romance with the game of tennis and covered the sport for NBC. He worked in the *New York Post*'s sports department from 1925 to 1932. He participated in the first transatlantic sports broadcast during the Davis Cup match between Allison and Borotra in Paris in July of 1932. Tunis died in 1975 and was hailed by the *New York Times* as a man who "helped educate a whole generation of Americans."

John Tunis' papers, manuscripts, etc., are in a collection at Boston University's Mugar Library. Among these papers is a sheet listing, character for character, his Dodgers and the real Brooklyn Dodgers. Roy Tucker's rabbi was Luke Sewell. Gabby Gus was Leo Durocher. Razzle Dazzle Nugent was Van Lingle Mungo. The Kid himself?—he is listed only as No. 36.

In the context of game theory, sports are, in the main, zero-sum games; that is, there is usually a loser and a winner. They are complicated, however, by something the game theorists call utility theory, which holds that there are choices which can be weighed and which often affect the outcome of games; parties in a game, for example, may have outside reasons for not competing at their best (as in throwing a fight for money). Pulp sports fiction has plenty of utility functions where effort is often not extended at maximum levels, but for more noble reasons than monetary gain.

Long before Tunis wrote his first sports book he was writing fact and fiction for *Sport Story Magazine*. The March 1931 issue has a timeless op. ed.-type piece by Tunis "Who Owns Football?" And in the January 1925 issue, 13 years before Tunis' first sports book, there is "The Limelight Kid."

A typical Tunis piece, the "Kid" in question is something of a hotdog and only concerned with his personal Yale athletic stats. In the big game with Princeton, Eddie Munroe (The Kid) suddenly decides in a split second on the football field that he cares more for the team than he realizes. The Princeton team fumbles the ball in the endzone and Eddie has a shot at recovering the fumble, but a teammate has a better shot. Eddie throws the key block, sacrificing personal glory for old Eli.

Tunis was an early critic of sports for its commercialism. In his book *$port$: Heroics and Hysterics*, he describes how concern for the dollar had infiltrated and diminished American professional sports and amateur sports down to the high school level as well. Taking his cue from Grover Cleveland Alexander, who had called baseball players "businessmen first and then baseball players," Tunis produced a book that was to sports of the day what Ralph Nader's *Unsafe at Any Speed* was to the automobile industry in the 1960s.

Contrary Opinion

Most pulp writers I have spoken to enjoyed their pulp experiences and appreciated the opportunity to write the type of freewheeling prose found in the pulps. Not so the anonymous writer of "A Penny a Word" who described his feelings about the experience in *The American Mercury* (March 1936):

> That is the real tragedy for us who came to the pulps for training. While we were writing this daydream in which some potential two-fisted barroom fighter or glamorous captivator or gun-slick bronco-buster can identify himself, we must believe it at the moment. We must inject some enthusiasm to give it false vitality and spurious reality. It is working oneself into this alien mood, this primitive emotional and cerebral pattern, that poisons the brain like a drug, atrophies the perspective, and dulls the spirit.
>
> And yet I myself have become a dependable purveyor to those five-million morons who pay a few nickels each month for their mechanized dreams. I am one of the camp followers of the writing profession, the ragtag and bobtail of the fashion parade, who, for a bare subsistence, scavenge in the garbage heaps of literature. I am one of those disillusioned hack authors whose hopes lie somewhere back in the dim golden years when everyone believed in self-expression.

Sources for Further Information on Robert E. Howard

de Camp, L. Sprague, Catherine Crook de Camp, and Jane Whittington. *Dark Valley Destiny — The Life of Robert E. Howard, the Creator of Conan*, Bluejay Books, Inc., 1983.
Fleisher, Nat and Sam Andre. *A Pictorial History of Boxing*, Castle Books, 1975.
Grant, Donald M. *The Iron Man and Other Tales of the Ring*, 1976.
The Gunfighters. Editors of Time-Life Books, Time-Life Books, 1974.
Lord, Glen, ed. *The Incredible Adventures of Dennis Dorgan*, Zebra Books, 1974.
____. *The Last Celt — A Bio-Biography of Robert Ervin Howard*, Donald M. Grant Publishers, 1976.
____. *The Second Book of Robert E. Howard*, Zebra Books, 1976.

References and Materials Cited in Chapter 6

Argosy Weekly, October 5, 1935.
Avallone, Michael. Personal correspondence.
Cox, William. Personal correspondence.
Inge, M. Thomas, ed. *Handbook of American Popular Culture*, Vol. 1, Ch. 12: Sports, by Robert J. Higgs. Greenwood Press, 1978.
L'Amour, Louis. Personal correspondence.
McCue, Andy. *Baseball by the Books — A History and Complete Bibliography of Baseball Fiction*, Wm. C. Brown Publishers, 1991.
Oriard, Michael V. *Dreaming of Heroes — American Sports Fiction 1868–1980*. Nelson Hall, 1982.
Parente, Audrey. *Pulp Man's Odyssey — The Hugh Cave Story*, Starmond House, 1988.
Phillips, Robert. *Louis L'Amour — His Life and Times. An Unauthorized Biography*, Paperjacks Ltd., 1987.
Weinberg, Robert. *The Louis L'Amour Companion*, Andrews and McMeel, 1992.
Weinberg & McKinstry. *The Hero Pulp Index*, Opar Press, June 1971.

7

Editors, Artists and Readers

Artists

The sports pulps differed from the other genre pulps which had cover art and interior art to illustrate the fiction. Taking their lead from the newspaper, the sports pulp began to use illustrated sports highlights or biographical illustration. Typically, a ballplayer's career would be sketched, cartoon style in some cases, in other cases with quite realistic renderings. Babe Ruth was so delighted with Mario Demarco's rendition of him that he sent a letter of appreciation. In one case a cartoon was used over a two-page spread to tell the story of the history of hockey. *Fight Stories* had a two-page spread called "Ringside Review" by artist Walter Galli, featuring boxer sketches with some lesser-known historical information:

> In 1917 the great Harry Greb defeated six fighters on six successive nights, including welters, middles, light-heavys and heavyweights.... No pushovers either!

In *The American Magazine*,* authors Janello and Jones define the purpose of magazine cover art:

> Its whole purpose is to communicate both explicit and subliminal messages about the riches within.

*Janello, Amy and Jones, Brennon, The American Magazine, Harry N. Abrams, Inc., N.Y., 1991.

In the July 1977 issue of the pulp fanzine *Xenophile*, editor Henry Steeger puts it more precisely:

> *Popular*'s covers were very specifically designed to appeal to a particular type. Each one was aimed at the audience I thought we had. A great deal of time was spent on covers and artists were accustomed to bringing them back for revisions over and over until the proper degree of competence had been reached. I devoted more time and attention to covers than to anything else because I figured our covers were our salesmen. It had to be just right because I figured we had only a matter of seconds to make our sale.

The sports pulps did have their cover art but, as good as it was (in some cases), it couldn't hold a candle to the cover art of the superhero or science fiction magazines. An air war pulp with a cover loaded with friendly and enemy aircraft shooting each other out of the sky would easily draw one's eye away from a close play at home plate, and this was certainly enough to tip the impulse buyer's scale.

Popular Publications editor, Henry Steeger, in a July 1977 interview in the pulp fanzine *Xenophile* (Pulpcon 6 Issue) talked about cover artists, recalling payments of $75–$100 in the beginning, and up to $250 later. Steeger took an active part in all facets of magazine production and even made a study of pulp cover colors:

> Yes, there were certain colors and color combinations used on covers which attracted buyers more than other colors. I made a complete study in considerable depth of every color in the artist's palette. I made all the possible combinations possible, then studied them at various distances to note and study eye appeal. In addition to this, I kept a newsstand in my office and arranged covers on the newsstand to see which ones stood out above the others. This study went on year after year. I became aware of the fact, for instance, that the hot colors like reds and yellows appealed to men, whereas the cooler colors appealed more to women. The magazine covers were planned accordingly and also the style of type was matched to the prospective purchaser. Men preferred block letters and women preferred serifs. This is, of course, the main principle, but we did use these themes with variations.

Editor Harold Hersey makes the following cover-art observations in his autobiography, *Pulpwood Editor**:

---

*Hersey, Harold, Pulpwood Editor, *Frederick A. Stokes Company, New York, 1937.*

> To the outside eye, a pulpwood cover often has the appearance of having been thrown hastily together. But, while I was glad to get flashes of inspiration in either sketch or final canvas, I labored unendingly in selecting paintings from a host of offerings, and never considered the layout of picture and text completed until the last press proof was delivered to the printer.

Hersey had a man working for him, W. M. Clayton, whom he used to manage the work of the artists:

> Clayton was one of the best cover men in the trade. He insisted that every original, engraver's proof and final copy be submitted to his inspection. And he always made some suggestion here or there that improved its appearance.

The fact remains that cover art was a competitive process and required the artist's best efforts. Covers by George Gross for the *All-American Football Magazine* were superior renderings of football action sequences, particularly his "Four Horsemen" cover on the Fall 1939 issue which pictured the four backs on the offense and a stadium in the low background with four white horses in the high background. In addition to his sports covers, Gross did covers for *Planet Stories* in the 1940s and paperback western covers for Dell in the 1950s. As late as 1980 he was still doing western covers.

Modest Stein, who did cover art for the Munsey magazines at the turn of the century, executed *Sport Story* covers as well as covers for other Street & Smith magazines (*Love Story, Astounding Science Fiction, Unknown*).

Charles De Feo did some excellent covers for the Popular Publications Group, especially the first issues of *Knockout Magazine* (January/February 1937) and *Sports Novels* (April-May 1937). The *Knockout* cover captures a left to the solar-plexis coupled with a head butt — a great action shot. Interior illustrations of this first issue of *Knockout* were equally good at portraying boxing skills accurately: guard up while the jab comes straight off the shoulder and with the feet properly positioned. Other good *Knockout* interior illustrations are by J. Flemming Gould.

Rafael M. de Soto worked in more pulps than he cares to remember, including *Dime Western, Ace Western, Red Seal Western, Star Western* and *Western Story Magazine*, as well as *Adventure, Detective Tales, The Spider, Black Mask* and many others. He was one of the best detective cover artists, if not *the* best, and he enjoyed doing western covers as well. In a personal letter he told me:

> They had to have action, color, six-shooter spitting fire, hero in trouble, but not defeated, and no girl kissing.

His cover for the January 1938 (Vol. 2, No. 1) issue of *Champion Sports* is an excellent rendering of New York Rangers' hockey player Murray Murdock, who was called the Lou Gehrig of hockey because of his string of 600 straight games played. The cover is a tribute to Murdock who is featured in the same issue in a piece by Jack Kofoed, "Hockey's Iron Man." Hockey was rarely used on sports pulp covers. The cover was the lure, and most potential buyers wanted baseball, football or boxing.

It wasn't very often that cover artists were identified but, starting with the second May 1939 issue, cover art credit was given in *Sport Story Magazine*. Cover artists by year are as follows:

1939: Arthur Jameson, Robert E. Lee, Hubert Rogers, George Gross, and Carleton Reed.
1940: A. Leslie Ross, George Gross, Graves Gladney.
1941: A. Leslie Ross, H. W. Scott, Llanuza.
1942: A. Leslie Ross (all but one cover), Modest Stein.
1943: A. Leslie Ross, H. W. Scott, Modest Stein.

H. W. Scott started his Street & Smith art career doing interior art for *Wild West Weekly* and *Western Story* and would become one of the best and most prolific pulp cover artists. *Life Magazine* ran a two-page spread on Scott (June 22, 1942) in which they called him the world's most prolific illustrator. The article noted that Scott had planned to be a pianist until a World War I compound arm fracture put an end to that ambition.

Hubert Rogers' work for *Sport Story Magazine* supplemented his 50-plus covers for *Astounding Science Fiction*. His covers were "nearly always superb," according to Alva Rogers in his history of that magazine (*Requiem for Astounding*). His baseball cover of a batter completing his swing for the first issue of *Dime Sports Magazine* was one of the better sport pulp covers (July 1935).

Leslie Ross did western, superhero, and *Sport Story Magazine* covers for Street & Smith as well as a number of science fiction pulps in the Columbia Publications Group (*Science Fiction, Science Fiction Quarterly, Dynamic Science Fiction* and *Future Science Fiction*).

In some cases the cover artist should have been thankful that he was not given credit. The Spring 1950 *Popular Baseball* cover depicts, in close up, a pitcher in windup. The pitcher is throwing with his left arm and has a left-hander's glove on his right hand!

Pulp cover artists generally preferred to work on the mystery, super hero, adventure, and science fiction magazines, where it was possible to be quite experimental and expansive. Baseball does not present these possibilities, nor does any other sport.

Among those pulp artists who have achieved some reknown are Rudolph Belarski, whose best covers decorated air, war, adventure, and detective pulps; Norman Saunders, whose work included some great western and science fiction covers and the Mars Attack Cards; Walter Baumhofer, whose best work is considered to be the Doc Savage covers; Graves Gladney for the Shadow covers; and among others who did science fiction covers, Frank Paul, J. Allan St. John, Edd Cartier, Hannes Bok, Howard Brown and Earl Bergey. Science fiction offered the cover artist the greatest opportunity to blast the potential reader's senses with imaginative, outrageous otherworld concepts.

One can't say enough about the work of these artists. Saunders, who died in 1989, left a legacy admired by all of the people who collect and research pulp history. He worked in the western, science fiction, detective, and weird genres and his renderings of sexy gals for the so-called saucy magazines had no equal. While much time has been devoted to his work in these areas for obvious reasons, little note has been paid to his work in the sports genre. His covers for *Sports Novels Magazine* are every bit as great as his covers for *Black Mask, Dime Detective, Ten Detective Aces, Mystery Adventure, Eerie Stories, Complete Detective, Thrilling Detective, Secret Agent X, Variety Novels*, the *Spicy* pulps, and others. After working in the pulps (1935–1953) Saunders worked for the men's magazines (*Stag, Argosy, True* and *Men's*). Many, unfamiliar with his pulp work, know of his artwork on the Mars Attack Cards.

The artwork that offered the sports illustrator the best opportunity to do imaginative work was the sports cartoon or the sports character/history pen and ink drawing. These drawings would, at their best, depict great sports moments and characters with eye-catching renderings. Not in the same category as a BEM (bug-eyed monster) carrying off a scantily-clad maiden, with the hero, ray gun in hand, in hot pursuit, but for the sports pulp, some of those cartoons and drawings were as good as it could get.

Earle Bergey rendered SF covers for *Startling Stories, Planet Stories, Space Science Fiction, Captain Future* and other SF pulps as well as doing covers for *Sport Story Magazine* in the 1930s and *Exciting Sports* in the 1940s. He is best remembered, however, for his SF covers which usually featured scantily-clad gorgeous gals being threatened by some evil being.

Mario DeMarco was one of the artists who provided illustrated features for the sports pulps. He drew for *Fight Stories, Baseball Stories, Football Action, All Sports, Thrilling Sports* and others. He recalled the pulp days in a recent letter to the author:

> Those were really great years drawing for the comic books and pulps during the mid-thirties. I first broke into the pulps by selling three western pages entitled "Western Stars" for five bucks each. At the time I was a sport cartoonist for my high-school paper, *The Mercury*, and figured I would do several pages of sports drawings, and I and my friend, Ray Houlihan bummed our way to New York. Next day we made the rounds of the comic-book houses. I met with Willard Mullin who sent me over to Street & Smith. He looked them over and the editor kept three pages. From then on I was doing regular sports cartoons for Street & Smith.
>
> In time I landed a sport cartoon job at Fiction House Publications, doing baseball, football and boxing cartoons plus illustrating some of their sport articles. This was really great because they let me send in what I wanted. At one time I did an illustration of Babe Ruth and sent it to him for him to autograph. Well, I never did get it back but received a nice letter from the Babe plus an autographed photo which I still have.
>
> Those were my real training years. I eventually sent material to Columbia, Popular Publications, Fox and several others. The average pay for a page at this time was twenty-five dollars, which was real great. I consider these years working for the pulps my "golden years."

Contrast the feelings Mr. DeMarco has about his pulp years with those of the anonymous writer of "A Penny a Word" (see page 156). I have suggested to Mr. DeMarco that he hold onto the auto-

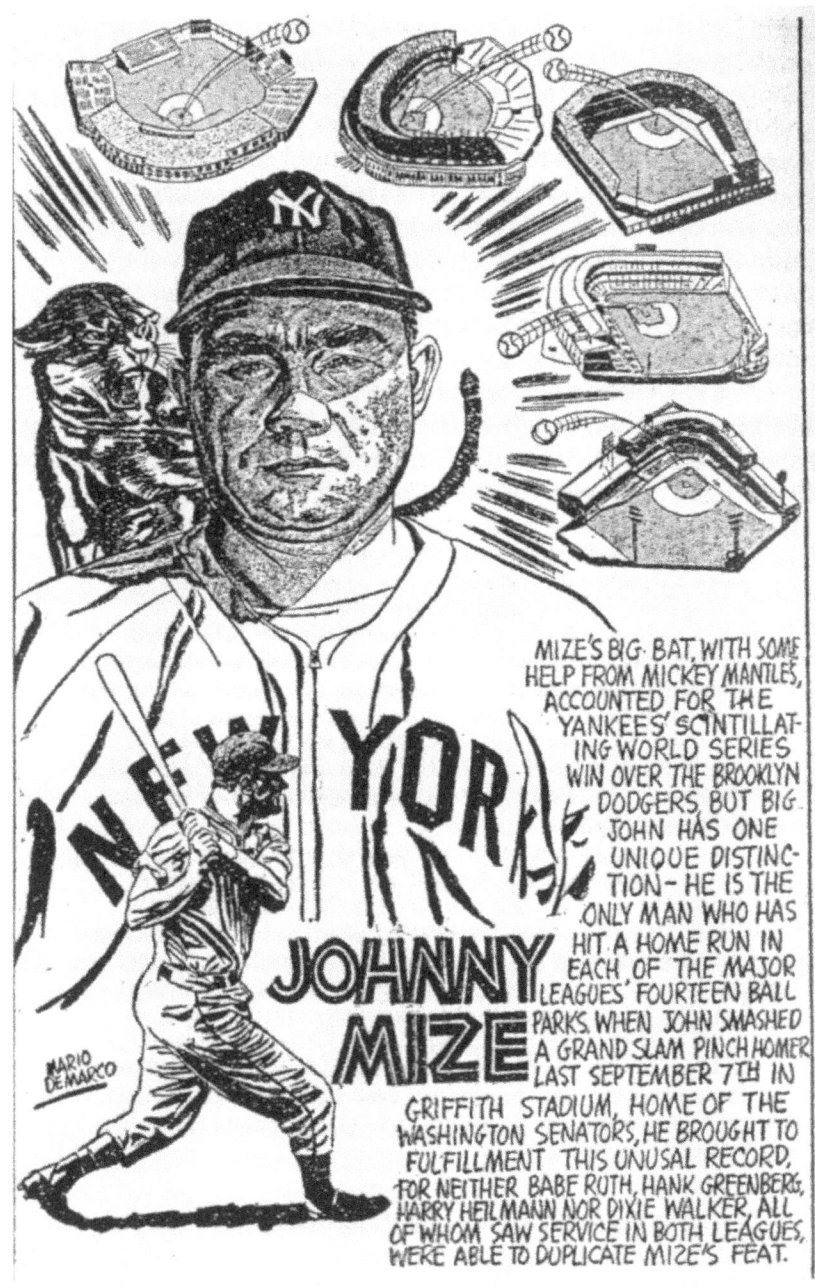

graphed Babe Ruth photo rather carefully as it auctions at a near-four-figure-price these days. Unfortunately for Mr. DeMarco, he never asked that the original drawings he sent off to the pulps be returned. Many of these drawings had the original signatures of sport figures like Dempsey, Cobb, Sisler, Tunney, and they are now sought by collectors willing to pay hundreds for such artifacts. The December 6 and 7 Leland's Auction Catalogue lists three similar items:

Item 512: 1953 N.Y. Yankees Team Signed Willard Mullin Print with Mantle, Mize, etc., signatures. Pre-auction estimate is given at $2000–$3000.

Item 499: Yogi Berra by Willard Mullin. Published pen and ink. This item is not autographed but the pre-auction estimate is given at $600–$800.

Item 506: Casey Stengel by Willard Mullin. Published pen and ink with South of the Border flavor. Mets going down to Mexico for some exhibition games. Again, not autographed but with a pre-auction estimate of $600–$800.

Things have certainly changed. Not only did the readers of the pulp sports magazine consider these drawings disposable, but freelance artists like Mario DeMarco never in their wildest dreams considered their work to have the potential to appreciate to these auction-house values.

Editors

Before MacKinlay Kantor earned a reputation as one of the country's leading Civil War writers he labored in the pulp vineyards for such editors as Edwin Baird of *Real Detective Tales*, Howard Bloomfield of *Detective Fiction Weekly* and Arthur Hoffman of *McClure's* (where he would write his first Civil War story). Like most pulp fiction writers he wrote with one hand and fended the wolf from the door with the other, always waiting, waiting for that check to come from the editor. Kantor described the "good" editor as "anxious to find a good author — all for his very own — as any bug catcher would be to catch a rare butterfly."*

In examining the role of the pulp editor one must consider the symbiotic relationship between the writer and the editor at a time when it was not uncommon for writers to hawk their wares in person. In his autobiographical foreword to *Brass Knuckles: The Life and Times of the Pulp Story*, Frank Gruber recounts some of his editor interactions:

> Cap Shaw [editor of *Black Mask*] killed writers with kindness. Yet writers swore by him. I have met and talked to writers all over the country about Shaw and a number of them spoke of him in a tone of awe, as if they were talking about God. The writers who revered Shaw, however, were the ones who lived away from New York.†

Gruber's experiences date to the heyday of the pulp magazine when he states that he would write anything and everything for a buck: "I wrote spicy sex stories, detective stories, love stories and sport stories." He goes on to say that he carried stories door to editorial door, much like a Fuller-Brush salesman. Making his way by the secretaries, he did get to see and know John Nanovic of Street & Smith, Duncan Norton-Taylor of *Detective Fiction Weekly*, Leo Marguiles of *Standard*, Rogers Terrill of *Popular*, and Harry Widmer of Magazine Publishers.

The sport fiction Gruber produced went to *Short Stories*, a pulp described by Gruber as "a closed market," but it opened to Gruber to the tune of two cents a word (a princely price at the time) after he was able to con editor Dorothy McIlwraith into accepting him into the *Short Stories* writers' stable: "I gave her one of my finest sales pitches, told her I had to have two cents a word, that the editors of *Argosy* and *Adventure* were laying siege to my door, but I liked *Short Stories* so much that I preferred to have my work appear in it."

Gruber would go on from these modest pulp beginnings to write hundreds of pulp fiction stories, dozens of suspense and mystery novels, about 30 historical westerns, a biography of Horatio Alger, Jr., a biography of Zane Grey, an autobiography (*The Pulp*

---

*Kantor, MacKinlay, Author's Choice — 40 Short Stories, Coward-McCann, Inc., 1944.
†All Gruber quotes from: Gruber, Frank, Brass Knuckles, Sherbourne Press, Inc., 1966.

Jungle), and to gather numerous television and film credits. Gruber also produced pulp fiction and books under an even-dozen pseudonyms. His sports fiction was produced for *Short Stories* over the years 1938–1957, for two issues of *Dime Sports* (August 1936 and January 1937), and for one issue of *Ace Sports* (May 1936). The sports fiction was mostly abandoned in favor of his more successful detective and western writing.

The July 1977 issue of the pulp fanzine *Xenophile* contains an extensive interview with Popular Publications co-founder and editor Henry Steeger. During the first 10 years of Steeger's editorial reign he produced 12 western titles, 11 detective/mystery titles, 10 character titles, 8 love, 5 adventure/general, 4 weird, 4 sports, 3 air-war and no science fiction/fantasy titles, and for as long as he could he tried to read every story himself. As the magazine count increased, this task became quite impossible, and editors like Howard Brown of the Ziff-Davis group of pulps have admitted to me that some issues would contain stories which were unscanned by editorial eyes. Robert Lowndes edited *All Sports*, *Sports Fiction*, *Super Sports*, and *Sports Winners* in addition to a number of other genre pulps. He told me, "My biggest problem was getting out the magazines each month and trying to get the time to look over the manuscripts."

The editor has his vision of what the magazine is and it may or may not impress the would-be writer. In his pulp-writing autobiography,* the giant among pulp writers, H. Bedford-Jones, says that "A few writers will honestly try to supply his wants but the majority will sneer at him and pay no attention." He goes on to talk about the difficulties and misunderstandings inherent in the writer-editor relationship and comes down on both sides of the issue: "The editor has every right to line up the sort of stuff he wants; the writer has every right to refuse to be bound down and trammeled."

One thing that is clear from the Bedford-Jones book is that in every writer's life there seems to have been a great editor:

> Many years ago, Gardner Hunting was editor of *People's Magazine*. Since that time, I suppose a dozen writers have mentioned to me their cordial relations with him, his very ungrudging assistance, his hearty endeavors to give them advice and help.

---

*Bedford-Jones, H., This Fiction Business, New York: Covici-Friede, 1929.

The book goes on in more detail to praise Hunting's editorial ministrations to pulp writers.

An editor at Popular Publications, Michael Tilden, was praised mightily by Elmore Leonard in my book *The Pulp Western*,* which reprints a thoughtful multi-page letter from Tilden to "Dutch," ostensibly commenting on a story of Leonard's but revealing much about the pulp business in the process. He indicates to Leonard that "some years ago" (the letter was written in 1951) Popular had conducted a reader survey and found that the average pulp reader was: "A young man in his middle 20s who had gone a couple of years to high school, was employed, usually by some large organization in which he used his hands pretty much. He had a wife and one and a fraction children, a small amount of money in the bank, a second-hand car, and hoped to own his own home."

Tilden is very professional but at the same time sympathetic to the plight of the part-time writer (which Leonard was at the time) and downright fatherly in his interest and cordiality. Sports pulp writer Bill Cox thoroughly enjoyed his relationship with Popular editor Rogers Terrill, and many of the writers I've interviewed talk fondly of their editors. Malcom Reiss, who edited *All-American Football*, *Football Action*, *Baseball Stories* and *Fight Stories*, is mentioned frequently as sensitive, intelligent and even-handed as a businessman.

Nat Fleischer was a rarity among pulp sports editors. An active player in the Dempsey-era fight game, he edited the bible of boxing (*Ring Magazine*), refereed fights (including some of Dempsey's) was a judge at fights and a constant presence at all championship fights of the era as a presenter of the *Ring Magazine* belt which symbolized the division title. Fleischer was editor of *The All-American Sports Magazine* and a frequent contributor. Over an eight-issue sequence (1933–1944) he wrote a Dempsey biography: "Jack Dempsey — The Idol of Fistiana."

Popular Publications co-founder and editor Henry Steeger was somewhat active in the pulp fanzine era and his passing in 1990 was noted with regrets by the *Pulp Collector* (Spring 1991). In addition to hero, western, detective, love, adventure and science fiction pulps, Popular produced four sports pulps: *Dime Sports Magazine, Fifteen*

---

*Dinan, John A., The Pulp Western, San Bernadino, CA: The Borgo Press, 1983.

Sports Stories, Knockout Magazine and *Sports Novels Magazines*. One of the pulp fans, Mark Leonard, recalled the man:

> One of my last memories of Steeger was of him walking down the aisles in the huckster room at Pulpcon. His eyes were bright and shining as he surveyed the boxes and boxes of those magnificent pulps which lined every table. Of course many of them were "his children," issues that he had begot through Popular. One can imagine the memories which were flooding back to him.

All was not love and roses in pulpdom. Some years ago I got a letter from Popular cover artist Graves Gladney who told me, a relative stranger, that he wouldn't mind "knocking the bejesus out of him," referring to Steeger. Gladney did not specify what experience(s) inspired him to make this statement. In the same letter he refers to Steeger "paying handsomely" for one of his pulp covers. Gladney died at his home in Clayton, Missouri, during the summer of 1976.

Pulp editor John Nanovic, best known for his editorial work on *Doc Savage*, *The Shadow* and other so-called "hero" pulps, got his start in the business by responding to a *Writer's Digest* ad calling for stories about college sports. Nanovic, a graduate of Notre Dame, responded with a piece ("Notre Dame, College of the Masses,") about three-quarters of which was Notre Dame football promo material. The piece earned Nanovic a job as editor of *College Stories* at Street & Smith and a check for $75. *College Stories* was a campus rah-rah-type magazine but it did contain some sports material, and when the magazine failed after five issues, the sports material was shuttled off to *Sport Story Magazine*. Some of the *College Stories* sport writers would be around for another 20 years in *Sport Story Magazine*, including Jack Kofoed, Jackson Scholz, T. W. Ford and Dabney Horton.

If anyone doubted that rodeo was a sport, the doubts would have been dispelled by reading editor Foghorn Clancy's stuff in *Rodeo Romances*. In a piece titled "In the Arena — Where Readers and Editor Meet," Clancy sets the readers straight (April 1947):

> Hi waddies. Here we are in the Arena once more to give out with news and gossip on that great sport of the cowboy, the rodeo, the sport which is typically American. In a span of 58

> years it has grown to be one of the leading sports of this country, with several million rodeo fans attending the various rodeos and the production of the contests hitting a new high from a big business standpoint. Everyone connected with the sport must be proud of the 1946 season, which was really a wonderful one, with the rodeo cowboys back from the war, big purses, big attendance, and consequently big gate receipts.

In successive issues of *Rodeo Romances* (Summer of 1948) Clancy ran a two-part "My Fifty Years in Rodeo" which tells of his first rodeo in San Angelo, Texas. Rodeo was then called "riding and roping contests." The year was 1898 and Clancy moved into the world of the rodeo riders, Wild West shows, and legendary rodeo characters like Pawnee Bill, Tom Mix, Will Rogers, and bulldogger Bill Pickett.

Writers who submitted their material to *Rodeo Romances* had best known their business. No pulpwood editor, sports or other, knew his subject more intimately than Foghorn Clancy, who modestly described himself as "America's foremost rodeo expert."

Some sports pulp editors came to their lot by default. Robert W. Lowndes (editor of Columbia sports pulps *Sports Fiction*, *Super Sports*, *Sports Winners*, *Ten-Story Sports*), an early science fiction fan, founded the Stamford, Connecticut, chapter of the Science Fiction League, and would later edit the Columbia SF pulps *Future Fiction* and *Science Fiction*. In 1942, he became Columbia Publications' managing editor. Some sports pulps, like *All-Baseball Stories*, not only did not have an editor's department but listed no editor's name on its masthead. *Rodeo Romances*, on the other hand, had a prominent role for the editor. *Rodeo Romances*' Foghorn Clancy wrote of the history of the sport, its current events and even those rodeo figures who had gone to that big arena in the sky (March 1946):

> Bobby Lee Coats died in North Hollywood, California, September 8th. His death was due to injuries sustained in bull riding at a rodeo more than a year ago. Interment was in Forest Lawn Cemetery. Pall bearers were Dick Slappert, Wag Blessing, Rocky Shahan, Burl Tatum, Clyde Kennedy, and Carol Henry, all buddies of the arena.

While the magazine was only published quarterly, it was one of only a few sources of information about the rodeo business and, consequently, served as an organ of sorts of the Rodeo Cowboy's Association whose activities, in the office and in the arena, it regularly reported.

Through the 1940s, editorial material in the sports pulps consisted of fact-based glimpses of sports teams and characters, and an occasional spotting of trends, as in this signed editorial piece by A. H. Norton in the August 1940 *Dime Sports Magazine*:

> Judging from the number of Major League Baseball players now participating in the game who were formerly gridiron men, it seems to be just a short jump from college football to baseball stardom. Seventeen of them will see action this present season (A.L. 9, N.L. 8). Upon observing this list, it will be easily seen that the majority of these players are stars on their own respective ball teams.

The piece (written under the editorial byline "The Score Board") goes on to analyze the trend in more detail, and this was about expansive as editors got. The politics of sports is common fare in today's newspapers but the subject would not surface until the pulp era was into its last days.

Best Sports routinely got into the politics of sports in the 1950s. Editor Robert O. Erisman and his associates Arthur Lane and Daniel Keyes took on the controversial issues in sports which heretofore had been avoided by the sports pulps, which chose instead to provide sports stats, trivia, biographies and such. In the May 1951 issue of *Best Sports*, under the editorial byline "Sports Bull Session," the editors take on several controversial issues, among them the need for protective gear in boxing and the blackball job done on baseball commissioner Albert "Happy" Chandler. The following passages are excerpted from the extensive editorial piece:

> Even though such a device may eliminate the knockouts and bloody brows the fight fans applaud eagerly, lives will be saved and the sport will have a final chance to save face before a growing feeling of contempt for such brutality from any quarters around the world.
> After all, Chandler was always a politician, and a good one, very early in life. And he was originally promoted into his job through the political machinations of an individual who is no longer connected with the game. A moral, perhaps, can be drawn from all this chicanery.

This was the sports pulp in its editorial maturity but today they are of little interest to the sports researcher except as they mark the beginnings of what we see as today's sports op/ed material.

It was the most enduring editorial/management sports pulp team of T. T. Scott and Malcom Reiss that provided sports fact material along with the regular sports fiction. As a team they produced *Basketball Stories, Fight Stories, Football Action, Football Stories, All-American Football Magazine* and *Baseball Stories* over three decades, using the same "Fact and Fiction" byline/format.

Through the thirties, Scott acted as president and general manager and Reiss as editor. In the late 1940s, Scott remained president, Reiss took over the general manager role, and Jack O'Sullivan was hired as editor. In all their years of publishing sports pulps, the editorial team of Scott and Reiss never had a "letters" department and never offered an editorial opinion.

The Readers

Frederic Wertham, M.D., internationally renowned psychiatrist and the man who made a big fuss about the Batman-Robin relationship, wrote a book titled *The World of Fanzines*.* A fanzine is described as a little-known, particular kind of publication which derives from the common term fan and the last syllable of the word magazine. Fanzines are noncommercial, nonprofessional, and published irregularly for a target audience comprised of hardcore devotees, researchers, and lovers of a particular brand of fiction. The first such group were the readers of science fiction. Wertham describes three of them:

> There is a difference between a long-standing science fiction devotee who has a hobby of editing, column writing, or reading, a young comics collector who comes to the same activities by a different route, and a Tolkien enthusiast with linguistic or medievalist interests. But they all chose the same means of creative expression and communication — the fanzine.

Such a passion has taken hold of those readers of pulp magazines who, now in their sixties and older, bought their pulps off the

---

*Wertham, Fredric, The World of Fanzines, *Southern University Press, 1973.*

newsstand, and those who were born in succeeding decades and had to pay premium prices to satiate their lust. They are pulp addicts all. Since the end of the pulp era (somewhere in the 1950s) they have banded together like a nomadic tribe so they may share the pleasures of pulps with their own kind. They speak a special language, the language of pulp lore, and their voice is the pulp fanzine. Once a year they migrate to a place where they speak of the magic of pulps among themselves.

In this place called the Pulpcon (Pulp Convention), they marvel at each other's wares and tell stories of conquest — like finding that obscure title in a junk store for something less than a king's ransom. And they sit at the feet of the pulp gurus, those men who edited, illustrated, and wrote for the pulps, and listen to those who were there at the creation.

The pulp fanzine has been around for many years; *Xenophile* and *The Pulp Era* were two early models and there were a few, such as *The Faust Collector*, dedicated to just one writer. (Faust wrote mainly western fiction under 17 pen names.) Each time one of these fanzines went out of print there was another pulpster ready to pick up the torch so that the old timers and those with newly-acquired tastes for the pulp had a focal point. Current fanzines include the following:

> *The Bronze Gazette*, Green Eagle Publications, 2900 Standiford Ave., Suite 136, Modesto, CA. Mostly Doc Savage Material.
> *Echoes*, Fading Shadows Inc., 504 E. Morris St., Seymour, TX 76380. Covers all pulp subjects.
> *Fantasy Commentator*, A. Langly Searles, 48 Highland Circle, Bronxville, NY 10708. Covers all pulp material with focus on fantasy and science fiction.
> *Pulp Collector*, The Pulp Collector Press, 8417 Carrollton Parkway, New Carrollton, MD 20704. Covers all pulp material.
> *Pulp Vault*, Tattered Pages Press, 6942 North Oleander Avenue, Chicago, IL 60631. Covers all pulp material.

This is now and pulps were then, things of the 1930s and '40s when a kid who couldn't afford a candy bar or admission to a sports event took pleasure in sneaking in to these events or hanging around an outfield wall in the hope of retrieving a baseball in fair condition to replace the one done over in electrician's tape that his gang had used for 30-odd inning games on hot summer days on dusty vacant lots. There was no television; radio broadcast games were dry incantations over the dit-dah-dit of the telegraph key.

Down at the local variety store you could stand in awe in the presence of a magnificent, multi-colored array of amazing, astounding, thrilling, exciting pulp covers which promised more than they could ever deliver. But what they could deliver was a brief trip to a fantasy world where you could make the key play, hit the game-winning home run and deliver yourself to a world where war wasn't on the horizon and the Great Depression wasn't doing its best to make your world a very grey place. For a while the magic of the pulp could make the world a better place. Yes, the simple-minded pulp story could do just that.

Reading the pulp story today one can, however imperfectly, briefly regress to where that barefoot boy with cheek of tan lived and remember the warm pleasure of knowing that your alter-ego would do himself proud in the big game. The sport story was more personal somehow. The western pulp was acted out in an alien land, as were the science fiction pulps, but the sports arena was a real place, a place where you could easily see yourself winning the day. Yes, this was more than possible.

The sports pulps were intended for an older audience as well, as the ad content — touting false teeth, neuritis and rupture relief — clearly indicates. I remember an old man in my neighborhood who needed help shaving because of palsy. A pal of mine and his older brother would help with a few chores. The apartment was a small two-room cellar dwelling, redolent of the masculine smell of pipe tobacco and the musty smell of the pulp magazines which lay around everywhere. His pleasures were few but enough that he could be tolerant of a couple of twitchy kids who are themselves now old men.

Evidence that the sport story pulp was more of a personal experience can be found in the so-called readers' segment of these magazines. While the science fiction and western pulps had very active readers' segments, most of the sports pulps did not. The one exception was *Sport Story Magazine* (its special departments are discussed in an earlier chapter). *Popular Sports Magazine* had a readers' segment but it seemed to have been created by the editors:

> I like a lot of variety in my sports magazines, and at first I thought I wouldn't get enough if you had such a long novel on one sport. But I found myself enjoying that long story every issue more than I've enjoyed any sport story in a long time. So why should I kick? In your other stories and features too. And then all the novels aren't about the same sport, so I get a huge mouthful every time of one particular sport!
>
> Incidentally, I also read *Thrilling Sports* and I can't kick about the variety there, with ten stories in every issue!—Malcolm Stuart [Fall 1940 issue]

These reader letters in *Popular Sports* always praised the format of the magazine, and its companion magazines were always touted. The readers' column of *Dime Sports Magazine* ("The Score Board") seemed more in tune with the spirit of the reader-magazine relationship:

> Dear Editor: Are you fellows hard up for stories? Who cares about Rabbit Maranville and the doings of Eddie Rickenbacker? Give us more fiction, and lay off those fact articles that you can pick up at space rates anywhere.—Ralph G., San Francisco, CA
>
> Ralph, old timer, you're not quite straight on your dope. When we get a story from Joe Cronin or Willy MacFarlane or Max Baer or Rabbit Maranville, we don't pick 'em up anywhere. We work blamed hard to get them and to get the kind we think and hope our readers want to see. If you think it's easy to do, just try walking up to a big league clubhouse some day and asking a featured star to talk to you for a while. They're busy fellows, Ralph, and they have a good many people asking favors of them.
>
> And if you think for a single minute that the kind of specialized and very valuable hand-to-hand talkfest with a big name is valued cheaply—you just try it! I'm glad to say that most of the fans don't feel that way. While I'm about it, I'd like to acknowledge helpful and kind letters from Ed Allen of Chattanooga, Tenn.; Joe French, Boston, Mass.; and many others about the Maranville yarn.—Sept. 1936

Sport Story Magazine segments were devoted to reader questions and there were other editorial attempts to draw in the reader such as giving badges of accomplishment for those readers who stated that they had accomplished some exercise regimen:

> The following readers have passed the National Amateur Athletic Federation of America Standard physical efficiency tests

under competent supervision and have been awarded the Sport Story Magazine Athletic Proficiency Badge...

A list of 50 or so awardees follows.

The *Sport Story* segment "Trainer and Coach" provided personalized physical training recommendations:

> I have only three weeks in which to train for a four-round boxing bout. I am in good general condition. Please tell me how I should train.
> — C.L.P., California
>
> Work out four or five days a week, as follows: Road work, one mile. Shadow boxing, three rounds. Bag punching, three rounds. Box four rounds with a partner once a week.

While most sport pulps had no reader department and a few had the typical letters-to-the-editor column, *Sport Story Magazine* experimented with their type and number over its 20-year history, peaking in the early thirties. The 1932 issues had the following departments: "Trainer and Coach," "From the Bleachers," "What Is the Answer?" "Now It Can Be Told," "Sports Miniature," "The Locker Room," "Between Rounds," "Here and There in Sports," "Off the Backboard," and a number of others.

In his autobiography Harold Hersey addressed the importance of these departments:

> They give the editor an opportunity to flatter his readers by printing their letters, answering questions, having heart-to-heart chats with his large family, talking about editorial policy, etc.

He concludes: "The precious contact must be preserved at all costs."

In *Pulpwood Editor*, Hersey speculates on the readers' motives and proves to be something of a prophet:

> Many intelligent people read unpretentious fiction because they are weary of pretense: others because they like to pretend. Naturally there are many who look down their long noses at a pulpwood yarn, but it is an error to assume that merely because they are intelligent it must follow that they scorn vicarious adventure and romance in their heart of hearts. Many of them prefer the

lazier habit of enjoying ready-made dream pictures, so they go to the movies — millions of them! And when television comes they won't even have to do that.

In the end, with or without the reader departments, the pulps would go the way of the dime novel, unable to survive television and the paperback. Confirming the Hersey dictum, the reader departments, in the form of "letters to the editor," survive in newspapers and magazines.

8

The Passing of the Pulps

No one questioned the popularity of the pulps; the sales figures told the story — eloquently. The public appetite for fast-paced pulp fiction resulted in hundreds of different titles in dozens of genres; the only limits were defined by the writers' imagination and the speed of the pulp presses. The pulp era was the peak of the Gutenberg revolution. The pulp years spanned an incredible period, encompassing a "great" depression and a world war, yet the time was a simpler one. One's passive entertainment pleasures were the movies, the radio and the pulp magazine. In spite of their widespread appeal at the time, only the pulps did not survive. The movies went on to become a more expansive experience and radio found a niche or two where it could survive.

Yes, popular literature did live on in the paperback and the hardcover book, but make no mistake about it, pulp fiction died and was buried. While there is an occasional resurrection of pulp fiction in the form of "The early works of" type of thing, usually a now-prominent writer cashing in on his pulp work, the sports pulp was permanently interred after taking one between the running lights:

> Manley shot again, into the dust, moving a leg, to support himself. Then the gun fell. He raised a hand to his chest and his left knee buckled. He fell, kneeling, and then pitched gently into the dust.

This description of the demise of a pulp gunman by Luke Short, aka Fred Glidden, is a fitting metaphor for the demise of the pulp genre.

There are several explanations for the end of the pulps, and with an exception or two, they have a common thread. The war years came along and piles of pulps were donated to the war effort at the same time that publishers were having their paper stock rationed. Publishers cut back their page count, went to monthly or quarterly production, converted to digest size, and took any measure they could to survive what was clearly going to be a long siege. Meanwhile, there were other publishing forces brewing, forces which would take their toll on each end of the pulp readers' age market.

Two forces that combined to set up the pulp knockout punch were the comic books and the paperbacks. The now-ubiquitous DC comic book empire was founded by one Major Malcolm Wheeler-Nicholson, a former U.S. Cavalry officer and frequent contributor to the pulps *Adventure* and *Argosy*. His fiction was of the world-adventurer variety, which was quite popular with the homebound pulp readers of the 1920s and 1930s.

Wheeler-Nicholson rented office space on New York's Fourth Ave. sometime in 1934 and began to publish comic books, the first of which was *New Fun*, which carried a February 1935 date. More tabloid than comic book as we now know it, *New Fun* didn't sell well and Wheeler-Nicholson was soon in financial trouble, having difficulty meeting his payroll. He struggled along until *Detective Comics* was introduced in 1936, at which time Wheeler-Nicholson took on pulp publisher Harry Donenfield as a partner. Later still, the publication of *Action Comics*, which contained the first Superman comic book story (June 1930), would start a super-hero land-rush. By 1941 *Action Comics* was selling 900,000 copies a month and would reach a circulation of 1,250,000 in 1940 — and the ball was just starting to roll.

The comic book would be a major blow to pulp sales. Easy to read eye candy, comics could be consumed effortlessly and what pulp publishers put into their covers, comic publishers put into every colorful page. The bottom end of the pulp age group was virtually swallowed up by the comic book revolution.

About the time the entry-age pulp reader was switching his dime to a comic book purchase, along came the paperbacks. In June of 1939, Robert Fair de Graf created a publishing house called Pocket

8. The Passing of the Pulps

Books. Starting off with 10 titles covering quite a range of tastes (Bambi to Shakespeare), the venture was an overnight success. Within a week the 10,000 copies of each of the 10 titles sold out. Throughout the early Pocket Book years de Graf published self-help, mystery, classics and popular fiction, and it was mostly the latter that would eat into the higher-age end of pulp readership. America was maturing and the de Graf paperback offered more sophisticated fare than the pulp magazines, which were now fighting the battle for readers on two fronts.

Pocket Book sport titles were, like the Armed Services Editions sport titles, a cut or two above the sport pulps. Popular sports commentators and writers like Red Smith, Bill Stern, and Bob Considine had Pocket Book titles and Ben Hogan and Red Auerbach had how-to books on their sports (golf and basketball). While GIs were reading the new, improved Armed Services Edition sports paperbacks, the home front was being treated to sports fact and fiction by some of sport's big names. The only sports pulp writer to have a Pocket Book title was Paul Gallico.

The pulps struggled through the 1930s and 1940s against this formidable competition. And if these two new publishing forces were not enough, a new popular reading format was looming in the not-too-distant future — the Armed Services Edition. A whole generation of men was taken away from the pulp market by the circumstances of World War II and, in addition to providing the G.I. with a weapon, three hots and a flop, Uncle Sam would provide reading material.

Between the fall of 1943 and the fall of 1947, 1322 different paperbacks of a unique design, designated as Armed Services Editions, were shipped by the crateload to American GIs all over the world. Over 122 million copies were printed in one of two sizes: 5½" × 3⅞" and 6½" × 4½". The shorter dimension was the height, giving these paperbacks a unique size which was ideally suited to a fatigue pocket. They were stapled rather than glued, a fact much appreciated by GIs in the South Pacific where temperature and tropical pests would soon wreak havoc on any glue then used in the publishing business. Each of these paperbacks had a seal on its cover identifying it as an Armed Services Edition.

These paperbacks sprung from the work of the Council on Books in Wartime, a group of booksellers, publishers and writers formed in March of 1942, whose purpose was to make "weapons in the war of ideas" and whose objective was to "use books to sustain morale through relaxation and inspiration." To achieve this objective they sought to mass-produce paperbacks at low cost, for overseas distribution at no cost to the GI. Because of their overseas distribution, few of these books made it back to the States, a fact which the home front publishers appreciated and a circumstance which resulted in few of these paperbacks being available to today's collector of popular American literature.

The subject matter was diverse, with westerns and mysteries having the largest number of titles; there were 160 westerns and 122 mystery titles. The most popular western writers were Ernest Haycox and Frederick Faust (most of Faust's titles were under his Max Brand pseudonym) — each with 18 different titles. In addition to the fiction which was then popular there were main-line fiction books by Saroyan, Greene, Conrad, Hemingway, Maugham, O'Hara, and dozens of others. There were biographies (86), historical novels (92), and humor books (130), but contemporary fiction had the greatest number of titles with 246. There were some science fiction titles, a few poetry titles, and a few anthologies assembled specifically for the Armed Services Editions.

ASE sports material was clearly a cut above the average pulp fare. Biographies of Joe Louis and Lou Gehrig, *The Best Sport Stories of 1944*, *Esquire's First Sports Reader*, Budd Schulberg's *The Harder They Fall*, J. P. Carmichael's *My Greatest Day in Baseball*, team histories of the Red Sox and Yankees, and Bob Feller's autobiography were among the more popular sports reading, which was to the average pulp sports story what the adult western was to the old "B" oater. However, two men with pulp sports roots were represented: Jon Tunis' *Keystone Kids* and *Rookie of the Year* and Paul Gallico's *Selected Stories* and *Farewell to Sport*.

Millions of GIs who were reading these stories were developing a taste for a higher level of writing than was generally found in the sports pulps, and when they returned home in the mid- to late 1940s they would no longer be reading pulp fiction of any kind.

The knockout punch was yet to be delivered. The pulps were struggling to maintain sales against the ever-increasing popularity of the comics and the paperbacks. World War II was winding down, as were the effects of the Great Depression. Live sports were coming out of the maintenance mode as returning ballplayers joined their old teams and the average fan found he could afford to attend professional sports events, something he couldn't do a few years earlier. He could also afford the down payment on a television set.

Boxing became a popular Wednesday and Friday night television event in the late 1940s, and between 1950 and 1960 the percentage of homes with television sets went from 10% to 94%. Instead of reading the pulp sports story with its ersatz drama, one could now see the real thing in person or on television. What pulp publishers suspected through the 1940s became unwelcome reality; times they were a'changing, and not for the better. Pulp sales in general and the sports pulps in particular were hard hit by the combined forces of the now-available live event, the now-popular comic book and paperback markets, and the crusher — televised sport events. Who in his right mind would prefer reading an issue of *Fight Stories* to seeing Rocky Graziano and Tony Zale go at it on television — for free? Who would prefer a copy of *Baseball Stories* to a trip to Fenway Park to see Teddy Ballgame perform when a bleacher seat could be had for the same 25¢ that the pulp cost?

The end of the sports pulp was as certain as the demise of Luke Short's gunman. It would struggle for a while and even make it into the 1950s before collapsing into the dust in a final death throe.

Street & Smith editor Daisy Bacon had some contrary opinions on the matter. Several years before her death I corresponded with Bacon and she was of the opinion that a major cause of pulp failure was that in the good years no funds were being spent to improve the magazines; that money ordinarily available for this purpose was being diverted to "other fields which would not be lasting and which indeed finally caused the name of Street & Smith to disappear altogether."

Street & Smith was a privately held company, so little hard data has been available on details of this position, but Bacon kept an eye on other, New York Stock Exchange–listed publishing houses, and claims that in one of these, executives spent most of their time making schedules for handing out press releases and that days were devoted to ascertaining the best time to communicate with their department heads in various European cities. Bacon was of the opinion that this particular publishing house had the idea that they were in the news service business.

Bacon speaks of the nefarious goings on at yet another misguided publishing house (unnamed), where the principal editorial pastime was meeting in out-of-the-way motels to plot against other editors. She felt that the editorial ranks of all of the publishing houses had been infiltrated by business manager types who were uniformed about the organization's publishing and distribution requirements.

Bacon was one of Street & Smith's premier editors. Quentin Reynolds said of her that she had "the zeal of a crusader" and possessed "an infallible instinct for choosing stories," and that she made the pulp *Love Story* Street & Smith's most valuable property. Perhaps the highest compliment Reynolds paid Bacon was his statement that neither Ormond nor George Smith ever interfered with her.

In one of the last letters from Bacon (dated 12/28/1977) she says, tersely: "Fell and broke hip, then been in hospital. Not able to get up to write." Later she wrote her last letter: "I didn't mean to be abrupt or superior but that letter was the best I could do. If I ever recover, I will be in touch."

In a time when the editor's job was man's work, Bacon excelled. She made her magazine Street & Smith's most profitable and the envy of the competition. Reynolds notes in his Street & Smith history that other publishers would not put out a competing magazine as all they would produce would be a cheap imitation of the real thing. Perhaps if there had been other Daisy Bacons the transition from the pulp era might have been different. Her attitude was that the collapse was not inevitable; that things could have, and should have, been done to improve the product. I have a feeling that had she run the show, things *would* have been different.

Perhaps one other factor played a part in this story. America was growing up. The depression and the war replaced a national psyche that embraced the simple pleasures with a darker view of life. The pulp world was clean and simple and pure, full of good guys, joy buzzers, and happy endings. The real world had evil lurking in the doorways; evil that took more than pureness of heart to defeat. Even when bad things happened in the pulps, everything would be okay in the end. This we knew. A world war and a depression turned this certainty into a sophisticated brand of cynicism which, in the final analysis, was probably enough, by itself, to doom the pulps.

Some years ago I talked to pulp writer Tom Curry about the

end of the pulps and his comment was based on his experience with Thrilling executive Leo Margulies and Thrilling editor Ned Pine: "When the thing finally collapsed, the publishers blamed the editors and the editors blamed the writers, and the only thing they could do was to go home and kick their wives."

Pulp Sources

It's safe to say that most pulps today are in private hands. Still, much material is on the shelves of private and public colleges and universities. Some material, such as Raymond Chandler's writings are widely dispersed. Some of the Chandler material is at the University of California-Los Angeles library, some is owned by *The Atlantic Monthly*, some is at Harvard, Indiana University, the University of Texas, and Boston University. Boston University has, in its Mugar Memorial Library, complete works and materials of many writers who have at some time worked in the pulps: Leslie Charteris, Thomas B. Dewey and Michael Avallone are three such.

The University of California-Los Angeles library has an extensive collection of pulps and pulp materials including many Volume 1, No. 1 pulps (*Nickel Detective*, *Great Detective*, *Mobsters*, and *The Avenger* are but a few.)

The Hess Collection at the University of Minnesota contains many dime novels and related materials including materials of characters such as Nick Carter who would bridge the gap to the pulps.

The George Arents Research Library for Special Collections at Syracuse University has exhaustive files and pulps from Street & Smith, one of the big pulp magazine publishers.

Brown University's John Hay Library has a large collection of the works, papers, pulps, etc., of H. P. Lovecraft.

There are a number of universities whose libraries hold the works of western pulp writers. Among them are the University of Texas, the University of Oregon, and the Western History Research Center at the University of Wyoming.

The University of Louisville (KY) and the British Library each have a large collection of detective pulp material. The Burroughs family has, in Tarzana, California, storerooms full of the works and materials of Edgar Rice Burroughs.

The following colleges and universities have extensive science fiction collections: University of Arizona, California State University-Fullerton, San Francisco Public Library, UCLA-Los Angeles, University of California-Riverside, Colorado State University, University of Colorado, University of Georgia, Northern Illinois University, Southern Illinois University, University of Illinois, Wheaton College (IL), Indiana University, Iowa Commission for the Blind Library, University of Kansas, University of Kentucky, Tulane University, University of Maryland, Boston University, Harvard University, Massachusetts Institute of Technology (a 30,000-item collection at the student center), Michigan State University, the University of Michigan, University of Minnesota, University of Southern Mississippi, Eastern New Mexico University, University of New Mexico (includes the Donald Day collection), Syracuse University, Duke University, East Carolina University, Bowling Green University, Case Western Reserve University, Ohio State University, University of Dayton, Pennsylvania State University, Temple University, Brown University, University of Tennessee, Sam Houston State University, Texas A & M University, Brigham Young University, University of Virginia, University of Wisconsin, University of Wyoming, Queens University (Ontario, Canada), Toronto Public Library, University of British Columbia, University of New Brunswick, and the University of Winnipeg.

Universities which have collections of detective fiction include Brooklyn College Library; Boston University Mugar Memorial Library; Humanities Research Center at the University of Texas (Austin); McMaster University of Hamilton, Ontario; State University of New York at Buffalo; Syracuse University's George Arents Research Library; State Historical Society of Wisconsin Library (Madison); the UCLA Library; the University of Minnesota George H. Hess Collection; the University of Rochester Library (New York); the Indiana University Lilly Library; the University of Pittsburgh Library; and the University of Wyoming Library (Laramie).

The pulp researcher has access to these materials as well as the extensive Library of Congress pulp magazine files. The LOC will provide photocopy and other assistance for a small amount of material and for larger jobs, the LOC will provide a list of local (Washington, D.C.) research people for hire. The LOC photoduplication service address is: Library of Congress, Photoduplication Service,

Washington, DC 20540-5230; telephone (202) 707-5640; Fax (202) 707-1771. Its statement of service is as follows:

> The Photoduplication Service provides expanded services, from a single-page photocopy to color slides and microfilm. These services are designed to assist scholars, publishers, and members of the public unable to visit the Library and use the Library collections in the reading rooms. Material is copied in accordance with U.S. copyright law and certain items cannot be copied; however, every effort will be made to respond to inquiries and fill requests in a timely manner. The service requires no appropriated funds and must recover all of its costs, including the cost of identifying and retrieving material, through service fees. Other information on products, services, and prices can be obtained by contacting: [address given above].

The Library of Congress had many of the sports pulp titles and is a researcher's best bet for obtaining sports pulp material. Most university collections do not include extensive sports material unless, as in the case of Syracuse University, they have obtained a publisher's entire stock (or at least as much of it as has survived).

Second only to use of the Library of Congress, the pulp researcher would be well served to become familiar with the pulp fandom/fanzine community, as many pulps are in private collections and pulp collectors are almost universally cooperative when asked for assistance, up to and including the loan of magazines.

The Future of Sports Pulps

Sports pulps, like all pulps, face an uncertain future. One can see the insidious pulp decay; the oxidation which starts at the extremities and works ever inward will someday turn its victim to dust. In addition to this physical decay there is the loss caused by the benign neglect that occurs when a class of popular writing is simply forgotten. Things not remembered decompose in the public consciousness. To prevent the inevitability of a pulp vanishing act, two things are necessary: preservation techniques must be used to stem the effects of age, exposure, and handling, and, as Willy Loman put it, "Attention must be paid."

The two-part solution, then, is to use microfilm to preserve the contents of the pulp and use the best available handling and storage techniques; and, to maintain interest and keep the fan/fanzine movement alive, to publish pulp research and information in printed form and on the internet. Colleges and universities play a large role in this process by providing special collections resources such as those at Boston University's Mugar Library.

As to the writing, what remains and what will survive of pulp sports material? There are two, distinct pulp influences here, the first of which is the hard-boiled private-eye story. A product of the detective pulps, the hard-boiled P.I. is alive and doing quite well in popular mystery fiction. A sports milieu is not uncommon in current treatments but is only peripherally plot-related. The second, and most promising future for pulp sports is the science fiction story.

Science fiction was not an original pulp form but the pulps took it to the level from which it could work its way to success as a mass fiction genre. The science fiction story offers the imaginative writer unlimited possibilities in which sport can be explored as anything from a test-tube experiment to an interplanetary confrontation, and this is truly in the spirit of the old science fiction pulp tale.

Much pulp fiction has been and is being republished, but this is not the case with the sports story. While science fiction and the mystery/adventure story from the pulps are popular and the early works of prominent pulp writers (Hammett, Asimov, Chandler, Lovecraft, etc.) find their way to frequent republication, the only sports material being reprinted is the series of eight Robert E. Howard fight stories paperbacks by Necronomicon Press.

The potential is there for a collection of pulp sports fiction and/or nonfiction. An editor considering a fiction collection would do well to consider some of the better sports stories by such writers as Paul Gallico and John Tunis, Louis L'Amour and John D. MacDonald. Someone might want to publish the very last story of the Merriwell brothers in such a collection, and a collection of pulp sports fiction by men like Robert Sidney Bowen, Jackson Scholz, Joe Archibald, Bill Cox, William Gault, and others who went on to write hardcover sports fiction could be of some interest. So also would be a collection of the Mr. Maddox stories, each of which set in a different racetrack or urban setting.

Non-fiction in the sports pulps is an untapped source of sports history and a collection of biographical pieces, team profiles, season and team histories and "as by" interviews with literally hundreds of sports figures over the decades of the 1920s, '30s and '40s should be of interest to the fan and the researcher.

Finally, the whole pulp magazine itself is an artifact worthy of preservation. Its stories and ads speak of a simpler day when joy buzzers and good guys were abroad in the land. The questions remain: 1) How long will the pulps (as physical objects) last? and 2) What can be done to stay the ravages of time? There is no precise answer to the first question but the clock, as they say, is ticking. As to what can be done, let's take a look at the current state of the art in pulp preservation techniques.

Pulp Longevity

How long will a pulp magazine survive? The answer to this question is central to the larger question of the future of pulp collecting.

Newsprint is the cheapest grade of paper used in the publishing business. In its crudest form it has been used by the pulp magazine business and these magazines are literally disintegrating before the eyes of collectors. In the mid–1800s manufacturers went from using rags and gelatins to the cheaper wood pulp and alum resins. Unfortunately, after just a few years, pulp paper reacts to exposure of air and light by forming tiny amounts of sulfuric acid and the books slowly combust. Examining a pulp magazine that has been so exposed, one can see that the deterioration starts at the extremities of the page with dark browning and brittleness, and merely touching the paper will cause it to crumble. The musty smell of the deteriorating pulp paper is not an unpleasant one and pulp collectors often refer, humorously, to these circumstances as causing "pulp lung."

Several things can be done to blunt the impact of the aging process but in time, as every quality engineer knows, everything fails. First of all, handling of the pulps should be restricted. If a paperback reprint of a pulp magazine is available to read, damage to the pulp can obviously be reduced. If you have to handle the magazine, it should be placed on a flat desk surface and the pages gently turned, with care not to stress the binding, e.g., by turning the page back only far enough to permit reading and no further. University collections and the Library of Congress are going to microfilm some of this material as a means of prohibiting all handling yet making the contents available to researchers.

Proper storage is essential to the longevity of the pulp magazine, and proper atmospheric conditions are the first consideration. Relative humidity of 50 percent and a temperature of 50 degrees are ideal, and exposure to fluorescent light or dust is to be avoided.

Clear plastic storage bags made of polyethylene, PVC, and polypropylene contain harmful chemical additives that adversely affect the pulp paper. Mylar (a registered trademark of the DuPont Company) storage bags contain no pulp-attacking acids and are used exclusively by the Library of Congress and should also be used by collectors. In pulp magazine size they can be purchased for about a dollar a bag. In addition to storing the pulp in the Mylar bag, an acid-free backing board should be used to ensure that structural integrity of the magazine is maintained in storage. For the more adventurous there are available on the market lightening solutions, tape removal kits, stain removal kits and dry cleaning pads for those who want to correct minor defects. However, amateur restoration efforts should be approached with the utmost caution, observing the physician's dictum "First, do no harm." It might be worthwhile, if the intrinsic value of the pulp justifies such an expense, to consider professional restoration. When the foregoing steps have been accomplished the magazines should be placed flat, alternating binding-page edges to eliminate any undue stress on bindings and the resulting edge roll, in acid-free boxes.

The last consideration is perhaps the most critical: what is to happen to your collection after your death. It is not uncommon to hear of collectors whose survivors know nothing of the value of a collection nor of the collector's wishes for the collection's future. Instructions for the disposition of his collection should be explicit, and conveyed in writing or verbally. If circumstances are such that next of kin are unable to carry out such instructions, the collector should consider the disposition of the collection during his/her lifetime.

Pulp Magazine Bibliography

Goodstone, Tony, *The Pulps: Fifty Years of American Pop Culture*, Bonanza Books, 1970. Brief genre overviews with representative genre fiction and some gorgeous color cover reproductions.

Goulart, Ron, *Cheap Thrills: An Informal History of the Pulp Magazines*, Arlington House, 1972. An informative overview of the pulps.

Gruber, Frank, *The Pulp Jungle*, Sherburne Press, 1967. A look at the pulp business from the writer's point of view.

Hersey, Harold, *Pulpwood Editor*, Frederick Stokes, 1938. A look at the pulp business from the editor's point of view.

Reynolds, Quentin, *Fiction Factory: Or from Pulp Row to Quality Street*, Random House, 1955. A history of Street & Smith from the dime novel era to the pulp era and beyond.

Pulp Magazine Preservation Information

Hall, F. Keith, "Wood Pulp," *Scientific American*, April 1974. A comprehensive discussion of pulp paper.

Rogers, Denis R., "Disposal of a Book Collection," *Dime Novel Roundup*, Vol. 49, No. 6, December 1980. A discussion of the process of controlling the future of your collection during and after your lifetime.

Wolseley, Ronald E., *Understanding Magazines*, The Iowa State University Press, 1965. "A discerning look at what goes on in the competitive and dynamic field of magazine publishing."

9

Appendix: Sports Pulp Titles

Ace Sports Monthly/Ace Sports
Magazine Publishers, Inc./Periodical House, Inc.
January 1936–January 1949 (168 issues estimated)

All-American Football Magazine
Love Romances Publishing Co., Inc.
Fall 1938–February 1953 (60 issues estimated)

All-American Sports
Atlas Fiction Group, Inc.
December 1940 (1 issue)

All-American Sports Magazine
All American Periodicals, Inc.
December 1933–May/June 1938 (49 issues estimated)

All-Baseball Stories
Interstate Publishing Corp.
October 1947 (1 issue)

All Basketball Stories
Atlas News Company, Inc.
Winter 1947 (1 issue)

All Football/All Football Stories
Interstate Publishing Corp.
Fall 1938–December 1947 (40 issues estimated)

All Sports Magazine/All Sport
Columbia Publications, Inc.
May 1940–February 1951 (130 issues estimated)

Athlete
Street & Smith Publications
August 1939–April 1940 (9 issues)

9. Appendix: Sports Pulp Titles

Baseball Stories/Fact and Fiction Baseball Stories
Flying Stories, Inc. (Fiction House, Inc.)
Spring 1938–Spring 1954 (50 issues estimated)

Basketball Stories
Fiction House, Inc.
Winter 1937–1938 (1 issue)

Best Sports/Best Sports Magazine
Stadium Publishing Corp.
July 1937–December 1951 (50 issues estimated)
(Finished in digest format)

Big Baseball Stories
Interstate Publishing Corp.
May 1948–December 1948 (3 issues estimated)

Big Book Sports
Exclusive Detective Stories, Inc.
November 1947–Winter 1948 (4 issues estimated)

Big Sports Magazine
Exclusive Detective Stories, Inc.
May 1948–June 1949 (12 issues estimated)

Blue Ribbon Sports
Blue Ribbon Magazines, Inc.
December 1937–Winter 1938 (12 issues estimated)

Bull's Eye Sports
Fiction House, Inc.
Winter 1938–Fall 1939 (4 issues estimated)

Champion Sports Magazine
Periodical House, Inc.
March 1937–May 1939 (15 issues estimated)

Complete Sports
Manvis Publications, Inc.; Skyline Publications, Inc.; Western Fiction Publishing; and Stadium Publishing Corp.
March 1937–November 1955 (40 issues estimated)

Dime Sport Magazine/Dime Sports Magazine
Popular Publications, Inc.
July 1931–June 1944 (81 issues)

Exciting Baseball
Better Publications, Inc.
Spring 1949–Fall 1950 (4 issues estimated)

Exciting Football
Better Publications, Inc.
Winter 1941–Fall 1951 (8 issues estimated)

Exciting Sports
Better Publications, Inc.
Winter 1941–Summer 1950 (30 issues estimated)

Fifteen Sports Stories
Fictioneers, Inc. (Subsidiary of Popular Publications, Inc.)
February 1948–April 1952 (30 issues)

Fight Stories
Fight Stories, Inc.
June 1928–Spring 1952 (200 issues estimated)

Five Sports Classics Magazine
Standard Magazines, Inc.
Spring 1941–Fall 1951 (90 issues estimated)

Football Action
Flying Stories, Inc. (Fiction House, Inc.)
Fall 1939–Fall 1953 (20 issues estimated)

Football Stories
Fiction House, Inc.
Fall 1937–Fall 1953 (50 issues estimated)

Jack Dempsey's Fight Magazine
Champion Associates, Inc.
May 1934–August 1934 (3 issues)

Knockout Magazine
Popular Publications, Inc.
January/February 1937–June/July 1938 (8 issues)

Life of Gene Tunney
Dell Publications, Inc.
December 1927 (1 issue)

New Sports Magazine
Popular Publications, Inc.
January 1947–July 1951 (33 issues)

Popular Baseball
Better Publications, Inc.
Spring 1949–Spring 1951 (24 issues estimated)

Popular Football
Better Publications, Inc.
Winter 1941–Fall 1950 (70 issues estimated)

Popular Sports Magazine
Better Publications, Inc.
June 1937–Spring 1951 (75 issues estimated)

Real Sports
Western Fiction Publishing Co.
January 1938–February 1938 (2 issues estimated)

Interstate Publishing Corp.
December 1946–November 1948 (20 issues estimated)

Rodeo Romances/Western Rodeo Romances
Best Publications, Inc.
April 1946–June 1948 (9 issues estimated)
Nedor Publishing Company
March 1943–March 1946 (16 issues estimated)

Sports Short Stories
Interstate Publishing Corp.
December 1947–June 1948 (7 issues estimated)

Sport Story Annual
Street & Smith Publications
1942 (1 issue)

Sport Story Magazine/Street and Smith's Sport Story Magazine
Street & Smith Publications
September 8, 1923–July 1943 (419 issues)

Sports Action
Manvis Publications, Inc.
December 1937–July 1943 (60 issues estimated)

Sports Fiction
Columbia Publications, Inc.
December 1939–June 1951 (45 issues estimated)

Sports Leaders Magazine
Stadium Publishing Corp.
April 1948 (1 issue estimated)

Sports Novels/Sports Novels Magazine
Popular Publications, Inc.
April/May 1937–April 1952 (86 issues)

Sports Winners
Blue Ribbon Magazines, Inc.
December 1937–December 1953 (60 issues estimated)

Star Sports Magazine
Western Fiction Publishing Co.
October 1936–January 1938 (20 issues estimated)

Super Sports
Columbia Publications, Inc.
October 1939–February 1957 (60 issues estimated)

Ten-Story Sports
Columbia Publications, Inc.
October 1948–June 1957 (50 issues estimated)

Thrilling Baseball Stories
Standard Magazines, Inc.
Summer 1949–Spring 1950 (6 issues estimated)

Thrilling Football Stories
Better Publications, Inc.
Standard Magazines, Inc.
Fall 1939–Fall 1950 (13 issues estimated)

Thrilling Sports
Beacon Magazines, Inc.
Better Publications, Inc.
Standard Magazines, Inc.
September 1936–Spring 1950 (40 issues estimated)

12 Sports Aces
Ace Magazines, Inc.
November 1938–July 1941 (30 issues estimated)

Variety Sports Magazine
Ace Magazines, Inc.
September 1938–February 1939 (6 issues estimated)

Index

Ace High Magazine 27, 36
Ace Sports 64, 85, 132, 168, 192
Ace Western 160
Acker, Frank 66
Action Comics 14, 180
Action Stories 13, 141, 149, 150, 152
Adams, Cleve 20
Adventure 12–15, 27, 55, 139, 160, 166, 180
Adventure Comics 14
Ainslee's 7
Air War 100, 143
Aldis, Brian 24
Alger, Horatio 7
The All-American Football Magazine 64, 76, 132, 160, 169, 173, 192
The All-American Sports Magazine 38, 64, 65, 70, 71, 72, 169, 192
All-Baseball Stories 38, 65, 192
All Basketball Stories 65, 81, 192
All Detective Magazine 26
All Football Stories 38, 65, 76, 192
All Sports Magazine 65, 163, 168, 192
All-Story Cavalier Weekly 8
The All-Story Magazine 7, 8, 12, 13, 26, 43
All-Story Weekly 8, 13, 15
Amazing Stories 24, 57, 58, 59, 61
American Autopsy 32
American Boy 141

The American Cyclist 5
The American Eagle 25
American Eagles 25
American Girl 40
American Golf 5
American Lawn Tennis 5
The American Magazine 17, 158
The American Mercury 6, 67, 156
The American Yachtsman 5
Ames, Joseph 68, 109
Anderson, Sven 20
The Angel Detective 25
Anthony Hamilton 25
Aquatic Monthly and Sporting Gazetteer 5
Archibald, Joe 19, 79, 188
Arena 5
The Argosy 7–9, 12–15, 17, 26, 27, 36, 37, 43, 77, 81, 95, 96, 137, 139, 145, 151, 162, 166, 180, 188
Argosy-All Story 9
Argosy All-Story Weekly 149
Armed Services Edition 181, 182
Army-Navy Flying Stories 32
Asimov, Isaac 58
Astounding Science Fiction 18, 61, 160–161
Athlete 64, 124, 125, 192
Athletic Journal 64
The Atlantic Monthly 185
Avalone, Michael 146, 147, 185
The Avenger 25, 126, 185

Bacon, Daisy 28, 128, 183, 184
Baird, Edward 165
Barbour, Ralph 46
Baseball Stories 38, 41, 64, 94–99, 132, 146, 163, 169, 173, 183, 193
Basketball Stories 38, 64, 81, 82, 173, 193
Baumhofer, Walter 22, 162
Beach, Rex 46, 47
Beadle & Adams 66
Bedford-Jones, H. 168
Belarski, Rudolph 162
Bellem, Robert Leslie 138
Bergey, Earl 162, 163
Best Detective Magazine 118
Best Sports 38, 41, 64, 74, 172, 193
Big Baseball Stories 38, 65, 94, 193
Big Basketball Stories 65
Big Book Sports 65, 83, 193
Big Chief Western 25
Big Sports Magazine 65, 193
Bill Barnes, Air Adventurer 25
The Black Bat 25
Black Book Detective Magazine 100
Black Mask 17–19, 48, 49, 51, 52, 78, 106, 113, 115, 140, 142, 147, 160, 162, 166
Black Mask Detective 49
Black Mask Detective Magazine 49
Bleiler, E.F. 16
Bloch, Robert 23
Blue Book Magazine 7, 12–15, 27, 36, 45, 139, 141
Blue Ribbon Sports 64, 193
Bok, Hannes 162
Bosworth, Allan R. 5
Bowen, Robert Sidney 143, 188
Bower, Bertha 7, 46
The Bowler's Journal 5
Bradbury, Ray 23
Brand, Max *see* Faust
The Bronze Gazette 174
Brown, Frederick 61
Brown, Howard 162, 168
Brown University 17
Bulletin 5
Bull's Eye Sports 38, 64, 193
Buntline, Ned 16
Burke's Peerage 44

Burks, Arthur 115, 116, 151
Burroughs, E.R. 7, 14

Cain, Paul 19
Campbell, John 58
Canadian Rodeo News 81
Cannon, Jeremy *see* Stoops, Herbert Morton
Captain Combat 25
Captain Future 25, 100, 163
Captain Hazzard 25
Captain Zero 25
Carleton, Warren 68, 109, 115
Cash Gorman 25
Cavalier 8, 12, 13, 42
Cave, Hugh 27, 43, 135
Chadwick, Paul 109
Champion Sports Magazine 64, 84, 85, 161, 193
Chandler, Raymond 19, 49, 185
Charteris, Leslie 15
Civil War Stories 32
Clancy, Foghorn 80, 170–172
Clayton, W.M. 160
Clues Detective Stories 19, 20
Coburn, Walt 27
Cohane, Tim 132
Cohn, Octavis Roy 107
College Stories 170
Collier's 5, 8, 139
Complete Detective 162
Complete Sports 38, 63, 64, 74, 75, 99, 132, 133, 193
Comprehensive Index to Black Mask (Hagemann) 49
Computer Life 18
Conan Doyle, A. 7, 12
Cosmopolitan 5
Costello, Peter 24, 58
Cowboy Stories 27
Cox, Bill 78, 81, 125, 126, 132, 139–141, 169, 188
Cox, J. Randolph 70
Coxe, George Harmon 19, 51
Crump, J. Irving 68, 109, 111
Csida, Joseph 49
Culture Publications 29
Curry, Tom 11, 17, 107, 109, 112, 114, 115, 184

Index

Daly, Carroll John 48, 106
Dan Dunn 25
Dan Fowler 25
Dan Turner — Hollywood Detective 138
Dare-Devil Aces 31
Dark Valley Destiny (deCamp) 148
Davies, Valentine 60
Davis, Robert H. 136
Day, Donald 25, 58
Day's Doings 5
DeGraf, Robert Fair 180
Delano, Gerry 28
DeMarco, Mario 96, 158, 163, 164, 165, 167
dePolo, Harold 106, 107
Derleth, August 23
Detective Book Magazine 143
Detective Comics 14, 180
Detective Fiction 17, 51
Detective Fiction Weekly 51, 52, 78, 135, 145, 165, 166
Detective Novels Magazine 54, 100
Detective Romances 130
Detective Story Magazine 137
Detective Tales 53, 160
Dime Detective 18, 47, 51, 52, 54, 142, 162
Dime Mystery Book Magazine 21
The Dime Novel and Its Successors (LeBlanc) 33, 133
Dime Novel Roundup 67, 128
Dime Sports Magazine 38, 47, 64, 139, 141, 145, 147, 148, 149, 153, 161, 168, 169, 172, 176, 193
Dime Western 160
Dinan, John A. 169
Dingle, A.E. 13
Dobyns, Stephen 48
Doc Savage 25, 170
Doctor Death 25
Dr. Yen-Sin 22, 25
Don Diavolo 25
Double Detective 135
Dusty Ayers and His Battle Aces 25, 31, 143
Dynamic Science Fiction 162
Dynamic Science Stories 21

Echoes 141, 142, 174
Eerie Stories 162

Eggenhoffer, Nick 28
Eight Dime Novels (Bleiler) 16
Ellery Queen Mystery Magazine 142
Ellis, Doug 135, 140
Ellis, Edward 7, 46
Ellison, Harlan 61
English, Edward L. 45
Everybody's Combined with Romance 6
Everybody's Magazine 6
Everyday Astrology 100
Exciting Baseball 38, 65, 94, 193
Exciting Detective 100
Exciting Football 65, 76, 193
Exciting Sports 65, 100, 144, 163, 194
Exciting Western 100

Fair, A.A. *see* Gardner
Famous Detective 20
Famous Spy Stories 25
Fanning, Cap 100
Fantastic Universe 60
Fantasy & Science Fiction 61
Fantasy Commentator 174
Faust, Frederick 15, 27, 45, 51, 116, 136, 137, 182
The Faust Collector 174
Fay, Bill 47, 139
Fiction Fantasy (Reynolds) 36, 103
Fiction House 36
Field and Stream 5
Fifteen Sports Stories 65, 169–170, 194
Fight Stories 38, 64, 87–91, 99, 132, 139, 148, 149–153, 158, 163, 169, 173, 183, 194
Fight Stories, Inc. 36
Fisher, Steve 147
Five-Novels Monthly 44
Five Sports Classics 38, 65, 194
Flash Gordon 25
Flying Aces 32, 85
Flynn's 51
Football Action 64, 7679, 132, 139, 163, 169, 173, 194
Football Stories 64, 76, 140, 141, 173, 194
Ford, T.W. 115, 117
Foreign Legion Adventures 32
Frontier 27

Future Fiction 171
Future Science Fiction 162

G-8 and His Battle Aces 16, 25, 31, 116
G-Men Magazine 25, 100
Galaxy 151
Galli, Walter 96, 158
Gallico, Paul 106, 107, 127, 181, 188
Gang World Stories 19, 32
Gangland Detective Stories 21
Gangland Stories 19
Gene Tunney: The Fighting Marine 86–87
Gernsback, Hugo 18, 24, 58
The Ghost 100
Ghost Stories 32, 149, 153
Gibson, Walter 115
Gipson, Leonard 59
Gladney, Graves 126, 161, 162, 170
Glidden, Fred 15, 27, 126, 180
Goldey's Ladies Book 14
Golf World 64
The Golfer 5
Golfer's Magazine 5
Good Housekeeping 6
Good News 134
Good Roads 5
Graham, Arthur 108, 120–122, 124
Grand Guignol Theatre 21–23
Great Detective 185
Grey, Romer Zane *see* Curry, Tom
Gross, George 160, 161
Gruber, Frank 55, 166, 168

Hammett, Dashiell 19, 49
Harper's Bazaar 5
Harper's Weekly 8
Harte, Bret 7, 12
Haycox, Ernest 106, 107
Hersey, Harold 11, 36, 159, 177, 178
History of American Magazines 1865–1885 Vol. III (Mott) 4
History of American Magazines 1885–1905 Vol. IV (Mott) 5
Hodgson, William Hope 12
Hoffman, Arthus 165
Hogan, Robert J. 116
Hopalong Cassidy 25
Hornig, Doug 48
Horror Stories 21

Horton, Dabney 115, 116, 119, 170
Hot Rod 64
Howard, Robert E. 23, 28, 35, 45, 46, 56, 85, 114, 132, 148, 150–153, 188
Hunting, Gardner 168, 169

The Incredible Adventures of Dennis Dorgan 150, 152
Independent 8
Index to Science Fiction Magazines 1926–1950 (Day) 25, 58
The Iron Man 152

Jack Dempsey's All-Sport Magazine 89
Jack Dempsey's Fight Magazine 38, 64, 85, 86, 89, 148, 149, 153, 194
Jackson, Edward Zane Carroll *see* Buntline, Ned
Jacobi, Carl 151
Jameson, Arthur 161
Jim Hatfield 25
Jones-Bedford, H. 7, 12, 14, 42, 45
Jules Verne — Inventor of Science Fiction (Costello) 24, 58
Jungle Stories 25

Kantor, MacKinlay 165
Ka-Zar 25
KI-Gor 25
Kinsella, W.P. 60
Kline, Otis Albert 58
Knockout Magazine 64, 89, 91–93, 140, 160, 170, 194
Know-Nothings 16
Kofoed, Jack 170
Kofoed, William 86, 90, 99, 101, 102, 114, 124, 126, 132
Kuhlhoff, Pete 43

L'Amour, Louis 28, 56, 143, 144, 188
Lariat 27
Lawn Tennis 5
Lawrence, John 49
LeBlanc, Edward 33, 67, 111, 133
Leonard, Elmore 28, 169
Leonard, Mark 170
Life Magazine 124, 161
The Life of Gene Tunney 38, 64, 89, 194
The Live Wire 8

Llanuza 161
London Morning Herald 100
The Lone Eagle 25, 100, 143
Lord, Glen 150
Love Adventures 130
Love Fiction Monthly 85
Love Stories 18
Love Story Magazine 18, 19, 28, 29, 103, 160, 184
Lovecraft, H.P. 23, 35, 188
Lowndes, Robert 168

McClure's Magazine 7, 12, 13, 17, 165
McCulley, Johnson 79, 137
MacDonald, John D. 145, 146, 188
McDonald, William Colt 25
McFarlane, Leslie 118, 120, 125
McGee, Doc 98
McGinnis, Vera 80
McIlwraith, Dorothy 166
McKenna, James 49
MacLean, Charles Agnew 47
Magic Carpet Magazine 149, 150, 153
Malamud, Bernard 60
Malzberg, Barry N. 61
The Man in the Red Mask 25
Mann, Arthur 116, 117, 119, 120, 125, 127
Manners, David 51
Margulies, Leo 17, 185
The Masked Detective 100
Masked Rider 100
Matalaa 25
Mayer, William 34
Men's 162
Merriwell, Dick 16, 17, 33, 65–69, 83, 103, 110, 130
Merriwell, Frank 16, 17, 33, 65–70, 83, 103, 110, 130
Mobsters 185
The Monthly Story Magazine 14
Morton, James F. 23
Moscowitz, Sam 23
Mother of a Champion 40
Motor Boat 5
Movie Detective 25
Movie Merry-Go-Round 85
Mundy, Talbot 12, 14
Munsey, Frank 7, 9, 14, 27, 42, 43
Munsey's Magazine 7, 8, 14, 15, 26, 43

Munsey's Weekly 7
Mystery Adventure 162
Mystery Book Magazine 145
Mystery Tales 22

Nanovic, John 166, 170
Nathan, George Jean 67
National Police Gazette 5, 8
National Recreation Association 10
Navy Stories 32
Nebel, Frederick 49
Nebel, Paul 19
New England Sportsman 5
New Fun 180
The New Republic 6
New Sports Magazine 65, 194
New York Clipper 5
New York Herald 8
New York Post 155
New York Times 8, 107, 154, 155
New York Weekly Dispatch 103
New York World 8
Newspaper Adventure Stories 32
Nick Carter 25
Nickel Detective 41, 185
Nickel Western 41
Nickell Magazine 5
Northwest Stories 27
Norton-Taylor, Duncan 166

The Ocean 8, 26
The Octopus 25
Oliphant, Roland 47
Onward 5
Operator 5 16, 25
O'Sullivan, Jack 173
Outdoor America 64
Outing 8
Outlook 8
Over the Top 32

Palmer, Ray 59
The Pathfinder 5
Patten, William Gilbert 16, 66–68, 108–110, 118, 131, 134
Paul, Frank 162
Peacock, Wilbur S. 43
Pearson's Magazine 7, 8, 12
The Pecos Kid Magazine 25
Pentacost, Hugh 145

People's Favorite 17
People's Magazine 15, 168
Periodical House 85
Peterson's 14
Phantom Detective Magazine 25, 54, 100, 143
Pine, Ned 185
Planet Stories 160, 163
Platt, Kin 48
Playboy 18
Pocket Love 29
Popular Baseball 38, 65, 94, 148, 162, 194
Popular Detective 19, 100, 143
Popular Football 65, 76, 144, 194
Popular Love 100
The Popular Magazine 12, 13, 15, 27, 45, 46, 47, 159, 166
Popular Publications 21, 49, 52, 72, 159, 166, 168, 169
Popular Sports Magazine 34, 38, 64, 94, 99–102, 132, 138, 143, 144, 175, 176, 194
Popular Stories 46
Popular Western 100
Powers, Jimmy 96, 98, 132
Price, E. Hoffman 50, 149
Pronzini, Bill 61
Public Enemy 19
Pulp Collector 169, 174
The Pulp Era 174
Pulp Vault 140, 145, 174
Pulpwood Editor (Hersey) 11, 36, 131, 159, 177
Putney, Walter 96

Railroad Detective Stories 26
Railroad Magazine 9, 26, 27
The Railroad Man's Magazine 8, 9, 26
Railroad Stories 9, 26, 32
Ranch Romances 27, 32
Range Riders Western 100
Rangeland Romances 130
Reading Football (Oriard) 8
Real Detective Tales 165
Real Love 29
Real Mystery Magazine 21
Real Seal Western 160
Real Sports 38, 64, 65, 74, 194
Red Hood Detective 25

Red Mask Detective 25
Red Seal Western 85
Red Star Western 25
Red Starr Adventures 25
Reed, Carlton 124, 161
Reel Humor 85
Reeves, Robert 48
Reise, Malcolm 173
Reynolds, Quentin 36, 47
Rinehart, Mary Roberts 47
Ring Magazine 56, 71, 72, 89, 90, 149, 169
Rio Kid Western 17, 100
Ritter, Simpson M. 100
Road & Track 64
Rodeo Romances 65, 79–81, 130, 137, 138, 144, 170–171, 195
Rogers, Alva 161
Romance 6
Romantic Range 29
Rosen, Jerome 22
Rosen, Richard 48
Ross, A. Leslie 126, 127, 161

Sabatine, Rafael 14
Sackett, Ada Taylor 111
The Saint 142
St. John, J. Allan 162
St. Nicholas 8
Sale, Richard 78
Sampson, Robert 15
Sanford, Holden 22
Saturday Evening Post 60, 148
Saucy Detective 29
Saucy Movie Stories 32
Saunders, Norm 22, 161
Scholastic Coach 64
Scholz, Jackson V. 43, 115, 120, 121, 124, 147, 170, 188
Schwab, Charles M. 8
Science Fiction 162, 171
Science Fiction by Gaslight 24
Science Fiction Quarterly 162
The Scorpion 25
Scott, H.W. 124, 126, 161
Scott, T.T. 173
The Scrap Book 8, 26
Sea Stories 17
Secret Agent X 25, 85, 143, 162
The Secret Six 25

Secrets 85
The Shadow 16, 25, 103, 170
The Shadow Magazine 25, 103, 116, 170
Sheena Queen of the Jungle 25
Short, Luke *see* Glidden, Fred
Short Stories 13, 15, 17, 27, 43, 44, 135, 142, 148, 166, 168
The Shudder Pulps (Jones) 21
The Silver Buck 25
Silver Buck Western 25
Sinclair, Upton 46
Sinister Stories 21
Ski Illustrated 64
Ski Magazine 64
Skiing 64
Sky Fighters 25, 30, 100
Sloane, T. O'Connor 58
South Sea Stories 32
Space Opera: An Anthology of Way-Back-When Futures (Aldiss) 24
Space Science Fiction 163
Speakeasy Stories 10
Speed Detective 50, 138
Spicy Adventure 29, 50
Spicy Detective 29, 32, 50, 138
Spicy Mystery 10, 29, 50
Spicy Western 29, 50
The Spider 25, 54, 160
Spirit of the Times 5
Sport 64
Sport Short Stories 65
Sport Story 133, 160
Sport Story Annual 65, 127, 195
Sport Story Magazine 1, 18, 33, 36, 38, 43, 63, 64, 68, 80, 99, 102–129, 131, 132, 136, 144, 147–149, 151, 153, 155, 160, 161, 163, 170, 175, 176, 177, 195
Sporting Life 5
Sports Action 38, 63, 64, 74, 195
Sports Afield 5
Sports Fiction 40, 64, 64, 133, 168, 171, 195
Sports Illustrated 64
Sports Leaders Magazine 38, 65, 74, 195
Sports Novels Magazine 38, 47, 64, 72, 74, 142, 160, 162, 170, 195
Sports Short Stories 65, 72, 73, 195
Sports Winners 38, 64, 168, 171, 195
Spy Novels Magazine 10, 32

Stag 162
Standard 166
Standish, Burt L. *see* Patten, William Gilbert
Star Sports Magazine 64, 195
Star Wars 24
Star Western 160
Startling Mystery 21
Startling Stories 100, 163
Steeger, Harry 20, 52, 159, 168, 169
Stein, Modest 127, 161
Stoops, Herbert Morton 13
The Strand 12
Strange Adventures Magazine 25
Strange Stories 100
Strange Suicides 10
Stratemeyer, Edward 133
Stratemeyer Syndicate 33, 134
Street & Smith 18, 29, 36, 46, 55, 66, 103–129, 162, 163, 166, 170, 184
Super Detective 78
Super Sports 33, 34, 40, 64, 68, 69, 133, 135, 146, 168, 171, 195
Super Western 85
Sure-Fire Western 85

Tailspin Tommy 25
Ten Detective Aces 85, 143, 162
10-Story Detective 143
Ten-Story Love 85
Ten-Story Sports 64, 65, 146, 171, 195
Terhune, Albert Payson 42
Terrence X O'Leary's War Birds 25
Terrill, Rogers 169
Terror Tales 21
Texas Ranger Magazine 17, 100, 115
Thompson, Walker A. 137, 138
Thrilling Adventure 100
Thrilling Adventures 55, 56, 144
Thrilling Baseball Stories 38, 55, 65, 196
Thrilling Detective 26, 55, 56, 100, 143, 162
Thrilling Football Stories 38, 55, 64, 76, 100, 144, 196
Thrilling Love 55, 100
Thrilling Mystery 55, 100
Thrilling Ranch Stories 55, 56, 100
Thrilling Sports 38, 55, 56, 64, 100, 163, 176, 196
Thrilling Spy Stories 100

Thrilling Western 55, 56
Thrilling Wonder Stories 100
Thurber, James 60
Tilden, Michael 169
Time 6
Tip Top Weekly 6
Tompkins, Walker A. 137, 138
Tonic, Al 8, 9
Top Notch Magazine 68
Torry, Roger 19, 140
Triple-X Western 27
True 162
True Love Stories 29
Truslow, Fergis 49
Tunis, John 40, 106, 107, 114, 131, 133, 153–156, 183, 188
Turf 5
Turner, Robert 53
Tuttle, W.C. 27
Twain, Mark 7, 12
12 Sports Aces 41, 63, 64, 133, 196

Uncanny Tales 21
The Underworld 19
Unknown 160

Van Every, Ed 86
Variety Novels 162
Variety Sports Magazine 38, 64, 196
Vogue 5, 18

Wallop, Douglas 60
Ward, H.J. 29
Webster, K. 49
Weird Tales 20, 22, 23, 112, 150, 151

Wellman, Manly Wade 151
Wells, H.G. 7, 12, 47, 58
Wertham, Frederic, M.D. 173
West 27, 100, 137
Western Aces 85
Western Adventures 27
Western Field and Stream 5
Western Magazine 100
Western Story Magazine 18, 27, 28, 103, 160, 161
Western Trails 85
Wheeler-Nicholson, Major Malcolm 180
Wheelman 5
The Whisperer 54
Whitfield, Raoul 107, 108, 112, 113, 147
Widmer, Harry 166
Wild West Weekly 28, 104, 124, 137, 138, 161
Williamson, Jack 58
The Witch's Tales 32
Witwer, H.C. 46
The Wizard 25
Worlds of Weird (Moscowitz) 23
Writer's Digest 51, 170
Wu Fang 22

Xenophile 159, 168, 174

Youth's Companion 8

Zane Grey Western 18, 115
Zeppelin Stories 32
Ziff-Davis 59, 168

www.ingramcontent.com/pod-product-compliance
Ingram Content Group UK Ltd.
Pitfield, Milton Keynes, MK11 3LW, UK
UKHW042006140426
5217IPUK00015B/1008